The Canon of the Śaivāgama and the Kubjikā Tantras of the Western Kaula Tradition

The Canon of the Śaivāgama and the Kubjikā Tantras of the Western Kaula Tradition

MARK S. G. DYCZKOWSKI

State University of New York Press

Published by
State University of New York Press, Albany

Printed in the United States of America

For information, address State University of New York Press, State University Plaza, Albany, N.Y., 12246

Library of Congress Cataloging in Publication Data

Dyczkowski, Mark S. G.
The canon of the Śaivāgama and the Kubjikā Tantras of the western Kaula tradition.

(SUNY series in Kashmir Shaivism)
Bibliography: p.
Includes index.
1. Agamas—Criticism, interpretation, etc.
2. Tantras. Kubjikātantra—Criticism, interpretation, etc. 3. Sivaism—Sacred books. I. Title. II. Series: SUNY series in Kashmir Śaivism.
BL1141.26.D93 1987 294.5′95 86-25116
ISBN 0-88706-494-9
ISBN 0-88706-491-4 (pbk.)

10 9 8 7 6 5 4 3 2 1

Contents

The Āmnāya Classification

The Āmnāyas of the Kaulatantras

The Āmnāya Classification and the Four Āmnāyas According to the *Ciñcinīmatasārasamuccaya*

Analysis

The Kaulatantras and Śaivāgama

The Paścimāmnāya—The Cult of Kubjikā

Kubjikā, the 'Crooked One'

The Origins of the Kubjikā Cult

PART THREE

Appendices

ACKNOWLEDGEMENTS

My greatest handicap in writing this monograph has been the paucity of manuscript material to which circumstance has allowed me access. Unfortunately, I have not had the opportunity to see more than a tiny number of the hundreds of manuscripts that most probably contain material to contribute to our knowledge of the Śaiva canon and, indeed, the Kubjikā cult. I can only hope that fate will be kinder to me in the future than it has been in the past and allow me access to the manuscripts in Nepal which for many years now I have dearly hoped to study.

I wish to acknowledge my debt of gratitude to a number of people who have helped and inspired me during more than fifteen years of study in India and in Oxford, where I had the privilege of working for my doctorate. One of the first who comes to mind is Mr. G. S. Sanderson, whom I consider not only a fine scholar but also a friend. I would also like to express my gratitude to Professor R. Gombrich, who was my supervisor during my years at Oxford and is one of the most sincere people I know. I cannot be grateful enough to Professor Vrajavallabha Dvivedi, former head of the Yogatantra Department of Sampūrṇānanda Sanskrit University. In our many conversations in Hindī and Sanskrit, he has been an inspiring guide to several areas of *Tantraśāstra*. Dr. B. P. Tripathi, head of the Research Department of the same university, has also helped me a great deal, not so much in the field of Tantric studies, but in Sanskrit grammar. His profound knowledge of Pāṇini and the Sanskrit language has inspired me to take delight in the Sanskrit itself, not just as a tool to read texts but as a language to speak and write for its own sake.

I should acknowledge the many suggestions made by Dr. Goudriaan, who is at present at the University of Utrecht, and Dr. N. Rastogi at Lucknow University. They were kind enough to read this monograph carefully and to bring to my attention a number of important points that have contributed concretely to the final form of this work. I should also thank Dr. Harvey Alper, the editor of the SUNY series of studies in Kashmiri Śaivism, for having chosen to include my work in the series and for his sustained encouragement throughout the long process of editing and publication.

Finally—and above all—I acknowledge my parents' contribution: their support in every way has been constant and unremitting; they, like my wife, have always had faith even when it failed me.

PART ONE

The Śaiva Āgamas

Preliminary Remarks

The past two decades have witnessed an unprecedented growth of interest in the Hindu Tantras both on the part of the layman and scholar alike. This vast area of study, so badly neglected in the past, is now slowly beginning to come into its own. The new interest, accompanied by a greater (although still very limited) knowledge of the Tantras, has led to a more critical and scholarly approach to the study of these sacred texts. Although scholars in the past were aware that important internal distinctions exist in the 'Tantric tradition',[1] they were largely glossed over in an attempt to penetrate the 'philosophy of the Tantras',[2] or the 'principles of Tantra'.[3] Important exceptions on the Śaiva side (we are not concerned here with Vaiṣṇava Tantra) have been the studies and critical editions made in recent years of the Siddhāntāgamas. This important work must be largely credited to the French Institute of Indology at Pondicherry and in particular to Pt. N. R. Bhatt and Dr. Hélène Brunner-Lachaux, who has contributed to it immensely by her extensive work on Siddhānta ritual.[4] Another area of research has been the Śrīvidyā tradition. Many of the major Tantras and allied works of this school have been edited and independent studies published. However, apart from these two major fields, hardly any other work has been done on individual Tantric traditions. The aim of this monograph is to pursue this line of approach further by presenting a preliminary study of another Hindu Tantric tradition, namely, the cult of Kubjikā, the details of which are recorded in the Tantras of the Western School: the *Paścimāmnāya.*

The *Paścimāmnāya* belongs to a category of Śaivāgama variously called *'Kulāgama'*, *'Kulaśāstra'* or *'Kulāmnāya'*, which we shall attempt to delineate in the second part of this monograph. Although not as extensive as the Siddhānta or as well known and diffused as the Śrīvidyā, the *Paścimāmnāya* is an important and substantial Tantric tradition. Up to now very little work has been done on the *Paścimāmnāya* (see appendix A). Hardly any texts of this school have been edited, although about a hundred independent works, some of considerable length, are preserved in manuscripts, almost all of which are in Nepal (see appendix D). At this preliminary stage of research we would do well, first of all, to locate this sacred literature in the vast corpus of the Śaivāgama. Such is the aim of this monograph. Thus, although we shall deal with the Tantras and cult of Kubjikā, we are here primarily concerned only with the contents of these Tantras that can help us to locate them in the Śaiva canon and construct their history. We are acutely aware that we are considerably handicapped in this task not only by our limited knowledge of the *Paścimāmnāya* but also by our scant understanding of the structure of the Śaiva canon. Even so, we feel that, however provisional it may turn out to be, at least an attempt should be made to plot, even if in the most general terms, the extent and divisions of the Śaivāgama. Forced as we are at present to work largely with sources in manuscript (many of which are corrupt), and given the vast amount of material that has yet to be studied and the even greater amount that has been lost, our endeavor is audacious, perhaps foolhardy. Even so, we shall be amply rewarded if this work leads to new insights into possible future avenues of research not only in the Kubjikā Tantras but, more generally, into the Śaiva canon.

The Śaivāgamas

The earliest known references to sectarian Śaivism are found in Patañjali's *Great Commentary* (*Mahābhāṣya*) on Pāṇini's grammar probably written in the second century B.C.. Patañjali refers to the *Śivabhagavats* which he describes as itinerent ascetics who wore animal skins and carried an iron lance.[5] The Śaiva symbols found on the coins of the Greek, Śāka and Parthian kings, who ruled in Northern India between the second century B.C. and the first century A.D., confirm that Śiva was already well established during this period as a sectarian god.[6] Unfortunately, however, no sacred texts of any pre-Āgamic Śaiva sect have been preserved. Possibly none were written during this early period. It is not unlikely that when Śaivism developed into a popular movement it relied at first on the Vedas and related literature along with the developing Epic and Purāṇic traditions as sounding boards for their sectarian views. We might also justifiably speculate that there must have existed numerous oral traditions that ultimately contributed to the development of a corpus of sacred Śaiva literature—the Śaivāgamas—that considered itself to be independent of the authority of the Vedas and had nothing to do with the Epics or Purāṇas.

Although it is not possible to say exactly when the first Āgamas were written, there is no concrete evidence to suggest that any existed much before the sixth century. The earliest reference to Tantric manuscripts cannot be dated before the first half of the seventh century. It occurs in Bāṇa's Sanskrit novel, *Kādambarī* in which the author describes a Śaiva ascetic from South India who "had made a collection of manuscripts of jugglery, Tantras and *Mantras* [which were written] in letters of red lac on palm leaves [tinged with] smoke." Bāṇa also says that "he had written down the doctrine of Mahākāla, which is the ancient teaching of the Mahāpāśupatas,"[7] thus confirming that oral traditions were in fact being committed to writing.

If our dates are correct, it seems that the Śaivāgamas proliferated to an astonishing degree at an extremely rapid rate so that by the time we reach Abhinavagupta and his immediate predecessors who lived in ninth-century Kashmir we discover in their works references drawn from a vast corpus of Śaivāgamic literature. It is this corpus which constituted the source and substance of the Śaivism of Kashmir, which Kashmiri Śaivites, both monists and dualists, commented on, systematized and extended in their writings and oral transmissions. The dualist Siddhāntins, supported by the authority of the Siddhāntāgamas, initiated this process by developing the philosophical theology of the Siddhānta. Subsequently, from about the middle of the ninth century, parallel developments took place in monistic Śaivism which drew inspiration largely, but not exclusively, from the Bhairava and other Āgamic groups which constituted the remaining part of the Śaiva corpus.

It was to this part of the Śaivāgama that the sacred texts of the *Paścimāmnāya* belonged. These Tantras, unlike those of the Siddhānta, advocated in places extreme forms of Tantricism that actively enjoined such practices as the consumption of meat and wine as well as sex in the course of their rituals.

Āgamic Śaivites who accepted these practices as valid forms of worship constituted a notable feature of religious life throughout India. Although many of these Śaivites were householders, the mainstays of these traditions were largely single ascetics, many of whom travelled widely and in so doing spread their cults from one part of India to another.

An interesting example of this phenomenon is Trika, nowadays virtually identified with monistic Kashmiri Śaivism. Abhinavagupta, who was largely responsible for developing Trika Śaivism into the elevated, sophisticated form in which we find it in his works, was initiated into Trika by Śambhunātha, who came to Kashmir from neighbouring Jālandhara. Sumati, his teacher and an itinerent ascetic like himself, was said to have travelled to the North of India from some "sacred place in the South."[8]

The Jain Somadeva confirms that Trika was known in South India during the tenth century. Somadeva identifies the followers of the *Trikamata* as Kaulas who worship Śiva in the company of their Tantric consorts by offering him meat and wine.[9] It is worth noting incidently that Somadeva was very critical of the Trika Kaulas. "If liberation," he says, "were the result of a loose, undisciplined life, then thugs and butchers would surely sooner attain to it than these Kaulas!"[10] Although Somadeva was a Jaina monk and so would naturally disapprove of such practices and tend to take extreme views, it appears nonetheless that Trika was not always as elevated as it now seems to us to be.

Although the *Paścimāmnāya* is entirely confined to Nepal at present, it was, according to one of its most important Tantras, the *Kubjikāmata*, spread by the goddess to every corner of India, right up to Kanyakumārī in the South, identified, by allusion, with Kubjikā the goddess of the *Paścimāmnāya.*[11] A long list of initiates into the *Paścimāmnāya* and their places of residence is recorded in the *Kubjikānityāhnikatilaka*, a work written before the twelfth century. It is clear from this list that the cult had spread throughout India although it was certainly more popular in the North.[12] That the *Paścimāmnāya* was known in South India in the thirteenth century is proved by references in Maheśvarānanda's *Mahārthamañjarī*[13] to the *Kubjikāmata*[14] as well as a work called *"paścimam"*[15] which may or may not be the same work but most probably belongs to the same tradition. An old, incomplete manuscript of the *Kubjikāmata* is still preserved in the manuscript library of the University of Kerala in Trivandrum.[16]

Despite relatively early references to the existence of Āgamic Śaivism in the South, it seems that the Śaivāgamas originally flourished in northern India, spreading to the South only later. *Madhyadeśa* (an area covering eastern Uttar Pradesh and west Bihar) was, according to Abhinavagupta, considered to be the "repository of all scripture"[17]—hence also of the Śaivāgama and the Kulaśāstra.[18] The importance of this part of India is indirectly confirmed by the fact that Benares, in the centre of this area, is to be visualized as a sacred place (*pīṭha*) located in the heart of the body in the course of the Kaula ritual described in *Tantrāloka.*[19] Similarly, Prayāga and Vārāṇasī are projected in the same way onto the centre of the body during the ritual described in the *Yoginīhṛdaya,*[20] a Kaula Tantra of the original Śaivāgama. The sacred circle (*maṇḍala*) shown to the neophyte in the course of his initiation into the cult of the *Brahmayāmala* is to be drawn in a cremation ground with the ashes of a cremated human corpse. In it are worshipped Yakṣas, Piśācas and other demonic beings, including Rākṣasas led by Rāvaṇa, who surround Bhairava to whom wine is offered with oblations of beef and human flesh prepared in a funeral pyre. The name of this circle is the "Great Cremation Ground" (*mahāśmaśāna*) and is to be drawn in Vārāṇasī.[21] Siddheśvarī is a quarter of Benares named after a goddess worshipped there; she was originally called Siddhayogeśvarī,[22] an important goddess of the Trika.

Although the *Paścimāmnāya* was not popular in Kashmir,[23] we must first examine the monistic Kashmiri sources to understand something of the development of the Śaivāgama and the relationship between the different groups which constituted it, including the Kaula group to which the *Paścimāmnāya* belongs. This is because Abhinavagupta's Trika encompassed the entire spectrum of Śaiva Āgamic cults ranging from these of the Śaivasiddhānta and the Siddhānta-type ritual of the Svacchanda cult[24] popular in Kashmir, right through to those of the *Bhairavatantras* and *Kulāgamas* to Trika. There are references to more than five hundred lost works within this range. Many of these Tantras and related works must still have existed in the thirteenth century when Jayaratha commented on the *Tantrāloka* and quoted extensively from these sources. From the manner in which he talks about these Tantras it appears that some at least of the rituals they described continued to be performed in his time.[25] However, outside the Himalayan region matters were different. Thus, although the Siddhānta flourished in the South, we can infer from the numerous references in Maheśvarānanda's *Mahārthamañjarī*, written about this time, that a good number of the primary Tantras familiar to Abhinavagupta were not known in the South. However, the secondary works associated with them (many still scripture in their own right) as well as Kashmiri works of known authors and texts belonging to the *Kramanaya* had been carefully preserved and even added to.

A great deal of this literature has been lost. There is no denying the fact that a relatively sudden interruption of the traditions associated with these texts has taken place: a break has occurred in the development of the Tantras. Within two or three centuries not only had the bulk of the *Bhairavatantras* and similar Tantric works been lost, but even Abhinavagupta and the monist Kashmiri authors seem, except in a few isolated cases, to have disappeared. It was only in the beginning of this century that the works of these authors started to be rescued from oblivion when their works began to be edited by Kashmiri scholars employed in a government research centre at Srinagar which published them as the *Kashmir Series of Texts and Studies*. The study of these texts made scholars aware of the loss of a large and rich corpus of Tantric literature. Indeed, this loss has been so great that all the developments in monistic Tantra after Abhinavagupta, with the important exception of the cult of Śrīvidyā, were fresh beginnings which had little direct connection with the older corpus, so much so that the younger scriptures are no longer called "Śaivāgamas" but "Tantras."

Thus the term "Tantra," which has anyway a wide range of connotations,[26] is used at times to denote a Śākta Tantric scripture to distinguish it from a Śaiva Āgama, whereas we find both words used in the early corpus without distinction.[27]

The reason for this loss has certainly much to do with the ethos of Hinduism itself and its history as a whole. The secrecy that these types of Tantras have always imposed on themselves is indicative of the uneasiness which these Tantric cultural elements must have aroused in many.[28] Thus the Purāṇas, which are from many points of view the bastions and guardians of Hindu orthodoxy, initially tended to reject the authority of the Tantras and so largely avoided quoting from them. However, insofar as the Purāṇas aimed to be complete compendiums of Hindu spirituality and practice, they later included long sections from Tantric sources, especially when dealing with ritual, the building and consecration of temples, yoga and related matters.[29] Thus there is much Tantric material to be found everywhere in the Purāṇas. The *Brahmavaivartapurāṇa* contains a brilliant theological exposition of the Supreme as the Goddess Nature (*Prakṛti*), which is a theme dear to Tantra in its later phases. The *Devī, Devībhagavata,* the *Kālikā* and large portions of the *Nārada* Purāṇas are extensively Tantric. The hymns eulogizing the names of the goddess, accounts of her actions, lists of female attendants of male gods, their Mantras, Yantras and much more show how strong the influence of Tantric ideas was on the Purāṇas. They also demonstrate that such trends were not only clearly apparent in the history of the development of Tantra but applied to them also. These developments, in other words, concerned the whole of the literate tradition, and so the Purāṇas could, without difficulty or self-contradiction, incorporate relevant material from the Tantras.

These incorporations were drawn from the entire range of Tantric sources available at the time in which they were made. It seems likely, in fact, that a possible way in which we can gain some idea of when these Tantric passages were added to the Purāṇic text is to establish the type of Tantric source from which they were drawn. No one has yet attempted to apply this method in an extensive or systematic way. However, the validity of this approach finds the support of R. C. Hazra, who in his work does attempt to date some Purāṇic passages on this basis.[30] The *Agni* and *Garuḍa* Purāṇas, for example, deal extensively with Tantric topics. Their treatment is based largely on the Śaivāgamas and Pāñcarātrasaṃhitās which belong to the early Tantric period, i.e., prior to the tenth century. As an example relevant to the study of the *Paścimāmnāya*, we may cite chapters 143-147 of the *Agnipurāṇa* where the goddess Kubjikā is extolled and the manner in which she is to be worshipped is described.[31] As Kubjikā is not worshipped in the way described in the *Agnipurāṇa* in later Tantric sources, we can conclude that this addition must be relatively early.

The changes in the Tantric material found in the Purāṇas also serve to underscore the fact that many of the early Tantras were lost and their cults superseded by others. Undoubtedly, this is partly due to the effects of the passage of time with its changing fads and interests. Manuscripts in India have a relatively short lifespan; if they are not copied, the texts they transmit soon become obsolete. Through the centuries much has been lost in this way from all the Indian *śāstras*. In the case of the Tantras, particularly the esoteric ones such as those belonging to the Bhairava and Kaula groups, this natural process was reinforced by the custom of disposing of the Tantric text once the teacher had explained its meaning to his disciple.[32] Moreover, the regional character of many of these Tantric cults entailed the scarcity of copies of their Tantras. Not infrequently, therefore, the speaker of a Tantra prefaces his instruction with an exhortation to hear the Tantra which is "very hard to acquire (*sudurlabha*)."[33]

There were, however, other factors at work apart from purely mechanical loss. Let us go back to the Purāṇas. Although the Purāṇas drew from Tantric sources, their attitude to the Tantras varied and was at times far from positive. The orthodox community, which the Purāṇas largely represented, was not always in favour of the Tantras, even though they somehow accepted them. The problem was that the Tantras often set themselves in opposition to the orthodox line. For one thing, the Āgamas as a whole rejected the authority of the Vedas. Some Āgamic schools took a mere tolerant view, others stuck to a harder line; even so the Āgamic tradition as a whole thought of itself as being quite distinct from the Vedic. This was particularly true of the Bhairava and the other classes of Tantras that suffered the greatest loss. Thus the *Ānandabhairava-tantra* declares:

> The wise man should not elect as his authority the word of the Vedas, which is full of impurity, produces but scanty and transitory fruits and is limited. [He should instead sustain the authority] of the Śaiva scriptures.

Abhinava remarks:

> That which according to the Veda is a source of sin, leads, according to this doctrine of the left, directly to liberation. In fact, all the Vedic teaching is dominated by Māyā.[34]

The Purāṇas basically sustain the authority of the Vedas. Understandably, they therefore reacted against these scriptures which so explicitly opposed themselves to it. Sometimes these differences were simply ignored; in other cases, however, the Purāṇas manifested an open hostility towards the Śaivāgama. The Purāṇic passages which represented the orthodox standpoint staunchly condemned these scriptures as inferior. They agreed that Śiva had revealed them, but his reason for doing so was to delude the apostate and distract him from the true path: they are the scriptures of darkness (*tāmasī*).[35] The *Kūrmapurāṇa* is particularly adamant in its opposition to these scriptures and repeatedly stresses that the Vedas are the sole source of right conduct and true religion (*dharma*).[36] The *Kūrma*, which is a Śaiva Purāṇa, wants to disassociate itself completely from Āgamic Śaivism. It displays an almost obsessive concern to condemn the scriptures of the heretical (*pāṣaṇḍa*) Śaivites, namely, those of the Kāpālikas, the *Bhairava* and *Vāma* Tantras, the *Yāmalas* and those of the Pāśupatas.[37] Similarly in the *Varāhapurāṇa*, Rudra himself denounces the Pāśupatas and the other followers of the Śaivāgamas as given to "mean and sinful acts" and as "addicted to meat, wine and women".[38] Their scriptures are outside the pale of the Vedas (*vedabāhya*) and contrary to them.[39] The *smārta* Śākta *Devībhagavata* unambiguously declares that Śiva made the scriptures of the Vāmas, Kāpālikas, Kaulas and Bhairavas with the sole intention of deluding them. Even so, it is more tolerant towards these scriptures than the *Kūrmapurāṇa*, and so prescribes that those portions of them that do not go against the Vedas can be accepted without incurring sin.[40]

These instances are just a few of many examples that clearly demonstrate that a marked tendency existed within Hinduism to reject these scriptures and condemn their followers. It is not surprising, therefore, that these Tantric traditions were at times actively repressed. We read, for example, in hagiographies of Śaṅkara's life of his encounter with the king of the Vidarbhas in eastern Maharashtra who asked Śaṅkara to suppress the heretical views of the followers of the *Bhairavatantras*—a request with which he gladly complied.[41] King Yaśaskara of Kashmir (938-48 A.D.) was concerned to enforce the rules regulating the caste and conditions of life (*varṇāśramadharma*) amongst his subjects and was therefore against the Tantric practices of the Śaivāgamas which had no regard for them. He was so opposed to these practices that he did not hesitate to imprison even the nephew of his foreign minister for attending Tantric gatherings (*cakramelaka*).[42]

This resistance within Hinduism to the Āgamas was not, however, the direct cause of their loss, although it must have been a crucial attendent factor. The interruption that occurred in the Tantric tradition was catastrophic: it took place suddenly and was totally devastating. We must therefore seek a cause which was immediate and directly effective. Nor do we have to look far. The eleventh century, which marks the beginning of this change in the Tantric tradition, coincides with a sudden reversal in the course of India's history, namely, the advent of Muslim rule. In the beginning of the eleventh century the brief incursions of Muslim raiders into Indian territories that had been going on for centuries turned, under the lead of Mahamūd of Ghazni, into a full-scale invasion. The onslaught of Islam forced Hinduism to retreat, challenging its resistance and stability as a whole. The Muslim scholar, Al-Birunī, who came to India with the invading armies noted that "the Hindu Sciences have retired far away from those parts of the country conquered by us, and have fled to places which our hand cannot yet reach, to Kashmir, Benares and other places."[43] Mahamūd of Ghazni did not manage to conquer Kashmir, although he plundered the Valley in 1014 A.D. and again attacked it, this time without success, in the following year. But even Kashmir, although outside the Muslim's reach for the time being, felt the intense impact of the Muslim presence in India. Kṣemendra, the Kashmiri polymath, describes in his *Acts of the Incarnations of Viṣṇu* (*Daśāvatāracarita*) written in 1066 A.D., the dire conditions that will prevail in the world on the eve of the coming of Kalki, Viṣṇu's last incarnation who was to finally herald the dawn of a new age of freedom. He says:

> The Dards, Turks, Afghans and Śākas will cause the earth to wither as do the leper his open, oozing sores. Every quarter overrun by the heathen (*mleccha*), the earth will resound with the sound of swords drawn in combat and her soil will be drenched with blood.[44]

The following centuries, during which the Muslims consolidated and extended their rule, witnessed the disappearance of Āgamic Śaivism in the north of India. The Āgamic Siddhānta survived these upheavals by fleeing to the South where the Muslim presence was not as powerful as in the North. Dunuwila writes:

> After the twelfth century the Siddhānta seems to have been losing popularity over most of India, giving way to more syncretic forms of Hinduism. The Siddhāntins also seem to have lost their posts as Royal Preceptors with the downfall of the dynasties that patronized them, as did the Kalacuris in the early thirteenth century. What remained of the Siddhānta was apparently annihilated by the ever-increasing Muslim incursions into Central India from the more northern regions of the country already under Muslim dominion. The Hindu will to resist the Islamic invaders, never very firm, was demoralized by Pṛthvīrāja III's

defeat at Tarian in 1192. Mālwā, the Siddhānta's homeland, was raided by the Mamluk Delhi Sultān Iltutmish in 1234-35, by his successor Balban in 1250, and by the Khaljī Sultān Jalāluddīn in 1292. The Muslims finally triumphed in 1305, when Alāuddīn Khaljī overran Mālwā, destroying, among other places, the sacred city of Ujjayinī and Bhoja's capital Dhārā. The Siddhānta had to take refuge in the Tamil country to survive.[45]

The Tantras of the *Paścimāmnāya* composed during this period are intensely aware of the harmful consequences of these developments. According to the *Manthānabhairavatantra*, the demon Rāvaṇa incarnated in this Age of Darkness (*Kaliyuga*) and descended onto the bank of the Indus, thus initiating the tyranny of the heathens' rule that extended its sway throughout the world.[46] Another Tantra of the Kubjikā school describes the dreadful state which prevails in the Age of Darkness as one in which the lower classes are oppressed by the proud Hindu aristocracy even though it has been defeated in battle and so must, presumably, accept foreign domination.[47] Just as the Siddhānta found refuge in the South, the cult of Kubjikā was similarly protected by the patronage of the Nepalese who eagerly adopted it as their own. Thus, it has survived to this day along with the huge royal libraries and many private collections large and small where virtually all that remains of the early Āgamic sources in North India is preserved.

It was not until the late thirteenth century that Kashmir finally succumbed to the Muslim invader and so we find, as we have already noted, that the Āgamas existed intact in the twelfth century when Jayaratha wrote his commentary on Abhinava's *Tantrāloka.* However, in Kashmir, which must have been one of the most flourishing centres of Āgamic Śaivism in India, the powerful internal forces within the monistic Āgamic traditions that led to the further development of monistic Śaivism in the hands of Kashmiri Śaiva theologians and exegetes, also helped to render obsolete the Āgamas, which were their original sources and foundation. The Kaula rituals which were controversial gradually ceased to be performed, giving way to tamer and milder cults, such as that of Svacchandabhairava, while the deeper philosophical, psychological and mystical insights behind the symbolic actions of the Kaula ritual were transferred entirely into the realms of philosophy and a mysticism of graded inner experiences. Thus the original scriptures, which were concerned with ritual, ceased to serve a purpose and all that remained was their philosophical and mystical exegesis. In Nepal on the other hand, where these sorts of developments did not take place, the Nepalese abandoned themselves to the opposite extreme—a formal ritualism which, though charged with meaning, had lost all significance for them beyond the ritual act itself. Thus the Nepalese, unlike the Kashmiris, did preserve the original Tantras they made use of in their rituals, but largely failed to see anything beyond their immediate content.

But apart from these extrinsic factors, a highly significant intrinsic factor contributed to the loss of these scriptures, namely, the internal development of the Śaivāgama itself. The Śaivāgamas, even those most Śaiva-oriented, accommodated within themselves the concept of Śakti.[48] This trend developed within some of the Śaivāgamas towards such a female-oriented view that at a certain stage, they simply ceased to be Śaiva. The *Śāktatantras* took over and, permeated with the earlier Kaula doctrine and ritual forms, preserved, along with those Tantras which continued to consider themselves to be Kaula (although not directly connected to their predecessors), the presence of this antinomian element within Hinduism. The old was transformed into something new, which replaced what had gone before so completely that all that remained was a dim memory of a glorious past in the form of the names of the ancient Āgamas now given to new works.[49] The most hardy survivor of these far-reaching changes was the mild Kaula cult of Śrīvidyā. The *Paścimāmnāya* is another Kaula cult that has managed to survive almost to the present day, although only within the narrow confines of Nepal.

Śaivāgama—Its Major and Secondary Divisions

At the outset of our exposition of the extent and divisions of the Śaivāgamic canon, with a view to ultimately determining the place of the *Paścimāmnāya* within it, it is important to note that although each Āgama does identify itself as a member of a cognate group, it is, ideally, complete in itself.[50] Indeed, the standard pattern in many large Āgamas of every type is the exposition of the essentials for a complete cult. These include the rites of initiation along with other occasional and obligatory rituals as well as the rules of conduct to be observed together with some theoretical considerations about the nature of reality and other matters. Many of the large temple complexes in South India, both Śaiva and Vaiṣṇava, affiliate themselves to one or other Vaiṣṇavasaṃhitā or Śaivāgama on the basis of which (in theory at least) they were built and worship in them is conducted. Abhinavagupta frequently refers to a Tantra as a teaching (*śāsana*) in its own right. Again, although he accepted all Śaiva scripture as authoritative to a degree, the *Siddhayogeśvarīmata,* (*A*)*nāmakatantra* and *Mālinī-*

vijayottara were singled out as the ultimate authorities for the Trika Tantricism he sponsored. He also sustained the *Siddhayogeśvarīmata*'s claim to being the most important of all the scriptures.

The primary textual tradition orders itself into canonical corpuses of sacred literature, which reflect upon themselves as belonging to a single group and so strive to concretely supplement and extend each other within the parameters chosen for themselves. We can observe this happening more commonly with primary texts belonging to the early formative period of Tantra. This tendency is more noticeable the more restricted the group becomes. Thus the scriptures of the *Paścimāmnāya*, which constitute a subdivision of a much larger category of scriptures, form a relatively coherent group. The rituals of the individual Tantras of the *Paścimāmnāya* do, in fact, share many common details. The basic Mantric system, for example, is fairly uniform in the majority of the Paścima Tantras, and matters which one Tantra deals with cursorily are taken up and elaborated in another.

In this way the huge body of primary texts consists of a manifold in which each member is independent although connected, more or less directly, through the mediation of common affiliations variously established, to others. It is not surprising, therefore, if we come across a certain amount of incoherence (not to say, at times, outright contradiction) even between texts belonging to the same group. Indeed, one of the functions of the Tantric master in the ordering and development of the Tantric tradition is to sort out these textual problems. Thus Abhinavagupta explains in his *Tantrāloka* that the Tantric master who teaches his disciples the meaning of the scriptures must, if necessary, proceed through them as a frog does, leaping from place to place within them. He must have an eye for every detail and observe it in its broader context, viewing the text as a whole, as does the lion strolling through the jungle who looks in all directions as he walks. Paraphrasing the *Devyāyāmala*, Abhinava says:

> The master should explain the statements [of the Tantra, demonstrating and] corroborating their consistency by means of their interconnection and apply this principle to the various sections of the text, its chapters, sentences, words and root meaning (*sūtra*). He should ensure that the preceding and subsequent sections of the scripture do not appear to contradict each other and so apply, as required, the principles [that one must move from one section to the next] as a frog leaps [omitting what is irrelevant], or as the lion who looks around [in all directions as he walks]. In this way he should coalesce the meaning of the scripture into a single coherent expression unconfounded with other teachings. Knowing well the meaning of each phrase as he expounds it, he avails himself of sound associations (*tantra*), repetition (*āvartana*),

exclusion (*bādha*), extensive application (*prasaṅga*) and reason (*tarka*), etc., taking care to distinguish one topic from another.[51]

The manner in which Śaivism developed in these early primary texts is analogous to the development of Hinduism as a whole: subsequent developments are viewed as being culminations of what has gone before in such a way that what is new appears not only as superior, but also incorporates all that has happened in the past. In this manner new scriptures can maintain their canonicity within (in this case, an amazingly rapidly) expanding corpus that encompasses what is old in a new system of classification in which the newcomers can reckon themselves to be amongst the members of the highest class.

We can observe this process happening in the sections of the Āgamas dealing with the Āgamic canon. These sections are an important part of the text because it is by means of them that the text can validate its own canonicity while at the same time present itself as belonging to a well-defined category of scripture. As new developments take place, these categories are extended, and subdivisions added or redefined. A particular Tantra may assert itself as a major member of a group and so institute new categories to make a place for itself or elevate old ones to a new, higher status. In other words, a text that records the structure of the canon is free to interfere with it. At times, this leads to a major change in the form of the canon. More often however, these changes are minor, indeed, sometimes none need be made if the text can accommodate itself amongst the others as a member of an already established group. Even so, the picture we get of the canon is, at times, perplexingly mutable. Moreover, matters are further complicated by the fact that more than one system of classification usually operates at one time. Thus a given text may fall into a number of classifications operating at different times. A text may understand itself, and the extent and nature of the group to which it belongs, in different terms than it is understood by another text—particularly if the latter is of a different class. Another factor which adds to the confusion is that some terms of reference to groups are broader than others. If all this were not enough, we also find that seemingly identical paradigms of classification are applied to different groups.

In order to understand the overall scheme of the Śaivāgama, we shall now briefly consider what different texts have had to say about their own location in it, and from that try to form a picture of its extent and parts. We shall begin by seeing what the Śaivasiddhānta has had to say.

According to the *Kāmikāgama*[52], spiritual knowledge was originally of two types, superior (*parā*) and inferior (*aparā*), according to the level of intelligence of those fit to comprehend it. *Śivajñāna*, which illumines the nature of Śiva, is superior while inferior is that knowledge which, starting from the Veda, illumines the nature of the fettered soul (*paśu*) and that which binds him (*paśa*). These two degrees of knowledge are as different from one another as the night vision of a cat and that of a man.[53] Śaiva scripture encompasses both the superior and inferior degrees of knowledge insofar as Śiva is considered to be the ultimate source of both. The higher knowledge is divided into four groups. These are, in descending order of importance: Śaiva, Pāśupata, Lākula and Somasiddhānta. Each is again divided into three: Right (*dakṣiṇa*), Left (*vāma*) and Siddhānta in such a way that the highest is Śaivasiddhānta.[54] According to a similar classification found in the Siddhānta manuals of South India, there are two basic categories: Śiva and Śaiva. These are subdivided as follows:[55]

- Śiva
  - Vāmaśiva
  - Dakṣiṇaśiva
  - Miśraśiva or Yāmalaśiva
  - Siddhāntaśiva
- Śaiva
  - Pāśupata
  - Somasiddhānta
  - Lākula

Clearly, the basic scheme consisting of four components, namely, Śaiva, Pāśupata, Lākula and Somasiddhānta, has not changed. All that has happened is that the first of these four has been further analysed. Indeed, this basic scheme recurs frequently in the Siddhāntāgamas[56] where it is generally integrated (as happens in the *Kāmikāgama*) into the larger scheme we shall discuss later. It appears to be one of the most basic classifications of the Śaivāgamic schools and so, possibly, one of the oldest. Let us therefore examine it a little more closely.

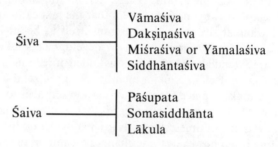

Important sources for us are the commentaries on *Brahmasūtra* 2/2/37 which states: "For the Lord there can be no creatorship for that leads to incongruity." Commenting on this aphorism, Śaṅkara simply refers to the Māheśvaras as those who worship Śiva as the supreme God. Vācaspati Miśra (c. 850 A.D.) divides the Māheśvaras into four: Śaiva, Pāśupata, Kāpālika and Kāruṇika Siddhāntins.[57] Yāmunācārya (c. 1050 A.D.), in his *Āgamaprāmāṇya*, lists the same basic four as Śaivas, Pāśupatas, Kapālins and Kālāmukhas.[58] Most later commentators follow this classification. Rāmānuja in his commentary on the *Brahmasūtra* lists the same four declaring, mistakenly, that they are Pāśupata sects because their followers agree that Paśupati is the instrumental cause of the universe.[59] Keśava Kāśmīrin agrees with this view,[60] while Śrīkaṇṭha correctly explains that they are all believers in the Āgamas revealed by Śiva, rather than just Pāśupatas.[61]

We find the same set of four in the Purāṇas and other independent sources. Lorenzen has collected a number of references to these groups and lists them in his book. Although Lorenzen's chart is somewhat lengthy, the material it contains is sufficiently relevant to our present discussion for us to quote most of it here.[62] See Table 1.

Table 1. Śaiva Sects Mentioned in the Purāṇas and Other Sources.

Kūrma Purāṇa	Kāpāla[63]	Pāśupata	Also Vāma, Bhairava, Pūrva-paścima and Pāñcarātra
	Soma[64] Lākura or Lāñjana or Vākula	Pāśupata	Also Vāma and Bhairava
	Soma[65] Lāṅgala (Lāguḍa)	Pāśupata	Also Vāma and Bhairava
Nāradīya P.[66]	Kāpāla Mahāvrata-dhara	Pāśupata Siddhānta-mārga	
Śiva P. Vāya-[67] vīya-saṃhitā	Kāpāla Mahāvrata-dhara	Pāśupata Siddhānta-mārga	
Skanda P.[68]	Kaṅkāla Kālamukha	Pāśupata Śiva	Also Mahāvrata
Skanda P.[69] Sūta-saṃhitā	Kāpāla Lākula	Pāśupata	Also Soma

Svayambhu[70] P.	Soma Vā(Lā)kula	Pāśupata Śaiva	
Vāmana P.	Kāpālikā[71] Kāladamana Mahāvratin[72] Kālāmukha	Pāśupata Śaiva Pāśupata Śaiva	 Also Mahāpāśupata and several others
Yogavāsiṣṭha[73] and Liṅga P.	Soma Nākula		Also Lokāyata and Bhairava
Ānandagiri[74]		Pāśupata Śaiva	Also Ugra, Raudra, Bhaṭṭa and Jaṃgama
Rājaśekhara[75]	Mahāvrata-dhara Kālamukha	Pāśupata Śaiva	
Śaktisaṅgama-[76] tantra	Kālāmukha	Pāśupata Śaiva	Also six others
Siddha-[77] siddhānta-paddhati	Kāpālika	Pāśupata Śaiva	Also Mahāvrata-dhara and five others
Malkāpuram[78] Stone Inscription	Śivaśāsana Kālānana	Pāśupata Śaiva	

We can draw the following conclusions from these lists. Firstly, despite the variant names and entries, they effectively establish the uniformity of this system of classification. Secondly, we can identify the groups generically called "Śaiva" with the Śaivasiddhānta in a restricted sense (as the *Nāradīya* and *Śiva* Purāṇas seem to do) and, more generally, with the Śaivāgama as a whole considered independently of the Pāśupatas etc.. This conclusion is supported by the distinction made between the 'Śiva' and 'Śaiva' groups in the South Indian Siddhānta manual we have referred to previously.[79] Moreover, the absence of this entry in the lists drawn from the *Yogavāsiṣṭha, Kūrma* and *Liṅga* Purāṇas apparently coincides with the addition of the Bhairava and Vāmatantras, which are major components of the Śaivāgamic canon. Thirdly, the entry *"Kāpālika"* (variants: Kāpāla, Soma, Saumya and Kaṅkāla) appears regularly in almost all the lists and so must be considered to be an independent group. This is true also of the "Pāśupata" and the "Lākula" (variants: Nākula, Vākula, Lāñjana, Lāguḍa and Lāṅgala). Finally, we notice that "Kālāmukha" (variants: Kālamukha, Kālānana and Kālāsya) sometimes appears to take the place of the Lākulīśa Pāśupata entry. The Kālāmukhas studied Lakulīśa's religion (*Lākulasamaya*)[80] and doctrines (*Lākulasiddhānta*).[81] Kālāmukha teachers are regularly praised in inscriptions by identifying them with Lakulīśa.[82] There can be no doubt, therefore, that the Kālāmukhas were Lākulīśa Pāśupatas. Even so, not all Lākulīśa Pāśupatas were Kālāmukhas; it would therefore be wrong to simply identify the two.

Let us now turn to a more detailed discussion of these groups individually. We shall deal first with the Pāśupata sects, then discuss the Kāpālikas, and then finally turn to the Śaivāgamas and their major divisions.

The Pāśupatas and Lakulīśa

The *Mahābhārata* refers to the Pāśupata as one of four doctrinal systems (*jñāna*)[83] along with the Veda, Sāṃkhya-Yoga and Pāñcarātra. Although the Purāṇas not infrequently condemn the Vaiṣṇava Pāñcarātra as advocating principles contrary to those of the Veda, it is the Pāśupatas who are generally considered to be the most subversive. In a myth often retold in the Epics and Purāṇas, it is Śiva, not Viṣṇu, who destroys Dakṣa's sacrifice in a fit of rage because he was not invited to it along with the other gods. In the Epic, one of the many variants of this important myth portrays this event as symbolic not only of the growing importance of Śaivism which seemed, as it developed, to be ousting the older Vedic religion but, more specifically, as an occasion to assert the growing power of the Pāśupatas. Thus, when Śiva in his terrible form of Rudra has destroyed Dakṣa's sacrifice, he declares:

> I, Rudra, for the first time created the mysterious religion of the Pāśupata, beneficent to all, facing in all directions, one that can take years or only ten days to master, one which although censored by the foolish because it is in places opposed to the order of the rules of caste and stages of life (*varṇāśramadharma*), is nevertheless appreciated by those of perfected wisdom (*gatānta*) and is in fact superior to it.[84]

It is not impossible that the reference in the *Mahābhārata* to the four doctrinal systems we have noted above was written at a time when the Śaivāgamas had not yet begun to be compiled and their cults had not yet developed, that is, when the major representatives of sectarian Śaivism were the Pāśupatas. It seems likely that these Pāśupatas, who considered themselves to be independent of the Vedic-Smārta tradition were, as such, the immediate precursors of Āgamic Śaivites. Consequently, the latter reserved a place for them amongst their own numerous groups and incorporated the Pāśupata into their own canonical categories.

We know very little about the oldest Pāśupata groups. According to the *Mahābhārata*, Śrīkaṇṭha, the Lord of the Elements (*bhūtapati*) and Umā's husband (*umāpati*), started the Paśupati cult.[85] Pathak has tried to establish that Śrīkaṇṭha is a historical figure,[86] his views however have been hotly contested and largely rejected. A more commonly accepted opinion is that Lakulīśa was the original founder of Pāśupata Śaivism.[87] Although scholars generally agree that Lakulīśa really existed, not everyone shares the opinion of some scholars that he lived in, or before, the second century.[88] There can be no doubt, however, that Lakulīśa must have lived before the sixth century because it is from this time onwards that images of him bearing standard iconographic features began to be produced.

Anyhow, however early Lakulīśa's date may be, it is far from certain that Pāśupata Śaivism starts with him. Indeed, it is far from certain that we can identify the Śivabhagavats mentioned by Patañjali as pre-Lākulīśa Pāśupatas, as Banerjee does.[89] Nor can we affirm without doubt that they are amongst the ascetic sects mentioned in Pali and other early sources.[90] Even so there are good reasons to distinguish between the Lākulīśa Pāśupata and other Pāśupata sects that have nothing to do with Lakulīśa. We have seen that the Pāśupatas and Lākulīśas are invariably distinguished in the Purāṇas, Āgamas and other sources. Lakulīśa had four disciples: Kuśika, Gārgya, Kuruṣa and Maitreya.[91] Each of these founded subsects. The ascetics of these orders considered themselves to be Lākulīśa Pāśupatas belonging to one or other of four lineages (*gotra*). They were not just Pāśupatas. We know also that other Pāśupata groups did exist, such as the Vaimalas and Kārukas. Although it is not possible to say whether they predate Lakulīśa, there are concrete indications that he did have predecessors. Thus a number of Purāṇas declare that Śiva had twenty-eight incarnations, which they list and portray as a lineage of Yoga masters ending with Lakulīśa. Dvivedi, who has collated these lists, believes that this tradition records, however imperfectly, the names of early Pāśupatas.[92]

Although we have no means at present of assessing how much, if any, historical basis there is for these names, there appears at least to have been a tradition which admits the existence of Pāśupata teachers prior to Lakulīśa. But, whether Lakulīśa was the first Pāśupata or not, he is without doubt an important founder figure whose contribution was so substantial that he came to represent Pāśupata Śaivism as a whole. Presumably this is why Abhinavagupta divides Śaivism (*Śaivaśāsana*) into two main currents (*pravāha*): one associated with Lakulīśa and the other with Śrīkaṇṭha, whose teachings (*śāsana*) consist of the five major streams (*srotas*) of the Śaivāgamas we shall discuss later.[93]

Unfortunately, no original Pāśupata scriptures have been recovered. Moreover we are hard pressed to find evidence to prove that such scriptures ever existed. We do come across expressions like *"Pāśupataśāstra"* and even hear of its fabulous size[94] but we have managed to trace only one concrete reference to a possible Pāśupata scripture. This occurs in Bhaṭṭotpala's tenth century commentary on Varāhamihira's *Bṛhatsaṃhitā*[95] where he says that the Pāśupatas worship Śiva according to the procedures enjoined by the *Vātulatantra*. All of the few works so far recovered belong to Lakulīśa's school. The oldest is the *Pāśupatasūtra* attributed to Lakulīśa himself. We also have a commentary called *"pañcārthabhāṣya"* by Kauṇḍinya, whose date, although far from certain, is generally thought to be sometime between the fourth and sixth centuries A.D.[96] Although we cannot be sure that the *sūtras* are, as the commentator says, by Lakulīśa himself, they do, in fact, appear to be quite old and bear many archaic traits. These are apparent particularly in the figure of Paśupati himself who is identified with Prajāpati and associated with the Vedic Rudra with whom he shares a number of Vedic names such as Aghora, Ghora, Śarva and Sarva. Apart from the *Pāśupatasūtra* the only other extant Lākulīśa Pāśupata work is the *Gaṇakārikā* by Haradattācārya and a tenth century commentary, the *Ratnaṭīkā*, by Bhasarvajña. These works, along with summaries of Lākulīśa Pāśupata philosophy found in medieval treatises on the philosophical systems, are the sole sources we possess.[97] It is possible that Lakulīśa's disciple, Musalendra, wrote a work called the *Hṛdayapramāṇa*[98] and there are numerous quotes from lost works both in the *Ratnaṭīkā* and Kauṇḍinya. Unfortunately, the sources are never named, and it is hard to say whether they are original Āgamas or not, or if they are specifically Pāśupata scripture or secondary works.

The spiritual discipline these works prescribe does not involve complex rites or require extensive intellectual development. It is, however, largely intended for the renunciate, rather than the householder. Thus lay worshipers have only to recite obeisance to Śiva (*namaḥ śivāya*) with folded hands while the celibate ascetic is given much more to do. He can be either fully naked or wear a single strip of cloth to cover his privities. He should practice austerities, such as the penance of sitting amidst five fires. After his morning ablutions he smears his body with ashes and does the same at noon and in the evening. After his bath he goes to the temple where he sits to meditate on Śiva. As he does so, he should sometimes laugh loudly, sing and dance. Before leaving and saluting the deity, he repeats the seed-syllable *"huḍuk"* three times and recites his mantra. When he bathes alone, he should pay homage to the lineage of Pāśupata teachers (*tīrtheśa*) headed by Lakulīśa. After his bath he should select a clean place for meditation and stay there to practice it through the day. In the evening the site is again cleared and purified with ashes. When he feels sleepy, he again spreads ashes on the ground and lies down to sleep.

When the Pāśupata yogi has developed a degree of spiritual insight (*jñāna*), his teacher permits him to practice antinomian behaviour.[99] At this stage of his spiritual discipline, he should act like a madman ignorant of right and wrong. Pretending to sleep, he snores loudly or rolls on the ground and talks nonsense. When he sees a beautiful woman, he should make lewd gestures at her. In this way he courts abuse in the belief that his disgrace will gain for him the double benefit of purifying him of his sins and gaining the merit of those who abuse him.

The Lākulīśa ascetic is, however, basically a disciplined, continent man. Moreover, although he is told to behave in a manner contrary to accepted norms, his conduct falls short of the total abandon extremist Tantrics allow themselves. He can laugh and sing in the temple but he is not allowed to offer Śiva anything else if it is not prescribed.[100] In fact, his behaviour is regulated by injunctions (*vidhi*) down to the smallest detail. For instance, he must offer garlands to Śiva, but they must not be made of fresh unconsecrated flowers.[101] He cannot simply abandon himself on his own initiative: he must wait for his teacher's permission to do so. His lewd gestures are just play-acting: in reality he must avoid woman's company whenever he can. He is specifically prohibited from even talking to women[102] and must be strictly celibate.[103] Women are a particularly dangerous source of temptation; they are not embodiments of the goddess and as such potential Tantric consorts through whom communion with Śiva could be attained. As Kauṇḍinya says:

> She whom people regard as woman is [in reality deadly] poison [which consumes a man's life like] fire [and is as dangerous as] a sword or an arrow. She is horror and illusion (*māyā*) incarnate. Fools, not the wise, revel in the body full of impurities and worms. Foul smelling and unclean, it is the ephemeral abode of urine and excreta. It is the sight of a woman, not wine, that maddens a man. Shun therefore woman whose

> mere sight, even at a distance, deludes. The world is bitten by the snake whose form is woman's sexual organ who, with mouth cast downwards, moves between [her] thighs, beyond all control [even that] of the scriptures.[104]

If the Lākulīśa Pāśupata works that have been preserved reflect Lakulīśa's own views, it appears that his path is a peculiar combination of the orthodox and extreme heterodox. As outlined in these works, it is, despite the antinomian elements, as closely linked to the orthodox 'Vedic' patterns as it is to the Tantric. If Lakulīśa was, in fact, a reformer who revived Pāśupata Śaivism, as some scholars believe, possibly this reform consisted in a restatement of Pāśupata ideals and the rationale behind the Pāśupata's behaviour in such a way as to make them more acceptable to the Brahmanical literate class. Alternatively, it is possible that Lakulīśa brought about a revival of an older, essentially Vedic, form of Śaivism that evolved out of the proto-sectarian ascetical orders of the Vedic world. These groups were sustained in their ideals by the peculiar figure of Rudra, a Vedic god whose appearance and character could serve as the focus of an alternative set of values sustained by the Brahmanical classes. Be that as it may, Lakulīśa himself is consistently portrayed, both in the Purāṇas and the Pāśupata texts, as a brahmin. The *Kāravaṇamāhātmya* says that he was an incarnation of Śiva born to a Brahmin couple in Ulkāpurī and later went to Kāyāvarohaṇa where he began to preach.[105] Kauṇḍinya says that he was an incarnation of Śiva who, taking the form of a brahmin, was born in Kāyāvataraṇa.[106] This place, also called Kāyāvarohaṇa, Kārohaṇa or Kāyārohaṇa, is identified with the village of Kārvān situated some twenty miles north of Baroda. Ulkāpurī is modern Avākhal in the same region.[107] According to the *Śivapurāṇa*, Śiva entered and revived the corpse of a brahmin lying in a cremation ground near Kāyāvarohaṇa. He did so for the benefit of all brahmins.[108] According to the *Kūrmapurāṇa* he, "the Lord of the gods," resides in the sanctuary of Kāyāvatāra.[109] He was the last of Śiva's incarnations, all of whom come into the world for the welfare of brahmins and to establish the Veda.[110] Kauṇḍinya repeatedly stresses that the followers of Lakulīśa must be brahmins. This is because Lakulīśa was himself a brahmin and taught his religion to brahmin pupils.[111] The *Pāśupatasūtra* itself declares that: "no brahmin returns to the world." Kauṇḍinya comments: "no brahmin, be he a householder, student, hermit or ascetic who reads one, two, three or four Vedas or even (merely recites) the *Gāyatrī* and who approaches close to Rudra by his conduct, returns to the cycle of rebirth."[112]

The *Pāśupatasūtra* prescribes that the aspirant should not even talk to a member of the lowest (*śudra*) caste.[113] If he happens inadvertently to do so or—worse—to touch one, he must purify himself by practicing breath control and repeating a Vedic mantra (here called Gāyatrī) addressed to Rudra.[114] In this way, his mind is freed from impurity (*kaluṣa*). Several teachers of the Kālāmukhas who, as we have noted, were Lākulīśa Pāśupatas, are referred to in inscriptions as brahmins.[115] Their monastic centres were places where these celibate ascetics could study every branch of orthodox Sanskrit learning, including the Mīmāṃsā and the Vedas with their auxiliaries.[116] The Pāśupatas of the *Pāśupatasūtra* were also close to their Vedic roots. The importance given to the recitation of "OṂ" (a practice normally forbidden to the lower castes) and the recitation of Vedic Mantras in honour of Paśupati clearly indicates the Brahminical character of this cult.[117]

However, not all Pāśupatas had to be brahmins. Dvivedi observes that some of the names of Pāśupata teachers listed as preceding Lakulīśa correspond to a list of members of the *Kṣatriya* aristocracy found in the *Mahābhārata*.[118] The *Vāmanapurāṇa* confirms that *Kṣatriyas* also followed the Pāśupata's path.[119] Possibly these references are evidence that Lakulīśa did, in fact, introduce changes in this respect into the earlier Pāśupata religion. Perhaps also, we can understand the specific injunction in the *Sūtras* not to look at urine and excreta as a reaction against the more extreme practices of the earlier Pāśupatas that required the handling and even consumption of these and other obnoxious substances.[120]

In fact, we must clearly distinguish between two basic types of Pāśupata traditions, namely, one that bases itself on the Vedic tradition (or better its classical *smārta* form as it appears in the Purāṇas, etc.) and one that, in the eyes of the former, runs counter to that tradition. We find extensive references to the former everywhere in the Purāṇas, particularly in the *Kūrma*, which can be said to be the most important Purāṇa for *smārta* Pāśupatas. In this Purāṇa the consort of the Great Goddess is Paśupati[121] and she enjoins that men should follow the ordinances of the Vedas and *smṛtis* concerning caste and the stages of life (*varṇāśrama*).[122] She loves those who do so.[123] Paśupati is invoked by reciting the *Śatarudrīya* section of the *Yajurveda* and other Vedic hymns along with the *Atharvaśirasupaniṣad*.[124] Indeed, Śiva is the embodiment of the Veda and can be known solely through the Veda, while the Veda's sole object of knowledge is Śiva.[125] Pṛthu's grandson, King Suśīla, went to the Himalayas and there praised Śiva with Vedic hymns. There appeared before him the sage Śvetāśvatara, a great Pāśupata. He imparted to the king a Vedic mantra and thus initiated him into the Pāśupata path. The king thus entered the last stage of life (*sannyāsa*) and, covering himself with ashes, dedicated himself to the study of the Vedas.[126] Everywhere in this Purāṇa, Śiva extols the importance of the Pāśupata vow:

> Tranquil, with the mind under one's control, the body covered with ashes, devoted to celibacy and naked, one should observe the Pāśupata vow. In former days I created the supreme Pāśupata vow, more secret than secret, subtle and the essence of the Veda, [for man's] liberation. The sage, devoted to the practice of the Vedas, wearing nothing but a loincloth or single piece of clothing, should meditate upon Śiva, the Lord of Beasts (Paśupati).[127]

But even though Śiva enjoins the observance of the Pāśupata vow, he goes on to say that scriptures of the followers of Lakulīśa and the Pāśupatas are amongst those that he has created which run counter to the ordinances of the Veda and so should not be followed.[128] We seem to be faced with a contradiction. The Lākulīśa Pāśupata path, as outlined in the *Pāśupatasūtra* and other extant works of this school, basically falls in line with the Pāśupata path described in the *Kūrmapurāṇa.* Yet both the Pāśupatas and the Lākulīśa Pāśupatas are repeatedly censored in this Purāṇa as heretics and outside the Vedic fold (*vedabāhya*). Similarly, the *Devībhagavata* stresses that knowledge of the Veda bears fruit only by applying ashes to the body as a sign of devotion to Śiva. It warns, however, that the ashes must not be prepared in the manner described in the Tantras nor should they be accepted from the hands of a Śudra, Kāpālika or other heretics including, presumably, non-Vedic Pāśupatas.[129]

The *Śivapurāṇa* distinguishes between two types of Śaivāgama, namely, Vedic (*śrauta*) and non-Vedic (*aśrauta*). The former consists of the essential purport of the Vedas, and is that in which the supreme Pāśupata vow is explained. The latter is independent and consists of the twenty-eight Siddhāntāgamas.[130] Why then does the *Kūrma* reject some Pāśupatas and not others? Again, what should we make of Abhinava's analysis of the Śaiva teachings (*Śaivaśāsana*) into two currents—one associated with Lakulīśa and the other with Śrīkaṇṭha?[131] Does he mean that Lakulīśa's current flows through the Purāṇas and Smṛtis? Probably not, otherwise he would not distinguish between the "Śaiva teachings" and those of the Vedic tradition, which he says are its very opposite.[132] The Śaivāgamas do, in fact, frequently refer with approval to the Pāśupatas and make room for them in their world view.

Thus the *Svacchandatantra*, as Dvivedi indicates in his article,[133] has homologized the places associated with Śiva's incarnations prior to Lakulīśa with the worlds located in the metaphysical principles (*tattva*) which constitute the cosmic order. The Āgamas in general, as we have already noted, accept both the Pāśupata and Lākulīśa Pāśupata as branches of the Śaiva teachings. Moreover, Abhinava associates them particularly with the monistic Tantric traditions which have contributed to the formation of Kashmiri Śaivism and sees them as being intimately related to the Kaula and Bhairava Tantras.[134] This association is apparently confirmed by the Purāṇas which treat the Pāśupatas and followers of the Vāma and Bhairava Tantras as groups of equally heretical Śaivites. We must therefore distinguish not only between two types of Pāśupatas in general but also, more specifically, between two types of Lākulīśa Pāśupatas as well. How these Smārta and Āgamic Śaivites are related to one another is a subject of further research.

The Kāpālikas

The Kāpālikas, so-called because they vowed to carry a human skull (*kapāla*), are as well known to the common Indian as they are obscure to them. Infamous for their extreme antinomian behaviour and for their supposed practice of human sacrifice, they caught the imagination of Sanskrit poets in the past just as they continue to fascinate the Indian mind to this day. Sometimes hardly more than an object of ridicule for his superficial hedonism and peculiar beliefs and way of life, the Kāpālika is more often portrayed as a villain dedicated to the exercise of his magic powers, which he acquires through his penance, Mantras and awesome, often violent, rites. Kṛṣṇa Miśra (c. 1050-1100) creates a Kāpālika in his play, the *Prabodhacandrodaya*, who proudly proclaims the essentials of his creed as he describes his way of life:

> "My charming ornaments are made from garlands of human skulls," says the Kāpālika, "I dwell in the cremation ground and eat my food from a human skull. I view the world alternately as separate from God (*īśvara*) and one with Him, through the eyes that are made clear with the ointment of yoga. . . We (Kāpālikas) offer oblations of human flesh mixed with brains, entrails and marrow. We break our fast by drinking liquor (*surā*) from the skull of a Brahmin. At that time the god Mahābhairava should be worshipped with offerings of awe-inspiring human sacrifices from whose severed throats blood flows in currents."[135]

One of the earliest references to a Kāpālika is found in Hāla's Prakrit poem, the *Gāthāsaptaśati* (third to fifth century A.D.) in a verse in which the poet describes a young female Kāpālikā who besmears herself with ashes from the funeral pyre of her lover.[136] Varāhamihira (c. 500-575 A.D.) refers more than once to the Kāpālikas[137] thus clearly establishing their existence in the sixth century. Indeed, from this time onwards references to Kāpālika ascetics become fairly commonplace in Sanskrit literature. However, only half a dozen or so inscriptions which unambiguously refer to the Kāpālikas and their ascetic organisations have so far been recovered. This is possibly because, unlike the Kālāmukhas, Siddhāntins and other Śaiva groups, the Kāpālikas maintained a more strictly itinerant way of life and did not found durable monastic institutions of any size.

The Kāpālikas are regularly referred to as "Somasiddhāntins," implying that they had formulated their own set of beliefs on a rational basis (*siddhānta*). However, they do not appear to have had any scriptures which were peculiarly their own, nor written independent works.[138] The Kāpālikas seem to have been ascetics who took the vow to live the Kāpālika's way of life; they were a distinct sect in this sense alone. Hindu Kāpālikas were invariably Śaivites who imitated in their own way the peculiar behaviour of Śiva, their mythical exemplar. It was possible for members of differing Śaiva sects to adopt the Kāpālika's vow. Even Buddhist ascetics could take similar vows in the context of their own Tantric practice. Thus Kanhapāda (Skt. Kṛṣṇapāda) who lived in the eleventh century and is well known as one of the Bengali Siddhas of the Buddhist Tantric Sahajīya school calls himself a Kapālin. He is such, he says, because he has entered into the higher path of Yoga and is sporting in the city of his body in non-dual form.[139] His anklets and bells (*ghaṇṭi*) are the two breaths which represent the opposites. His earrings (*kuṇḍala*) are the sun and moon. The ashes he smears on his body are the ashes of passion, aversion and error. His pearl necklace is the highest liberation.[140] These are the same insignia that distinguish the Śaivite Kāpālika as well, namely, the necklace (*kuṇṭhikā*), neck ornament (*rucaka*), earrings (*kuṇḍala*), crest jewel (*śikhāmaṇi*), ashes (*bhasma*) and sacred thread (*yajñopavīta*).[141] Most important of all is the skull the Kāpālika carries, which distinguishes him from other ascetics and symbolizes his antinomian way of life.

The Aghori is the Kāpālika's modern counterpart. Committed to a spiritual discipline which aims at freeing him directly from every contrast between the opposites of prescribed and forbidden conduct, his disregard for the conventional norms of behaviour has earned him, as it did the Kāpālika, an ambiguous reputation. On the one hand, the conventions of the world do not touch him and so in India, where the subjective sense of personal freedom is considered to be a measure of spiritual development, the Aghori is a saint. At the same time, as one would expect, he is considered (especially by the higher castes) to be unclean and vulgar. Nonetheless, he is respected and even feared for the powers (*siddhis*) he acquires by the strangeness of his way of life. A modern observer who has spent time with these ascetics in Maṇikarṇikā, the main cremation ground at Benares, writes that the Aghori:

> .... may go naked or clothe himself in a shroud taken from a corpse, wear a necklace of bones around his neck and his hair in matted curls, his eyes are conventionally described as burning-red, like live coals; his whole demeanour is awesome, and in speech he is brusque, churlish and foul mouthed. ... The Aghori sleeps over a model bier (made from the remnants of a real one); smears his body with ashes from the pyres, cooks his food on wood pilfered from them and consumes it out of the human skull which is his constant companion and alms-bowl. ... The 'true' Aghori is entirely indifferent to what he consumes, drinks not only liquor but urine and eats not only meat but excrement, vomit and the putrid flesh of corpses.[142]

A *liṅga* is installed in an open shrine in the cremation ground called, significantly, Kapāleśvara—the Lord of the Skull. Kapāleśvara is worshipped here by the resident Aghori, who acts as the officiating priest for his cult. He is joined at dawn every morning by a small group of householders who are followers of Rāma Avadhūta, a well-known Aghori belonging to the Kīnārām sect, named after the Aghori who founded it in the eighteenth century in Benares. These householders call themselves Kāpālikas although, technically, they are not so.

Travelling back in time we observe that Śaiva sects in the past have also associated themselves with the Kāpālikas because they resembled them. We should stress here that this resemblance did not necessarily imply that they advocated such a shocking life style. In fact, we more often find that the Kāpālika is thought to be a man who has shaken off all worldly ties (*avadhūta*) and his antinomian behaviour is understood to be a meaningful visible expression of the liberated life (*jīvanmukti*) he leads. This is how the Kāpālika and his code of conduct are viewed in the Nātha tradition that has associated itself in the past, although somewhat peripherally, with the Kāpālikas. Our source is the *Gorakṣasiddhānta-saṃgraha*, a late medieval Sanskrit work. The anonymous author quotes from the *Śābaratantra* a list of twelve sages to whom the Kāpālika doctrine was revealed, namely: Ādinātha, Anādi, Kāla, Atikāla, Karāla, Vikarāla, Mahākāla, Kālabhairava, Baṭuka, Bhūtanātha, Vīranātha and Śrīkaṇṭha. These twelve each had a disciple who propagated the path. They were: Nāgārjuna, Jaḍabhārata, Hariścandra, Satyanātha, Bhīmanātha, Gorakṣa, Carpaṭa, Avadya, Vairāgya, Kanthādhārī, Jālandhara and Malayārjuna.[143] Several of these names appear in the Nātha lists of eighty-four Siddhas and nine Nāthas, notably that of Gorakhanātha himself, who is also associated with the *Śābaratantra*,[144] and Ādinātha, who is generally accepted by Gorakhanāthīs to be Matsyendranātha's teacher who was Gorakhanātha's preceptor.[145] Although we cannot expect to glean much of real historical value from this list, its existence indicates how easily the Kāpālikas are aligned with other Śaiva groups. It is not surprising, therefore, that the Kāpālikas were frequently confused with other Śaiva groups, such as the Kaulas whose scriptures we shall discuss in the second part of this book.[146]

The Kāpālikas worshipped Bhairava, the wrathful form of Śiva who, because he decapitated Brahmā, was forced to carry a skull as penance. According to the *Vāmanapurāṇa*,[147] it was because Śiva was a Kāpālin that Dakṣa did not invite him to the sacrifice he had prepared for the gods. In this version of the myth, the orthodox tradition represented by Dakṣa does not appear to be concerned to exclude Śiva from the pantheon as much as Bhairava—the Skull Bearer and the god of many Śaiva Āgamic cults, including those of the Kāpālikas.

The Kāpālikas who, as we have already noted, do not appear to have had scriptures of their own, looked to the *Bhairavāgamas* as their authority. Mādhava in his *Śaṅkaradigvijaya* describes a meeting between Śaṅkara and Krakaca "the foremost of Kapālin teachers." Krakaca mocks Śaṅkara for being a half-hearted Śaivite who smears his body with ashes but even so prefers to carry an 'impure' clay bowl rather than a human skull:

> "Why," he then asks, "do you not worship Kapālin? If he does not receive your worship as Bhairava with liquor (*madhu*) and the blood-smeared lotuses which are human heads, how can he be blissful when embraced by Umā, his equal?"

In this way Krakaca is said to "prattle the essence of the *Bhairavāgamas*."[148] A battle then ensues between Krakaca's Kāpālika followers and Śaṅkara's disciples. Seeing his army routed, Krakaca approaches Śaṅkara and says:

> "O devotee of evil doctrines, behold my power. Now you will reap the fruits of this action!" Closing his eyes (Krakaca) placed a skull in the palm of his hand and briefly meditated. After that master of the *Bhairavāgamas* had thus meditated, the skull was immediately filled with liquor (*surā*). After drinking half of it, he held (the remaining half) and thought of Bhairava.[149]

Bhairava then appears as Mahākapālin, the Bhairava of Universal

Destruction (*Saṃhārabhairava*). But instead of killing Śaṅkara, as Krakaca orders him to do, Śaṅkara convinces him to kill Krakaca instead.

Krakaca and his disciples are expressly said to be Kāpālikas and distinguished from the followers of the *Bhairavatantras* that Mādhava says Śaṅkara vanquished before he met Krakaca.[150] Even so, Krakaca evidently derives his power from the *Bhairavatantras* in which he is well versed. It is not surprising, therefore, that the adepts of the *Bhairavatantras* and other Tantras like them, such as the Vāma and Kaula groups, are similar to the Kāpālikas in many respects. Thus Bāṇa, the seventh century poet, describes a Bhairavācārya in his *Harṣacarita* who, as Lorenzen remarks, "performed a Tantric ritual appropriate for a Kāpālika."[151] His lip hung low "as if overweighted by the whole Śaivite canon (*Śaivasaṃhitā*) resting on the tip of his tongue."[152] He worships Mahākālabhairava, the god for whom Tantric rites are performed. The Bhairavācārya is engaged in magically subduing a *Vetāla* by offering black sesame into a fire burning in the mouth of a corpse upon which he sits in the dense darkness of a moonless night.[153] But, however striking the resemblance may be, he is not a Kāpālika.

The *Bhairavāgamas* do, in fact, outline many rituals and patterns of behaviour that can serve as the basis for the Kāpālika's practices. We have already noted the form of the initiation prescribed in the BY.[154] (See pp. 128-133 for abbreviations.) In the same Tantra (which belongs to the Bhairava group) a lengthy section is devoted to a ritual known as the "Sacrifice of the Skull" (*tūrayāga*) in which the deity is invoked and worshipped in a human skull.[155] According to Abhinavagupta, this rite can take the place of the more conventional worship of Śiva's *Liṅga*[156] which, although more extensively treated in the *Siddhāntāgamas*, is also prescribed in the *Bhairavatantras*. This rite, which involves ritual sex and the offering of wine and meat (even beef and human flesh), is clearly based on the power the skull possesses to invoke the awesome presence of Bhairava and the other gods and goddesses worshipped in it. We are reminded here of Krakaca's skull and the magical powers (*siddhis*) he possesses by virtue of his penance, that is, the vow he makes to carry a skull (*Kapālavrata*).

Although the Sacrifice of the Skull and the Kāpālika's vow are independent of each other, they belong to the same world: the culture of the cremation ground where death and decay are not just reminders of the transitoriness of life but awesome sources of yogic power and, for those who seek it, liberation. Carrying the skull of a brahmin, thus imitating Bhairava's penance for having severed Brahmā's head,[157] the votary of the Vow of the Skull gains the god's cosmic power. This vow is one of a number, including that of the Pāśupata, that the initiates of the

Bhairavāgamas can undertake.[158] Even so, the Āgamas distinguish between the Kāpālikas, as Votaries of the Skull (*Kapālavratin*), and other Śaivite yogis, ranking them separately in a group of their own along with the Pāśupatas. This group is called the Higher Path (*atimārga*).[159]

According to the *Svacchandatantra*, the Higher Path is so called because it is beyond all intellectual notions and the knowledge of it transcends the world. The worldly are the fettered who travel the path of creation and destruction, whereas the ones who adhere to the Vow of the Skull and the Pāśupatas are established on the Higher Path beyond it and so are no longer subject to further rebirth.[160] Another reason why this group is called the "Higher Path" can be understood if we examine how the Āgamas in general, and the Siddhānta in particular, conceive of the relationship between themselves and other technical and sacred literature (*śāstra*). According to the *Kāmikāgama*,[161] all existing *śāstras* are divided into five groups which, although ultimately uttered by one of Sadāśiva's five faces, are created through the mediation of a *Karaṇeśvara* who is one of five deities collectively called the Five Brahmās (*pañcabrahma*). See Table 2.

Table 2. The Treatises and Scriptures Spoken by Sadāśiva's Faces.

Direction	*Face*	*Karaṇeśvara*	*Śāstra*
West	Sadyojāta	Brahmā	Laukika
North	Vāmadeva	Viṣṇu	Vaidika
South	Aghora	Rudra	Ādhyātmika
East	Tatpuruṣa	Īśvara	Atimārga
Upper	Īśāna	Sadāśiva	Mantratantra

The *Laukikaśāstras* are the secular arts and sciences, including politics, medicine, dramaturgy and horticulture. The *ādhyātmikaśāstras* are the Sāṃkhya and Yoga while, according to Kṣemarāja, the knowledge taught on the Higher Path is "beyond the well-known path of the Veda, Sāṃkhya and Yoga, etc.. It refers here to the means [to liberation and the acquisition of power] explained throughout the Supreme Lord's scripture in general, namely, the many rituals, *maṇḍalas* and gestures (*mudrā*). It is not independent of the [other] four."[162] It is quite clear that what Kṣemarāja is saying here is that the Śaiva groups that belong to the Higher Path draw from the sacred texts and treatises belonging to the other categories and do not possess a corpus of scripture of their own. We are reminded here of the Pāśupata Kālāmukha teachers who are praised in

South Indian inscriptions as erudite scholars in all the major branches of Sanskrit learning and who, by their knowledge of the Supreme Soul's scripture (*paramātmāgama*), the *Lākulāgama*, contributed to the Lākulīśa Pāśupata system.[163]

Essentially, therefore, the Śaivāgamas are the *Mantratantraśāstra* manifested by Sadāśiva through Īśāna, his upper face. Insofar as each face is supposed to possess all five faces, the *Mantratantra* group is also divided into five. See Table 3.

Table 3. Divisions of the Mantratantra.

Direction	*Face*	*Class of Āgama*
West	Sadyojāta	*Bhūta*
North	Vāmadeva	*Vāma*
South	Aghora	*Bhairava*
East	Tatpuruṣa	*Gāruḍa*
Upper	Īśāna	*Siddhānta*

This system of classification is common to the *Siddhāntāgamas* as a whole[164] and appears to have originated with them. Moreover, Jayaratha tells us that all Āgamic Śaivites generally accept that the Śaiva teachings are divided into these five major currents of scripture.[165] The *Siddhāntāgamas* stick closely to this basic scheme while many major Āgamas of other types modify it in various ways and sometimes also integrate it with other systems of classification for their own purposes. A good example of how these modifications take place can be observed in the way *Trikatantras* prevalent in Kashmir present the Śaiva canon from their own perspective. Thus the *Śrīkaṇṭhīyasaṃhitā*, which Abhinava treats as his major authority in these matters, divides the scriptures into three groups belonging to Śiva, Rudra and Bhairava respectively. The first two constitute the *Siddhāntāgamas* and the third is related to the *Bhairavatantras*. This division into three groups suits the ŚKS purpose which is to establish that the three aspects of Trika are the source and essence of the scriptures. But although the currents of scripture are reduced in number, they are still said to originate from Sadāśiva's five faces which produce them by combining in various ways.[166] Consequently, Abhinava still considered the original five-fold division of the scriptures to be the most basic and fundamentally linked to the very structure of reality as a manifestation of the five powers of universal consciousness. Abhinava writes:

> The phenomenal aspect [of reality] born of consciousness shines radiantly and spontaneously through the Five Brahmās in the five individualized powers of its own nature, the forms of which are consciousness, pulsation, will, knowledge and action. (Thus) assuming the nature of scripture, it unfolds five-fold.[167]

The Siddhānta, which universally categorizes itself as the "upper current" and hence as the highest class,[168] consists of twenty-eight principal Āgamas, of which ten are *Śivāgamas* and eighteen *Rudrāgamas*. The list of these twenty-eight Āgamas is well known and recurs regularly, not only in the Āgamas of the Siddhānta but also in those belonging to other groups,[169] thereby indicating the Siddhānta canon's stability and the authority it managed to establish for itself at a relatively early date. The Siddhānta canon is, in this respect at least, reminiscent of the Purāṇic canon. Once the number of Purāṇas had been fixed at eighteen, they remained eighteen and every major Purāṇa thought of itself as one of them. The Āgamic texts were not, however, generally subject to the manifold additions, subtractions and other changes that occurred regularly in Purāṇic texts. The Āgamas simply increased in number. In the case of the Siddhānta, where the number remained fixed, addition took place by the accretion of subsidiary Āgamas (called *upāgamas*) which attached themselves to the principal Āgamas. However, other Āgamic groups—particularly the *Bhairavatantras*—continued to undergo major developments in their structure through the addition not just of Āgamas that submissively tacked themselves on to others, but of scriptures that asserted themselves as primary, root texts. Thus the way these Āgamas classified the scriptures had to keep changing in order to accommodate these additions and the altered understanding of their own identity that was entailed.

In order to understand what changes have taken place in the Śaiva canon and how they have occurred, let us see first of all what we can make out of the basic division of scripture into five currents. Below is a list of these Tantras. The *Siddhāntāgamas* are sufficiently well known to be excluded from our present discussion. Originally in the *Pratiṣṭhalakṣaṇa-sārasamuccaya*, Dvivedi has, in his *Luptāgamasaṃgraha*, reproduced this list in alphabetical order.[170] Here the original order in which these Āgamas are listed has been restored because, as we shall see, it tells us a great deal. See Table 4.

Table 4. The Tantras Listed in the Pratiṣṭhalakṣaṇasārasamuccaya.

East:	*Gāruḍatantras*	*North:*	*Vāmatantras*
1.	Haram	1.	Nayam
2.	Huṅkāram	2.	Nayottaram
3.	Bindusāram	3.	Mūkam
4.	Kalāmṛtam	4.	Mohanam
5.	Devatrāsam	5.	Mohanāmṛtam
6.	Sutrāsam	6.	Karapūjāvidhānam
7.	Śābaram	7.	Vīṇātantram
8.	Kālaśābaram	8.	Jayam
9.	Pakṣirājam	9.	Vijayam
10.	Śikhāyogam	10.	Ajitam
11.	Śikhāsāram	11.	Aparājitam
12.	Śikhāmṛtam	12.	Siddhanityodayam
13.	Pañcabhūtam	13.	Jyeṣṭham
14.	Vibhāgam	14.	Cintāmaṇimahodayam
15.	Śūlyabhedavinirṇayam	15.	Kuhakam
16.	Kālakaṣṭham	16.	Kāmadhenukadambakam
17.	Kālāṅgam	17.	Ānandam
18.	Kālakūṭam	18.	Rudram
19.	Paṭadrumam	19.	Bhadram
20.	Kambojam	20.	Kiṃkaram
21.	Kambalam	21.	Anantavijayam
22.	Kuṃkumam	22.	Bhoktam
23.	Kālakuṇḍam	23.	Daurvāsam
24.	Kaṭāhakam	24.	Bījabheda
25.	Suvarṇarekham		
26.	Sugrīvam		
27.	Totalam		
28.	Totalottaram		

West:	*Bhūtatantra*	*South:*	*Dakṣiṇatantra*
1.	Halāhalam	1.	Svacchandabhairavam
2.	Hayagrīvam	2.	Caṇḍabhairavam
3.	Karakoṭam	3.	Krodhabhairavam
4.	Kaṭaṅkakam	4.	Unmattabhairavam
5.	Karoṭam (Kavāṭam)	5.	Asitāṅgabhairavam
6.	Maṇḍamānam	6.	Rurubhairavam
7.	Kaṅkoṭam	7.	Kapālīśam
8.	Khaḍgarāvaṇam	8.	Samuccayam
9.	Caṇḍāsidhāram	9.	Ghoram

10. Huṅkāram
11. Hāhākāram
12. Śivāravam
13. Ghorāṭṭahāsam
14. Ucchiṣṭam
15. Ghurghuram
16. Duṣṭatrāsakam
17. Vimalam
18. Vikaṭam
19. Mahoṭkatam
20. Yamaghaṇṭam

10. Ghoṣaṇam
11. Ghoram
12. Niśāsañcāram
13. Durmukham
14. Bhīmāṅgam
15. Ḍāmararāvam
16. Bhīmam
17. Vetālamardanam
18. Ucchuṣmam
19. Vāmam
20. Kapālam
21. Bhairavam
22. Puṣpam
23. Advayam
24. Triśiram (Triśirobhairavam)
25. Ekapādam
26. Siddhayogeśvaram
27. Pañcāmṛtam
28. Prapañcam
29. Yoginījālaśambaram
30. Viśvavikaṇṭham
31. Jhaṅkāram
32. Tilakodyānabhairava

This list is important for several reasons. Firstly, we know that the author of the PLSS, Vairocana, was the son of the Bengali Pāla king Dharmapāla who reigned from 794 to 814 A.D..[171] Thus this list furnishes an *ante quem* for these works which can be ascertained with reasonable accuracy. Moreover, it is the only list we know of at present in which the *Dakṣiṇatantras* are related to those of the Siddhānta in the basic five-fold scheme and in which all the Āgamas are clearly enumerated. Thirdly, it appears that this was an early standard list (or one of them) and that it does present a faithful picture of these currents of scripture (*srotas*) at an early stage of their development, as the following discussion will hopefully establish.

In the *Mṛgendrāgama* we find that the Śaivāgama is divided into five major currents and eight secondary ones. Unfortunately, the reference is very concise; even so it supplies us with a number of facts. Here it is:

> The currents [are as follows]: the Upper [current consists of the Āgamas] starting with *Kāmikā.* [The Āgamas] starting with *Asitāṅga*

> belong to the South, those starting with *Saṃmohana* are in the North. To the West is the extensive [group] starting with *Trotala*. Eastern are those starting with *Caṇḍāsidhāra* of Caṇḍanātha.[172]

Here, as usual, the Upper Current is that of the *Siddhāntāgamas*. Although the *Kāmikā* normally heads the list of these Āgamas, its explicit mention is particularly relevant here because the *Mṛgendra* is closely related to it.[173] The *Dakṣiṇasrotas*—the current of the Southern Face—is characterised by the *Asitāṅgāgama* which, although admittedly not at the head of the PLSS list, does figure as a member of this group. Moreover, the *Kāmikā* considers Asitāṅga to be one of the forms of Śiva that spoke these Tantras.[174] According to the *Mṛgendra*, the *Saṃmohanatantra* heads the next group, namely, the *Vāmatantras* belonging to the North. The *Saṃmohana* probably corresponds to *Mohanam*, the fourth Tantra in the PLSS list. The *Kāmikā* confirms that there are twenty-four Tantras belonging to this group. Moreover, it considers the *Nayasūtra* to be the first of the *Vāmatantras* which tallies with *Nayatantra*, that heads PLSS's list.[175] We know from the *Brahmayāmala* that the *Saṃmohana* and *Nayottara* along with the *Śiraścheda* belong to the *Vāmatantras*.[176] This is supported by the *Jayadrathayāmala* (also known as the *Śiraścheda*) which says:[177]

> Belonging to the Current of the Left are the perfect [Āgamas including] the frightening *Śiraścheda*. The three: *Nayottara, Mahāraudra* and *Mahāsaṃmohana* have, O goddess, emerged in the Current of the Left.

A further important piece of evidence that these Āgamas belong together is furnished by a Cambodian inscription dated *Śāka* era 974 (1052 A.D.). It refers to the introduction of these Āgamas into Cambodia during the reign of Jayavarman II, who came to re-occupy the throne in Cambodia in 802 A.D. after a period of exile in Java. His priest was a brahmin called Hiraṇyadāma who, with the king's consent, revealed to Śivakaivalya, a fellow priest, the Four Faces of Tumburu, namely, the *Śiraścheda, Viṇāśikhā, Saṃmohana* and *Nayottara*.[178] The king also invited Hiraṇyadāma to perform a ceremony meant to bring about the independence of Cambodia from Java and establish himself as emperor. The ceremony was performed according to the *Viṇāśikhā*. During the ritual Hiraṇyadāma recited all four Tantras so that Śivakaivalya could write them down and learn them.

According to the *Netratantra*, Tumburu is the form of Śiva that presides over the *Vāmasrotas*[179] although, like Sadāśiva, he has five instead of four faces.[180] Even so, most other independent sources do describe him as having four faces.[181] In the NT, as in other sources, Tumburu is accompanied by four goddesses. These goddesses are commonly found together in a group in both Purāṇic and Tantric texts and need not necessarily be associated with Tumburu, although they are usually his chief companions when he is represented along with his attendants.[182] The names of these goddesses are significant for us, as they correspond (in the feminine) to four *Vāmatantras* in the PLSS list, namely, Jayā (*Jayam*), Vijayā (*Vijayam*), Ajitā (*Ajitam*) and Aparājitā (*Aparājitam*). These four Tantras appear together directly below the *Vīṇātantra* and thus could well be the *Vīṇāśikhā* mentioned in the Cambodian inscription.

A manuscript of the *Vīṇāśikhatantra* is preserved in Nepal and has been edited by Goudriaan.[183] As one would expect, Tumburu is the chief deity of this Tantra and is portrayed along with the four goddesses.[184] It is, however, surprisingly short and the rituals it describes are relatively simple. Even so, there can be no doubt that this VŚT is closely associated with the *Śiraścheda, Saṃmohana* and *Nayottara* to which the goddess refers at the beginning of the Tantra while expressing the desire to know more.[185] The *Nayottara* is mentioned as a source of basic rituals the votary of the VŚT should perform.[186] Similarly other rituals were drawn from the *Sarvatobhadra* and *Mahāsaṃmohana* Tantras.[187]

The Āgamas regularly characterise the *Vāmatantras* as being concerned with the acquisition of power: *Siddhi.*[188] According to the Cambodian inscription, Hiraṇyadāma, "an expert in the science of *siddhis*,"[189] revealed a unique *siddhi* to King Jayavarman and taught it to Śivakaivalya,[190] along with the means to acquire it. In fact, the VŚT, which Śiva proclaims bestows *siddhi*,[191] is primarily concerned with this. Even the worst sinner, one who has killed a brahmin, can attain this *siddhi* by performing the rituals of the VŚT.[192] Here *"siddhi"* does not mean success in Yoga or yogic powers, but rather the successful completion of magic rites and the powers acquired thereby. These rites are of two types, either cruel (*raudra*) or pure (*śuci*). Amongst the former are those meant to subjugate others, defeat and kill one's enemies or create discord between friends. The latter include those performed for peace and the pacification of malevolent spirits. Even when the Tantra deals with higher esoteric practices that can potentially lead to communion with Śiva,[193] it prefers to devote itself to magic and the acquisition of power. For example, according to this Tantra, when Śiva, in the form of the vital breath, moves along the path of the nerve *Piṅgalā*, his nature is fiery and bestows the powers to perform the cruel acts (*raudrakarman*). When Śiva moves along

Iḍā's track, he is nectar and gives the power to perform the pure acts (*śucikarman*). Between these two nerves lies *Suṣumnā*, which is the way of release (*mokṣamārga*).[194] The Tantra, however, almost exclusively deals with the first two paths. Anyway, the rituals and Mantras taught in the VŚT lead to both worldly success and release.[195] Once the adept has fully enjoyed all the worldly pleasures the Tantra can bestow, he ultimately reaches Śiva's abode.[196]

Other Tantras of the Vāmasrotas

A number of manuscripts of a Tantra called the *Jayadrathayāmala*, which identifies itself as the *Śiraścheda*, are preserved in Nepal. Possibly the same *Śiraścheda* to which the Cambodian inscription refers, it is a long and complex text. According to the *Jayadratha*'s colophons, it belongs to the *Bhairavasrotas*. However, it affiliates itself to a Middle Current of scriptures between those of the Right and the Left[197] while affirming that it belongs equally to both.[198] Although the JY's association with the Right Current is well established, there are numerous links that connect it to the *Vāmatantras* of the Left. One is the sage Śukra who, the JY says, received this Tantra (from Bhairava?) and transmitted it to men.[199] The VŚT affirms that one of the rituals it describes was taught by this sage, who extracted it from the *Sarvatobhadra* and *Nayottara* Tantras,[200] while according to the JY, Śukra, along with Aṅgiras, received the *Nayottara* and brought it into the world.[201] Apparently the JY's syncretistic character and complex affiliations with both the Right and Left currents made it possible for it to be linked with both as well as either of the two.

The JY probably postdates the *Nayottara* and other major Tantras of the Left. This seems likely not only because it refers to them but also because its system of classifying the Tantras displays a degree of sophistication that presupposes previous extensive developments (see below). There can be no doubt, however, that the JY precedes Abhinavagupta (c. 975-1050 A.D.) who refers to it as a major authority. Known to the Kashmiris as the *Tantrarājabhaṭṭāraka*, the JY was an important source for the ritual worship of Kālī. There can be no doubt about the identity of these works because we know that the *Mādhavakula* was an important section of the *Tantrarājabhaṭṭāraka*[202] and it is indeed a major section of the JY.

The *Ānandatantra* is a lengthy Tantra[203] known in Kashmir as the *Ānandaśāsana, Ānandādhikāraśāsana, Ānandeśvara* and *Ānandaśāstra.*

It may possibly correspond to the *Ānandam* listed as no. 17 of the *Vāmatantras* in the PLSS. Abhinava expressly states that the *Ānandatantra* teaches the "doctrine of the left" (*vāmaśāsana*).[204] It is also one of the Tantras Abhinava cites when he describes *Vāmācāra* ritual,[205] one of the characteristics of which is the offering of a drop of libation with the left hand to *mātṛcakra* in the sacrificial vessel.[206] According to the *Gamatantra*, the fourth finger and thumb are to be joined when making this offering because these two fingers represent power and the possessor of power which, as Jayantī and Tumburu, unite together.[207] Elsewhere the deity of this Tantra is referred to as *Vāma*.[208]

Of course, although the *Gamatantra* prescribes ritual procedures for those who practice *Vāmācāra*, this does not necessarily mean that it was a *Vāmatantra*. The Left-hand Practice, *Vāmācāra*, is a pattern of spiritual discipline and the Tantras of the Left a category of scripture: they need not have anything to do with each other. Even so, the *Ānandatantra*, which was probably a *Vāmatantra*, does discuss *Vāmācāra*, while the references to Jayantī and Tumburu in the *Gamatantra* may indicate that it was, at least in this ritual context, influenced by the scriptures of the Left.

The Gāruḍa and Bhūta Tantras

No *Gāruḍa* or *Bhūta* Tantras have been found; the list of these Tantras recorded in the PLSS can, however, be established to be authentic by references from several sources. The *Śrīkaṇṭhīyasaṃhitā* states that the number of *Gāruḍatantras* was traditionally said to be twenty-eight which agrees with the number in our list.[209] The *Kāmikā* confirms that the number of *Bhūtatantras* was twenty.[210] Again the passage from the *Mṛgendratantra* quoted above states that the *Gāruḍa* group in the East is headed by the *Trotalatantra*.[211] The *Totalam* and *Totalottaram* are, in fact, at one end of our list, although not at the beginning. Again, these Tantras are found listed together as a pair in a list of sixty-four Tantras found in the *Nityāṣoḍaśikārṇava*.[212]

While the *Vāmatantras* are traditionally said to be concerned with the acquisition of *siddhi*, the *Gāruḍatantras* are supposed to deal with magical remedies for snakebite and poisons, and the *Bhūtatantras* with the exorcism of ghosts and malevolent spirits.[213] Unfortunately, we have not recovered any of these Tantras; even so it is possible to get an idea of the sort of rites they described from other sources. In the case of the *Gāruḍatantras*, in particular, our scant knowledge can be supplemented by the

Garuḍapurāṇa. The *Garuḍa*, like the *Agnipurāṇa*, appears to have drawn its Tantric material from relatively early sources. It is not at all improbable that *Gāruḍatantras* were amongst them. Thus, chapter 19 of this Purāṇa deals with a system of Mantric formulas belonging to Garuḍa technically called the "*Vidyā* of the Lord of the Vital Breath" (*prāṇeśvaravidyā*), which is expressly said to have been taught by Śiva. Could this teaching have been imparted in a *Gāruḍatantra*?

In fact, the *Garuḍapurāṇa* contains many incantations and magical rites designed to counter snakebite and the effects of poison, all of which are connected with Garuḍa. Worth noting in passing is that some of these rites are Vaiṣṇava, in which case Garuḍa is represented as a form of Viṣṇu, while others are Śaiva with Garuḍa portrayed as an aspect of Śiva.[214] It is Viṣṇu who originally granted Garuḍa the power to overcome snakes and, because of his sincere devotion, took him as his vehicle.[215] Thus Garuḍa's Vaiṣṇava associations are obvious. Even so, the Śaiva Garuḍa Mantras and rites are, as a whole, more extensively treated in the *Garuḍapurāṇa* than are the Vaiṣṇava ones. Could this be because these matters were of greater concern to the Śaiva Āgamas than to the Vaiṣṇava Saṃhitās?[216]

The way in which Gāruḍa Mantras are applied is basically the same in both Śaiva and Vaiṣṇava forms. The body of the ailing person is first transformed into a cosmic body of Mantric energies by the projection of Mantras and seed-syllables onto it. The sick man must then think that he is one with Garuḍa and so be cured. Abhinavagupta declares that a man who identifies with Garuḍa is freed from the effects of poison,[217] thus confirming that these, or similar, techniques were known to Āgamic Śaivites.

Sometimes this process of identification involves long and elaborate visualizations. An interesting example is a practice Garuḍa himself is said to have taught to Kaśyapa. It is outlined in chapter 197 of the *Garuḍapurāṇa*. The adept first visualizes the five elements in the form of symbolic figures (*maṇḍala*) of various shapes and colours. They are then imagined to be located in separate parts of the body. Letters and syllables are then projected into these figures, which thus become charged with their Mantric powers. Finally, the divine beings they embody are worshipped and the adept's body is fully transformed into a microcosm in the centre of which is the Lotus of the Heart wherein resides the Self (*ātman*), the adept's authentic nature. This he must identify with Garuḍa in the following way:

> Contemplate your own nature that creates and destroys [all things], beautiful and of the form of passion, as pervading [literally 'flooding'] the entire universe and encircled with garlands of flames burning radiantly from [the abode of] Brahmā up to this world. To be successful in all

> [your] undertakings, remember [that you are] Bhairava who is Garuḍa.[218] [Contemplate yourself as Bhairava] who has ten arms and four faces. His eyes are a tawny-brown and he carries a lance. His terrible teeth are exposed in a fearful grimace. Extremely terrible, he has three eyes and bears the [crescent] moon on his head. To destroy snakes contemplate [yourself as] Garuḍa, awesome and frightening. At his feet lie the hells, the quarters are his wings, he bears on his chest the seven heavens and the universe (*brahmāṇḍa*) on his throat while his head contains all space. Garuḍa, the Lord of the World, is Śiva himself who bears Sadāśiva with [his] three powers in his topknot. In all your undertakings think of Garuḍa brilliant like the Fire of Time, his body Mantra, his face frightening, devouring, three-eyed and his form terrible, the destroyer of snakes and poison. Having performed the projection in this way, whatever one thinks becomes [easily] attainable and man becomes in truth Garuḍa. Seeing him, ghosts, spirits, *yakṣas*, snakes, *gandharvas, rākṣasas* and all the fevers are destroyed.[219]

As we can see from this example, rites designed to counter the effects of poison can also be effective against malevolent spirits. It is not surprising, therefore, if the *Gāruḍa* and *Bhūta* Tantras, which specialized in these matters, had, like the *Vāma* and *Dakṣiṇa* Tantras, much in common. This supposition is supported by the only known extant Tantra which associates itself with these two groups, namely, the *Kriyākālaguṇottara*, manuscripts of which are deposited in the National Archives in Nepal. Kṣemarāja quotes this work extensively in the course of his commentary on chapter 19 of the *Netratantra*,[220] which deals with the various types of possession by ghosts and spirits including *Piśācas, Mātṛ, Daityas, Yakṣas* and *Rākṣasas.* It is clear from the introductory verses of this work quoted in the Nepalese catalogue that this Tantra subsumes under a single category of concerns the matters treated in both the *Gāruḍa* and *Bhūta* Tantras and deals with them all equally.[221] That there was much common content in the Tantras of these two groups is further confirmed by the citations from the *Totulāgama* Kṣemarāja quotes, along with the *Kriyākālaguṇottara*, in his commentary on the *Netratantra*.[222] Although the *Totalatantra* is listed in the PLSS in the *Gāruḍa* group, these passages refer to possession (*bhūtāveśa* and *yakṣagraha*), rather than magical antidotes for poison.

The *Totala* and *Totalottara* are the only *Gāruḍatantras*, and the *Caṇḍāsidhāra* the only *Bhūtatantra*, to which we find references.[223] It seems, therefore, that most of these Tantras were lost at quite an early date. The reason for this is possibly because the matters they dealt with could be accommodated into the wider perspective of other less specialised Tantras. Thus the *Netratantra*, as we have seen, contains a long chapter dealing with possession as does the *Śrītantrasadbhāva* which Kṣemarāja quotes in his commentary on this part of the *Netratantra*.

The Dakṣiṇatantras

The Tantras that issued from Sadāśiva's Southern (*dakṣiṇa*) Face are the Tantras of the Right Current of scriptures (*dakṣiṇasrotas*), while those that issued from the Northern (*vāma*) Face are those of the Left (*vāmasrotas*). The Tantras of the Right are called *"Bhairavatantras"*[224] because Bhairava is their supreme god and is, in most cases, the one who teaches them to the goddess, his consort. The *Siddhāntāgamas* belonging to the Upper Current and the *Bhairavatantras* of the Right became the most important of all the Āgamic groups.[225] As we have already noted, the *Gāruḍa* and *Bhūtatantras* were largely lost at a relatively early date. The *Vāmatantras* must have been valued and studied, as their presence and influence in distant Cambodia testifies. Even so their corpus did not grow as did that of the *Dakṣiṇatantras* which, on the contrary, developed extensively. The *Siddhāntāgamas* largely superseded all the other Āgamas in the South of India. In the North, in Kashmir and Nepal—the only regions about which we have sufficient source material to make relatively detailed assessments—the *Vāmatantras* were mostly ignored (in Nepal) or relegated to a secondary place (in Kashmir).

The *Bhairavatantras* neither dwindled in importance nor acquired the stability of the *Siddhāntāgamas* but kept on growing both in terms of their number and internal categories. We cannot be absolutely sure that similar extensive developments did not take place in the other currents of the Śaivāgama without examining their Tantras or discovering further notices of them in other sources; even so this possibility seems remote. The fact of the matter is that, in the regions in which the Āgamas have been preserved, we are left with two basic categories of Āgamic text. One includes the *Siddhāntāgamas* and their numerous subsidiary Āgamas (*upāgama*) which are preserved largely in South India.[226] The other, preserved in Nepal, includes the *Bhairavatantras* and numerous groups closely affiliated to them, the most important of which are the *Kaulatantras* we shall discuss in Part Two of this study. Let us see now how these developments are reflected in the Āgamic accounts of the Śaiva canon.

Before the ninth century, the division into five currents of scripture gave way to a new basic three-fold division into Left, Right and Siddhānta.[227] This scheme is found in the *Netratantra*, which presents the mantra of Śiva, the Conqueror of Death (*Mṛtyuñjaya*), as one by which the gods of each Current (*srotas*) can be worshipped and so finds occasion to deal briefly with these divisions.[228] Here the presiding deity of the Left is Tumburu; of the Right, Bhairava; and of the Siddhānta,[229] Sadāśiva. They are presented as aspects of Śiva, the Lord of Ambrosia (*Amṛteśa*), in chapters 9, 10 and 11 respectively. A similar division into three currents is found in the *Brahmayāmala*. Although it is not the first Tantra to make use of this system of classification,[230] it is not as well defined here as it is in the NT, indicating that it probably precedes it. According to the BY, each of these three currents is presided over by one of the three powers (*śaktitraya*) that together pervade the "three worlds."[231] The Right Current is considered pure (*śuddha*), the Left mixed (*miśra*), while the Middle one is said to be affected by every form of impurity.[232] The Middle Current is like rice in its husk, the Left Current is like rice when the husk has been removed, while the Right Current is like rice when it has been washed and made ready for cooking. These three together constitute the Stream of Knowledge (*jñānaugha*).[233] The Right Current is then expressly identified with Bhairava, while the *Vāmatantras* are said to belong to the Left Current and the *Siddhāntāgamas* to the Middle. The latter are of two types, namely, *Śivāgamas* and *Rudrāgamas*, both of which are said to originate from the Upper Face (*ūrdhvavaktra*) just as they do according to the Siddhānta. The BY identifies a category of scripture belonging to the Right Current which it calls "the division into eight times eight" (*aṣṭāṣṭaka-vibhāga*), also known as the *"Eight times Eight Bhairavatantras"* (*bhairavāṣṭāṣṭaka*). Moreover, there is a fourth, the Lower Current (*adhaḥ srotas*) to which belong the Tantras that deal with the worship of *Nāgas* and Narasiṃha as well as those of the Pāñcarātra together with the *Gāruḍa* and *Bhūta* Tantras and the Tantras dealing with alchemy (*rasāyana*). In this way the BY eliminates the Eastern and Western currents of scripture to which the *Gāruḍa* and *Bhūta* Tantras belong. They thus lose much of their identity, barely surviving in the Lower Current to which are relegated odd classes of scripture that cannot be accommodated elsewhere.

The account of these divisions in the BY tells us a great deal about the development of the Śaivāgama, particularly if we compare it with that of the *Śrīkaṇṭhīyasaṃhitā* and our original list of Tantras belonging to the four currents. The ŚKS's system of classification basically agrees with that of the BY, although there are important differences also. Thus, the ŚKS also divides the scriptures into three groups but these are said to be the ten *Śiva*, eighteen *Rudra* and sixty-four *Bhairava* Āgamas. This division into three allows the ŚKS to establish that these groups correspond to three levels of doctrine, namely, dualism (*bheda*), unity-in-diversity (*bhedābheda*) and monism (*abheda*),[234] which are represented as the three powers of universal consciousness constituting Trika and worshipped as the three goddesses: Aparā, Parāparā and Parā.[235] In this way the *Vāmatantras* have been eliminated as a major current of scripture.[236] We notice, however, that some of these Tantras are found amongst the sixty-four *Bhairavatantras*, particularly in a group of eight called *Śikhabheda*.[237]

It appears that the ŚKS's categories are more compact units than those of the BY, possibly because the ŚKS postdates the BY. Moreover, the ŚKS lists the sixty-four *Bhairavatantras* in full whereas the BY does no more than barely refer to their existence collectively as a group. Again, according to the BY the sixty-four *Bhairavatantras* are just a part of the *Vidyāpīṭha*, which is itself only a part of the Right Current of scripture. The ŚKS removes the Siddhānta from the older division into five currents and relegates the remaining four currents to a secondary level equivalent, broadly speaking, to the BY's Lower Current. In the process, the sixty-four *Bhairavatantras* have become an isolated group which assumes a new and particularly important status.

The sixty-four *Bhairavatantras* are also treated as an important group in the JY's system of classification (see appendix C), where it assumes such a markedly independent character that it is not attached to any particular current of scripture. Thus, although described in detail, it is not fully integrated into the JY's system of classification, but appears there as an addition or an afterthought. The names of the eight groups correspond exactly in the JY and the ŚKS, and they are enumerated in the same order. However, in the ŚKS there is a discrepancy between the order of these groups when stated in brief, at the beginning of its detailed exposition of their members, and the order in which they are listed when the Tantras of each group are named individually. As the order of enumeration tallies with that in the JY in the first instance, there can be no doubt that the order in which these groups are presented has been altered when the ŚKS deals with them in detail. Moreover this fact proves that this is a well-established and standardized system of classification. Finally, a detailed comparison of these lists (see below p. 121-3) reveals that more than half of the names of these Tantras correspond. It is quite clear, therefore, that this group came to be considered a fully formed corpus in its own right with its own subdivisions which was independent of the original classification into currents of scripture. Even so, it remained closely related to it as a whole and directly connected to the current of the Right in which it originated and developed.

In order to understand a little better how the sixty-four *Bhairavatantras* are related to the original thirty-two *Dakṣiṇatantras*, we will now compare some lists of these Tantras. What interests us here particularly are the first eight *Bhairavatantras* of the Right Current. According to the ŚKS each group of eight is associated with eight Bhairavas. These eight Bhairavas occur again in almost the same order as the names of the Tantras of the first group of eight, namely, the *Bhairavāṣṭaka.* The Tantras belonging to this group are listed below along with another group of eight *Bhairavatantras* found in the BY and the first eight Tantras of the Right as recorded in the PLSS. See Table 5.

Table 5. The Bhairavāṣṭaka.

PLSS	Bhairavāṣṭaka (ŚKS)	Bhairavāṣṭaka (JY)	Eight Bhairava Tantras (BY)
1. *Svacchandabhairava*	*Svacchanda*	*Svacchanda*	*Svacchanda*
2. *Caṇḍa*	*Bhairava*	*Caṇḍa*	*Krodha*
3. *Krodha*	*Caṇḍa*	*Krodha*	*Unmatta*
4. *Unmatta*	*Krodha*	*Unmatta*	*Ugra*
5. *Asitāṅga*	*Unmatta*	*Asita*	*Kāpālī*
6. *Ruru*	*Asitāṅga*	*Ruru*	*Jhaṅkāra*
7. *Kapālīśa*	*Mahocchuṣma*	*Jhaṅkāra*	*Śekhara*
8. *Samuccayam*	*Kapālīśa*	*Kapālīśa*	*Vijaya*

Listed below are the names of the eight groups of the sixty-four *Bhairavatantras* according to the ŚKS (see Table 6). In the first column (A1) are listed the names of each group of eight Tantras in the order in which they are enumerated in the ŚKS prior to their detailed exposition. Their corresponding Bhairavas are listed in the second column (B1). In the third column (A2) these same groups are listed in the order in which they appear when the Tantras of each group are named individually in the ŚKS. Their corresponding Bhairavas make up the fourth column (B2).

Table 6. The Eight Groups of Bhairavatantras.

A1 *Original Order of the Groups Enumerated in the ŚKS*	B1 *Bhairava*	A2 *Order of Detailed Presentation*	B2 *Bhairava*
1. Bhairava	Svacchanda	Svacchandarūpa	Bahurūpa
2. Yāmala	Bhairava	Yāmala	———
3. Mata	Caṇḍa	Mata	Caṇḍa

4. Maṅgala	Krodha	Maṅgala	Krodha
5. Cakra	Unmatta	Cakra	Asitāṅga
6. Śikhā	Asitāṅga	Bahurūpa	Ruru
7. Bahurūpa	Mahocchuṣma	Vāgīśa	Kapālīśa
8. Vāgīśa	Kapālīśa	Śikhā	Unmatta

What we want to establish is that the eight Bhairavas who are said to preside over the eight groups of Tantras are in fact the eight Tantras that belong to the first of these groups, namely, the *Bhairavāṣṭaka.* Once we have done this, we can go on to compare this group with the eight Tantras that head the list of *Dakṣiṇatantras* in the PLSS. First of all, we can assume that the order of these groups is as we have it in column A1. This is a reasonable assumption insofar as this order coincides exactly with the one we find in the JY. Now if we compare these lists, we find that entries 3) A1+B1 and 3) A2+B2 as well as 4) A1+B1 and 4) A2+B2 correspond exactly. To 8) A1+B1 corresponds 7) A2+B2. It is clear that *Kapālīśa* has been displaced from his position as no. 8. Again, the empty space created by the absence of a Bhairava for the *Yāmala* group[238] seems to have moved *Caṇḍa* and *Unmatta* of list B1 down one place. If this is so, the order of the first five *Bhairavatantras* in the *Bhairavāṣṭaka* of the ŚKS and JY corresponds exactly to those of the *Dakṣiṇasrotas* according to the PLSS. Again 6) and 7) B2 are *Ruru* and *Kapālīśa* who follow one another as no. 6 and 7 in the list of the *Dakṣiṇatantras.* The original order given in the ŚKS (column B1) places *Kapālīśa* in the eighth place with *Mahocchuṣma* in the seventh. It seems, however, that the seventh and eighth were originally *Ruru* and *Kapālīśa* respectively because their corresponding divisions, *Bahurūpa* and *Vāgīśa*, are the seventh and eighth in list A1. If this is so, then *Mahocchuṣma* is dislodged from its position as no. 7 in column B1 and moved up to the place of no. 6. In this way this Tantra preserves its place next to *Asitāṅga.* The resultant order then is: *Svacchanda, Caṇḍa, Krodha, Unmatta, Asitāṅga, Mahocchuṣma, Ruru* and *Kapālīśa.* If this order is correct, then all that needs to be done to the list of *Dakṣiṇatantras* is to eliminate *Samuccayam*—which is not the name of a Bhairava—and *Mahocchuṣma* can then be accommodated in the gap left in position 6. It is clear, therefore, that the *Bhairavāṣṭaka* and the first eight Tantras of the *Dakṣiṇasrotas* were originally the same. In other words, what came to be known as the *Bhairavāṣṭaka* was a standard group in the *Bhairavatantras* of the *Dakṣiṇasrotas* which, possibly because it headed the list of these Tantras, came to be considered as the basis of the sixty-four *Bhairavatantras.* The *Kāmikāgama* says: "The *Bhairavatantra* originated two-fold from the Southern Mouth."[239]

Can it be that the two types mentioned here were the first eight *Bhairavatantras* as one group and the remaining *Dakṣiṇatantras* as the other? That the *Bhairavāṣṭaka* existed as a group in its own right is confirmed by the *Nityāṣoḍaśikārṇava* which refers to it as constituting eight of the sixty-four Tantras that it enumerates (see below). The list of eight *Bhairavatantras* in the BY is further proof that this is so. Thus, if we identify *Ugra* with *Caṇḍa* and restore him to his place as no. 2 in the list, then the first four correspond exactly, while of the three not found in the *Bhairavāṣṭaka* only one is not found in the list of Tantras belonging to the *Dakṣiṇasrotas*.[240] Finally, it is worth noting that, apart from these eight, not a single Tantra in the ŚKS's list corresponds to any of the *Dakṣiṇatantras* noted in the PLSS. The reason for this seems to be that the first eight Tantras of the *Dakṣiṇasrotas* have been extracted from it to serve as the basic model for the *aṣṭāṣṭakabheda*, which although originally just a part of the *Dakṣiṇasrotas* assumed an independent status in a different sphere from the original *Dakṣiṇasrotas*. This appears to be clearly the case when we consider that the ŚKS retains the older classification as subsidiary to its own Trika-based exegesis of the Śaivāgamic corpus in which the *Dakṣiṇasrotas* now figures as consisting of twenty-four Tantras and not thirty-two. Is this not because the *Bhairavāṣṭaka* has been removed from it?[241]

The *Bhairavāṣṭaka* is not the only group which has acquired an identity of its own. Another important group is that of the *Yāmalas*. In the *Kāmikāgama*, the *Yāmalas* (without specifying their number) figure as a separate category which was not even specifically connected with the *Śaivāgama* although the possibility that Śaivas could practice according to them was allowed for.[242] In the BY they form a group of eight along with the eight *Bhairavatantras* and other Tantras in the *Vidyāpīṭha* to which the BY itself belongs.[243] The *Yāmalas* are represented as forming a group of their own also in the JY; so too in the NSA[244] which is probably older than the BY.[245] There can be no doubt, however, that there were a good deal more than eight,[246] and judging from the original *Yāmalas* still preserved, many were probably of considerable length. Finally, *Bahurūpa* and *Mata* are two divisions of eight found both in the ŚKS and the NSA indicating that they were also considered to be groups in their own right.

Let us consider next the sixty-four Tantras as a whole. A comparison of the lists of sixty-four Tantras found in the NSA and in the ŚKS proves to be highly instructive from many points of view, both because of their similarities as well as differences. Firstly, it is a striking fact that there are hardly two titles common to both lists. This could perhaps be justified by saying that the ŚKS lists the sixty-four *Bhairavatantras* while the NSA lists what it calls the sixty-four *Mātṛtantras*. In this case, however, the expression *"mātṛtantra"* should not be understood in a technical sense, because the Tantras listed are far from forming a uniform group. Despite the wide divergence between these two lists of Tantras, there are also striking similarities between them. Thus, four groups of eight—as groups—coincide, although the members of these groups, as far as we can tell, are not the same. Indeed it seems that the layout in the NSA is a crude form of that found in the ŚKS. It is as if a neat scheme of eight by eight is what it is tending towards, having got barely half way with its three *aṣṭaka-s* named as such and the *Mata* Tantras which, although they do in fact constitute another group of eight, are listed individually. Moreover, it seems that the ŚKS's list is more contrived, less natural than that of the NSA which does seem, on the contrary, to be just a list of important Tantras prevalent at the time and place of its compilation, although the number sixty-four is certainly a symbolic figure. Thus in the ŚKS, titles are apparently added in places merely to fill out the eight by eight scheme; for example, the whole of the *Cakrabheda* does not appear to be a genuine record of *Cakratantras.* The names recorded are: 1) *Mantra*, 2) *Varṇa*, 3) *Śakti*, 4) *Kalā*, 5) *Bindu*, 6) *Nāda*, 7) *Guhya* and 8) *Khacakra.* One could very reasonably argue that we have here not a group of Tantras, but a mystical ascent of consciousness in ordered stages (*krama*) expressed in the typical symbolic language of these texts.

It seems, therefore, that the NSA list is the older of the two, which is certainly possible, as the NSA is older than the BY.[247] That the system of classification in the BY is cruder than that of the ŚKS also suggests that the BY precedes it. Moreover, one could argue that the scheme of eight by eight Tantras rather than just sixty-four had not yet been formulated at the time of the redaction of the NSA but because the cult of Śrīvidyā continued to be sustained by a living scriptural tradition, the NSA furnished the model for the subsequent enumeration of the Tantras into sixty-four rather than eight by eight.[248]

If the NSA is indeed as old as the evidence seems to suggest, then we must assign a relatively early date to the *Paścimāmnāya* insofar as the *Kubjikāmata* figures in the NSA's list of Tantras. This means that the *Paścimāmnāya* existed at the time of the redaction of the NSA, which is in all probability the first Tantra dealing with Śrīvidyā and the sixteen Nityās.[249] This is not at all impossible because the Kaula scriptural tradition is certainly quite old—the *Siddhāntāgamas* are well aware of it (see below) as are the Tantras of other groups. The NSA itself lists three Tantras which can be said to be *Kulatantras*, namely, the *Kulasāra, Kuloḍḍīśa* and *Kulacūḍāmaṇi.*[250] It is difficult to assign dates to these texts. However, if we accept that they do succeed each other chronologically in this way, it is not improbable that the *Paścimāmnāya* originated at least two centuries before Abhinavagupta, that is, in the eighth or ninth century and is probably older. This is the most we can say at present.

Before we proceed to the next section of our exposition, a few remarks remain to be made about some other Tantras listed by the PLSS as belonging to the *Dakṣiṇasrotas.* There are three Tantras we notice here in this list that we know to be *Trikatantras*, namely, the *Triśiram* (called *"Triśirobhairava"* or *"Triśiromata"* in Kashmir), the *Niśisaṃcāra* and the *Siddhayogeśvaram* (or *Siddhayogeśvarīmata*).[251] Their presence in this list establishes that these Tantras are old members of the Śaivāgama. If we accept that these are amongst the *Dakṣiṇatantras* which existed at the time of the compilation of the *Siddhāntāgamas*, there are good grounds to argue that they are older than some of them, at least. Thus, it transpires that Tantras teaching Trika doctrine and ritual already existed at the time of the formation of the Siddhānta as a coherent group of Śaivāgamas. Moreover, it may also be argued, in broader terms, that the Siddhānta's notion of itself as a group presupposes the existence of an older classification into four divisions to which it has added itself as an upper fifth. This is a standard pattern of development of the canon as we shall have occasion to observe again when we come to deal with the *āmnāya* division of the Kulatantras and the place of the *Paścimāmnāya* in it.

The Pīṭha System of Classification

The word *"pīṭha,"* in a non-technical sense, means a stool, seat or bench and, by extension, the pedestal upon which an idol is installed. In the Tantras it commonly means a sacred place. In this present context, however, it means a "collection," or "aggregate" (*samūha*) with reference to group of scriptures[252] and so denotes a class of Āgamas. It also signifies a range of matters that, taken collectively, concern a single Tantric topic. The two usages of the word are closely related: sometimes one applies, sometimes the other and, occasionally, both. In order to understand how the *pīṭha* system of classification works, we should first distinguish these two uses of the word. In order to do so, before we attempt to outline the contents of the *pīṭhas* understood as categories of scriptures, let us see what *pīṭha* means as a Tantric topic.

There are four *pīṭhas,* namely, *Vidyā, Mantra, Mudrā* and *Maṇḍala-pīṭha.* According to the BY, Tantras that concern themselves with one or other of these topics belong to the corresponding *pīṭha.*[253] Abhinava adds that, insofar as the essential contents of the Tantras are basically the same, the ascription of a particular Tantra to one or other of the *pīṭhas* indicates the most dominant feature of its contents. In this sense, therefore, one can say that each *pīṭha* contains all the others.[254] Thus the *maṇḍalapīṭha* is a topic considered separately in its own right in the SYM,[255] and *mudrā-pīṭhādhikāra* is the name of chapter 52 of the BY, although both Tantras belong to the *Vidyāpīṭha*.[256] Similarly, in the *Tantrāloka*, Abhinava deals with the basic Mantras, Maṇḍalas and Mudrās of Trika Śaivism individually in chapters 30, 31 and 32 respectively.

In this way the *pīṭha* division can serve as a device by which a Tantra, although formally affiliated to one or other *pīṭha*, could say that it contains in itself the essential doctrines of all the other Tantras because it deals with all these matters. So we find that some Tantras, like the *Svacchanda*, claim that they consist of all four *pīṭhas* and bestow the fruits of them all.[257] We notice this same claim being made in the *Paścimatantras*. We are told that another name for the goddess Kubjikā is "Samayā" the feminine form of the word *"samaya"* which means rule. As such, she is the Rule that is observed equally in both the Tantras of the Left and Right as well as in all four *pīṭhas*.[258] As *Kuṇḍalinī*, she is the essence of the Kaula tradition and so the same 'rule' which prevails in all the *pīṭhas*.[259] We do, in fact, come across references to matter drawn from various *pīṭhas* in the *Paścima-tantras*. Thus, for example, the *Kularatnoddyota* contains Mantras described as belonging to the *Mantrapīṭha*.[260] Again, the KMT explains that the *Mudrāpīṭha* is characterized by the joining of the two hands flat together. The left hand symbolizes creation (*sṛṣṭi*) and the right, destruction (*saṃhāra*). The union of the two is the 'Kuṇḍalinī of the Self' which is the Supreme Power, the primordial energy 'Beyond Mind' (*manonmanī*). It is the Supreme Gesture (*mudrā*) that brings about universal pervasion, and he who knows it, knows the entire universe. When the hands are joined, the emissive power of consciousness (*visarga-śakti*) rises up out of the genital region and comes to reside in the foundation of this Gesture by uniting creation and destruction.[261]

The *pīṭha* classification served an important function in the formation of the Śaivāgamic canon. Affiliated through this system of classification, Tantras not otherwise related could belong together in a group which expressed the coherence of the basic principles they taught. Affiliation to a *pīṭha* was a sign of an alignment not of schools or traditions, but of practice and application of method. Thus Rūpaśiva in his commentary called *"Vidhāna"* on the *Manthānabhairavatantra* which is the root collection (*mūlasaṅgraha*) of the doctrines of the Kubjikā school, associates the antinomian behaviour prescribed in *Kulācāra* with the *Mudrāpīṭha*.[262] Parts of the Kaula ritual (*kulaprakriyā*) described by Abhinavagupta in chapter 29 of the *Tantrāloka* are ascribed to two traditions (*sampradāya*), one linked to the *Mantra* and *Mudrā pīṭhas* and the other to the *Vidyā* and *Maṇḍala pīṭhas.*[263] The rituals relating to all four *pīṭhas* are described here because, Jayaratha tells us, the scripture in this context is of these four types.[264] Presumably what Jayaratha means here is that the *pīṭha* classification includes all the Śaivāgama although it refers in a special way to that part of it which is Kaula-oriented. Accordingly, in a short tract dealing with Kaula yoga called "*Yogapīṭha,*" of which there are early manuscripts in Nepal,[265] the Lord of Kula is adored at the beginning as the consort of the goddess who is the presiding deity of the four *pīṭhas.*[266] It appears, therefore, that in some important aspects the *pīṭha* classification became the focus of a new and higher understanding that an important part of the Śaivāgama had of itself as Kaula-oriented. At the same time it allowed for the existence within this broad system of categorization for the existence of scriptures which did not expressly consider themselves to be Kaula as such and so served to link the two.

The Tantras of the Four Pīṭhas

We turn now to the second aspect of the *pīṭha* classification, namely, "*pīṭha*" understood as a category of scripture. The BY makes use of this system of classification, integrating it somewhat awkwardly with a division of the scriptures into Left, Right and Middle currents. The BY's account of the *pīṭhas* is sketchy and unsystematic—a sign that this system of classification is still at an early stage in its development. In the JY, on the other hand, the *pīṭha* classification is well worked out and the contents of each *pīṭha* clearly defined. Indeed, it has developed to such a degree that it has superseded the division into *srotas*, which is relegated to the level of a secondary, subsidiary classification. A detailed account of the JY's description of the contents of each *pīṭha* is found in appendix C, to which the reader is referred. Here we shall deal with the basic structure of these *pīṭhas* and how they are related to each other and to other systems of classification.

It appears that the *Vidyāpīṭha* was the most extensive and important of the four *pīṭhas.* Abhinava considered this *pīṭha* to be the highest, after which comes the *Mantrapīṭha* sustained by it.[267] Again, the *Mudrā* division follows the path of *Mantra*[268] and is said to be its reproduced image (*pratikṛti*),[269] while the *Maṇḍalapīṭha* is the lowest.[270] This is also the order in which they are graded in the BY. The JY deals with the *Mantrapīṭha* first although the contents of the *Vidyāpīṭha* are more extensive.

The *pīṭhas* are also generally linked together in pairs. The BY treats the *Vidyā* and *Mantra pīṭhas* together and similarly considers the *Mudrā* and *Maṇḍala pīṭha* to be a pair.[271] This agrees with Abhinava's exposition of the division of the *pīṭhas* found in the *Ānandaśāstra* which states:

> '*Pīṭha'* [is a term referring] to a class [of Tantras]. It is of two types: right and left, called *Mantra* and *Vidyā* respectively, from which are derived the two associated with *Mudrā* and *Maṇḍala*.[272]

Accordingly, we can represent the four *pīṭhas* schematically as follows. See Figure 1.

Figure 1. The Four Pīṭhas.

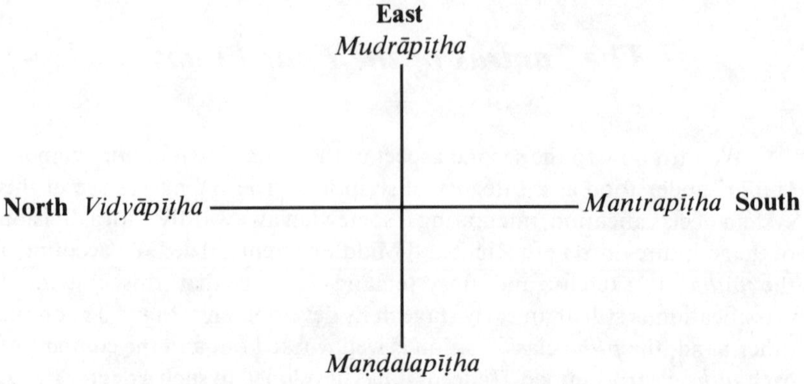

The *Mudrā* and *Maṇḍala pīṭhas* seem to have been the least well defined of the four *pīṭhas*. The BY enumerates the Tantras of the *Vidyā*— and *Mantra—pīṭhas* as belonging to the current of the Right but then simply states that the other two *pīṭhas* include all the *Mudrās* and *Maṇḍalas* of the Tantras in all the currents of scripture.[273] Similarly, the JY refers to only one root Tantra in the *Maṇḍalapīṭha* and then simply states that this *pīṭha* is part of the contents of all the *pīṭhas*. The *Mudrāpīṭha* contains only three root Tantras of which one is the *Kubjikāmata*.[274] The *Mantra* and *Vidyā pīṭhas* are thus generally considered to be the most important pair and we shall therefore limit our discussion to them.

The Mantrapīṭha

We start with the *Mantrapīṭha* because it is less extensive than the *Vidyāpīṭha* and is a more compact category. The BY lists seven Tantras belonging to this *pīṭha: Vīra, (Ugra?) Bhairava, Caṇḍabhairava, Guḍaka, Bhairavī* (?), *Mahāvīreśa* and *Bhairava.*[275] The BY appears to be uncertain of the contents of this *pīṭha.* It lists two titles that are virtually the same (i.e., *Vīra* and *Mahāvīreśa*), and two entries—*Bhairava* and *Bhairavī*—seem to be incomplete. That the *Caṇḍabhairavatantra* is listed here is significant because this Tantra usually belongs to the standard group of eight *Bhairavatantras*, namely, the *Bhairavāṣṭaka* we have already discussed. In fact, it is this group that in the JY comes to constitute the *Mantrapīṭha.* According to the *Sarvavīratantra*, four of these Tantras belong to the *Mantrapīṭha*, namely the *Svacchanda, Caṇḍa, Krodha* and *Unmatta.*[276] Kṣemarāja thinks that the *Svacchandatantra* belongs to this *pīṭha* and quotes the *Sarvavīra* as an authority to support this view.[277] The *Svacchanda* itself, incidentally, nowhere aligns itself specifically with any *pīṭha* although it knows this system of classification.[278] The JY quotes the *Sarvavīra*[279] and appears to take the lead from this Tantra in its exposition of this *pīṭha.* Thus the JY takes the four Tantras mentioned above as the main Tantras of this *pīṭha* and links them systematically with the remaining four Tantras in the group of eight *Bhairavatantras* thus:

Svacchanda	—	*Asitāṅga*
Caṇḍa	—	*Ruru*
Krodha	—	*Jhaṅkāra*
Unmatta	—	*Kapālīśa*

If we place the right-hand column below the left, we have the eight *Bhairavatantras* in the order in which the JY enumerates them. It seems, therefore, that we can trace a line of development here from the BY through the *Sarvavīra* to the JY. These Tantras must, therefore, also succeed each other chronologically.

The Vidyāpīṭha

The *Vidyāpīṭha*, as the JY presents it, virtually contains the three currents of scripture, viz., Left, Right and Middle. The JY has, however, rearranged their contents. The *Siddhāntāgamas* have been entirely excluded from the *pīṭha* classification.[280] Therefore, the Middle Current is now vacant and a new category is created to take its place, namely, the *Śaktitantras.* However, this is just a new name for old familiar Tantras amongst which are the *Siddhayogeśvarīmata*, the *Sarvavīra* and the JY itself. It is worth noting that the SYM is regularly assigned to this *pīṭha.* The BY does so and Abhinava tells us that it is this *pīṭha* which dominates in this, the root Trika Tantra, and hence also in the *Mālinīvijaya*, which presents the essentials of the former.[281] In fact, the SYM itself tells us that it belongs to the *Vidyāpīṭha.*[282]

The BY locates the *Vidyā* and *Mantra pīṭha* in the current of the Right[283] while the JY extends the *Vidyāpīṭha* to include the Tantras of the Left amongst which are the *Mahāsaṃmohana* and *Nayottara.* Although the *Vīṇāśikhā* is not amongst the major Tantras, it may be the *Śikhātantra* listed as one of the secondary Tantras associated with the *Saṃmohana.*[284] The Right Current of the *Vidyāpīṭha* consists of the *Yāmalas* amongst which the BY is considered to be the most important. The JY thus allots a major category to the *Yāmalas* and they are, as we have already had occasion to remark, treated at times as a category on their own. The Tamil poem, the *Takkayāgapparaṇī* by *Oṭṭakkūttar* written in the twelfth century, frequently refers to the "*Yāmalaśāstra.*" According to this work there are ninety-one secondary *Yāmalas* and Tantras associated with the main *Yāmalas* of which one of the most important is the BY.[285] It is indeed an extensive and interesting work which deserves to be edited and carefully studied.

The *Mantra* and *Vidyā pīṭhas* are closely related, so much so that Jayaratha says that they stand for Śiva and Śakti.[286] Similarly, the JY states that the *Mantrapīṭha* is associated with masculine words and the *Vidyāpīṭha* with feminine ones.[287] Perhaps we can understand this to mean that the Tantras in the former group are more Śiva-oriented than those belonging to the latter. The *Svacchandatantra*, which is said to belong to the *Mantrapīṭha*, is indeed markedly more 'Śaiva' than the *Siddhayogeśvarīmata* of the *Vidyāpīṭha* which is more 'Śākta'. Moreover, Abhinava's statement that the *Vidyāpīṭha* sustains and strengthens the *Mantrapīṭha*[288] is exemplified in the context of the Trika exegesis of Śaiva scripture by the secondary and yet vitally important place given to the *Svacchandatantra* which supplies, amongst other things, along with the *Mālinīvijaya*, the cosmology of the Trika.

In Kashmiri circles the *Vidyāpīṭha* was considered to be the most important of the *pīṭhas.* Abhinava quotes the *Kularatnamālātantra* to say that Trika, as a Kaula school which embodies the essence of the doctrines of the Tantras of the Left and the Right currents, is superior to them all.[289] He does this immediately after he has extolled the superiority of the *Vidyāpīṭha*, implying perhaps in this way that Trika as a whole belongs to this *pīṭha*. Thus Abhinava exalts the *Vidyāpīṭha* as the ultimate essence of the other *pīṭhas* by stating, on the authority of the *Ānandaśāstra*, that all the *pīṭhas* ultimately derive from the *Vidyāpīṭha* in such a way that, as Jayaratha puts it: "there is only one *pīṭha* which is of the nature of them all."[290]

The *Vidyāpīṭha* is also important in Nepal. Most of the Tantras preserved there, which affiliate themselves to a *pīṭha*, belong to this one. Amongst them are two texts which represent themselves as elucidating the essentials of the doctrines of this *pīṭha*. One is called *"Vidyāpīṭha"* and is quite short[291] while the other, the *Śrīvidyāpīṭhamatasāra*, claims to be 12,000 verses long.[292] The *Vidyāpīṭha* and its importance in Nepal is particularly relevant to our present study because major Tantras of the Kubjikā cult affiliate themselves to it. The *Manthānabhairavatantra*, which is amongst the most important Tantras of this school, belongs to this *pīṭha*[293] and tells us that the goddess of this tradition resides in it.[294] Certain manuscripts of the KMT bear long colophons that are very similar in form and content to those of the MBT and include a reference to the affiliation of the KMT to the *Vidyāpīṭha*. As these colophons are not uniform in all the manuscripts, it is hard to say on the basis of this evidence alone whether the KMT did, in fact, originally affiliate itself to this *pīṭha*. Although, as we have noted above, the KMT does consider its doctrines to be the essential teachings of all these *pīṭhas*,[295] it does not expressly say that it belongs to any *pīṭha*. Possibly the JY is right to assign it to the *Mudrāpīṭha*. If this is so, it appears that later tradition shifted the KMT's affiliation to the *Vidyāpīṭha*. Anyhow, many later Tantras of the Kubjikā cult most certainly do belong to this *pīṭha*. Thus the *Śrīmatottaratantra* which is considered to be a direct successor of the KMT (which is also called *Śrīmata*) is a *Vidyāpīṭhatantra*,[296] and so is a Tantra closely associated with it, namely, the *Kādibheda* of the *Gorakṣasaṃhitā*.[297]

To conclude the first part of this monograph, let us recall what K. C. Pandey wrote more than three decades ago concerning Śaivāgamic studies: "How can any correct conclusion be possible unless all of (the Āgamas) or at least a respectable number of them be carefully read?"[298] Indeed, we cannot say much about the structure, history and form of the Śaiva canon without having access to, and carefully studying, the extant material in manuscripts which, although a tiny fraction of this vast corpus of sacred literature, is vast in itself. This is a major area of Indology which has, sadly, not even gone past the stage of preliminary assessment.

Part Two

The Kaula Tantras

The Kulāgama

The *Kaulatantras* belong to such an extensive and important category of Āgamic scripture that they can be considered to constitute a corpus in their own right which we can conveniently label *"Kulāgama"*. But although, as we shall see in the following pages, the *Kulāgama* can be treated as an independent unit with its own subdivisions and internal distinctions, its link with the greater Āgamic corpus is very close and consistently maintained. Thus, the *Kaulatantras* consider themselves to be essentially Śaiva and venerate Bhairava as the highest God.[1] Moreover, many *Kaulatantras* are not only affiliated to their own Kaula groups but also have a specific place of their own in the greater Śaiva canon, usually as members of the *Bhairavasrotas*. Even so, one of the most striking features of these Tantras is their markedly Śākta character. Indeed, Kaula traditions are sometimes distinguished from one another, and their Tantras classified, according to the goddess who is at the focus of their complex Tantric system of Mantras, rituals and yogic practice.

Kaula rites are generally private and, ideally, performed in secluded places such as lonely forests, mountains, deserts, cremation grounds or sacred centres where adepts, male and female (*siddhas* and *yoginīs*), traditionally assemble. The deity worshipped is often (but not always) fearsome and adored with offerings of meat (including at times beef and human flesh) and wine as well as the male and female sexual fluids (*kuṇḍagolaka*) produced during ritual intercourse. The deity may be invoked to take possession of the worshipper so that he can gain its awesome power through which he perceives the deity's pervasive presence (*vyāpti*) in all things. Many practices such as this one are designed to be fearful (*bhayāvaha*); others, and these were particularly important for the refined Kashmiri Trika Kaula, are meant to delight the senses and mind (*sukhāvaha*). The sacrificial offerings and ritual, in this case, induce the emergence of the innate bliss of consciousness (*ānanda*). This inner, spiritual joy is cultivated as the adept's consciousness unfolds until he lays hold of his own innate nature (*svasvabhāva*), when consciousness reaches its most fully expanded state (*pūrṇavikāsa*). This process, therefore, entails a change in the modality of the adept's consciousness which takes place by the actualization of the latent inner spiritual power technically called "*Kuṇḍalinī.*" When *Kuṇḍalinī* awakens, it rises in the form of the Upward Moving Breath (*udānaprāṇa*), penetrating, as it does so, through successive levels of the cosmic order homologized to the microcosm of the adept's body. Finally, it merges, in the form of the vitality of the vital breath (*prāṇaśakti*) and Mantra (*mantravīrya*), into the universal breath (*prāṇana*) and divine resonance of consciousness in the highest state of bliss, to then permeate all the lower levels it traversed in its ascent. In this way the delight of the senses becomes a means to liberation: one who is on the Kaula path drinks wine, eats meat and performs ritual intercourse in order to make the innate bliss of his own nature manifest—not out of greed or lust.[2]

The bliss the Kaula experiences is entirely spiritual and not at all worldly. The Kaula savours the objects of the senses not just for his pleasure but to use this pleasure to make consciousness more fully manifest and in so doing unite it with its object. When *Kuṇḍalinī* rises, the fettered soul is elevated out of his state of bondage (*paśutva*) in which the experience of sensory objects deprives him of his authentic subjectivity and so becomes, like a sacrificial beast (*paśu*), a helpless victim of the forces of his own contracted consciousness. Accordingly, some Kaula traditions advocated symbolic substitutes for the meat, wine and sex, declaring that the essential point of Kaula practice is the arousal of *Kuṇḍalinī* and the expansion of consciousness. The followers of these Kaula schools were, however, condemned by others such as the Kashmiri Trika Kaulas who, possibly closer to the original spirit of Kaula doctrine, insisted that these were essential and hence irreplaceable elements of Kaula ritual.[3]

The flow of *Kuṇḍalinī* up through the lower levels, reabsorbing them as it goes into their ultimate source—the Nameless (*anāmaka*) absolute Beyond Mind (*unmanā*), and its return back down, recreating as it does so all the lower levels now experienced as one with consciousness, constitute the sequence of absorption and emanation (*saṃhāra-* and *sṛṣṭikrama*) which are the two aspects of the dynamic power of consciousness, here called Kula.[4] At the same time, as the pure consciousness which is the innate nature of all things and their universal cause, it is the source of this flow and the abode of rest where it reposes.[5] As such, it is said to be the Supreme Bliss of one's own essential nature.[6] This authentic Being is Akula—the male principle, while his cosmic outpouring (*visarga*) is Kula, his divine power—Śakti, the female principle.[7] These two are worshipped as Kuleśvarī and Kuleśvara. The union of these two principles—Kula and

Akula—is called the Supreme Kaula (*paraṃ kaulam*) which is both at rest in itself (*śānta*) as well as rising out of itself (*udita*) in the form of its cosmic manifestation. Both these, Kula and Akula, are combined in Kaula doctrine.[8] The philosophical standpoint of the *Kaulatantras* and that of their exegetes is essentially monist. Ultimate reality is *Kaula*—the fusion of opposites in which subject and object are united in the unfolding of consciousness which expands out into itself to assume the form of its universal manifestation.[9] This reality can be realized by the performance of Kaula ritual without succumbing to doubt (*śaṅkā*),[10] that is to say, in a state of consciousness free of thought-constructs (*nirvikalpa*) in which the opposites, particularly the dichotomy of pure and impure, prohibition and injunction, are transcended.

Kaula doctrine and practice is not confined exclusively to those Tantras which explicitly consider themselves to be Kaula: it is an important element of other Tantras as well—particularly those of the *Vāma* and *Dakṣiṇasrotas* with which the *Kaulatantras* are closely related. Kula doctrine originates in these two currents of scripture and so is said to flow from them and extend them at their furthest limit.[11] At the same time, it is present in all the Śaiva scriptures, pervading them as their finest and most subtle element, like the perfume in flowers, taste in water or the life in the body.[12] In fact, the expression "Kaula" can be used to refer to a typology of practice outlined in the Tantras as a whole, as well as to an identifiable part of them which is sometimes even specifically said to be such by the Tantras themselves. Thus the *Netratantra* describes the worship of Sadāśiva, Tumburu and Bhairava in three separate chapters as representative of the three *Śaivasrotas*, while the *Kulāmnāya* is treated separately in a chapter on its own.[13] This chapter, according to Kṣemarāja, deals with *Kulāmnāyadarśana*[14] which he says is the "undivided essence of the upper, left and right currents."[15] Although the NT deals with Kaula ritual separately in a category of its own, this does not mean that the Kaula tradition is a newcomer whose Tantras need to be somehow accommodated into an older, already well-defined corpus,[16] for we come across references to Kaula schools already in the *Siddhāntāgamas* as distinct groups alongside the Śaivāgama.[17] The Kaula traditions were, in a sense, set apart from other Āgamic schools due to their strictly esoteric character. As a Śaivite one could be initiated into Kaula practice, although this was to be kept as secret as was one's own Kaula identity.[18] In fact, *Kulaśāstra* seems to have been developing alongside the Tantric schools of the Śaivāgama from an early period, influencing them while being influenced by them. It made sense, therefore, in view of this close symbiosis, that Kaula rites should find a place in Tantras which did not consider themselves to be specifically Kaula. We observe this phenomenon particularly in the *Vāma* and *Bhairavatantras*, while the Siddhānta, on the contrary, is virtually free of this Kaula element. An instance of the application and integration of this important dimension of the *Vāma*, and more particularly of the *Bhairavatantras*, led to the development of Kashmiri Trika which, even though it originated in the *Dakṣiṇasrotas*, came to think of itself as Kaula.

Kula schools seem to have proliferated to an astonishing degree.[19] The number of Kulas were so many that they are referred to in juxtaposition with the Tantras of the Śaivāgama as if the Kulas were as numerous as the Tantras themselves.[20] In this context, "Kula" meant a line of transmission (*santati*) from master to disciple or a tradition (*sampradāya*)[21] that was handed down in small monastic centres (*maṭhikā*) and so was also called *"maṭhikā."*[22] The *Tantrāloka* records one of the basic patterns of classification of these Kaula traditions, namely, the *Siddhakrama* (or *Siddhasantati*) originally established by four Kaula masters, each said to have been incarnated in one of the four Ages (*yuga*). They are, in due order: Khagendranātha, Kūrmanātha, Meṣanātha and Matsyendranātha.[23] Each of these teachers had consorts while the last couple gave birth to (or initiated) twelve 'princes' of whom six were fit to impart Kaula doctrine and founded six distinct Kaula traditions.[24]

Following another system of classification, Jayaratha distinguishes between four basic types: *Mahākaula, Kaula, Akula* and *Kulākula*.[25] A more common distinction is that made between *Kula* and *Kaula*, which the *Niśisañcāra* and *Bhairavakulatantra* consider to be of ascending order of importance, with Trika as superior to both.[26] The *Paścimāmnāya* also recognizes the distinction between *Kula* and *Kaula* and thinks of itself as separate from both.[27] At the same time, it considers itself to be a Śaiva (*śāmbhava*) tradition which combines both Kula and Kaula.[28] In this tradition, both the male and female principle are worshipped, and so it is Kaula and leads to the blissful experience of both Śiva and Śakti.[29] What this means, apparently, is that the *Paścimāmnāya* is closely associated with the Śaivāgama although its roots are in the Kula tradition, emerging as it does as both Kula and Kaula.[30] Thus this tradition can say, without contradiction, that it is equally Kula as well as Kaula.[31]

This Kula / Kaula school is said to be of six kinds.[32] These six are listed in the *Kularatnoddyota* as follows: *ānanda, avali, prabhu, yaugika, atīta* and *pāda*, which correspond to the Kaula traditions established by the six princes generated from Matsyendranātha.[33] The grouping together of these traditions (*santati*) is one of the many features the *Paścimāmnāya* shares in common with the Trika (see below). The Kaula schools generally set themselves apart from one another[34] but the *Paścimāmnāya*, like the

Trika, prides itself in being higher than other Kaula schools because it includes them all within itself and does not make unnecesssary distinctions between them, although, of course, it maintains its own independent existence as a *śāstra* to be followed without resorting to others.[35]

The Mouth of the Yoginī

A characteristic feature of all Kaula traditions is that they consider themselves to be originally oral transmissions imparted in secret,[36] and the *Paścimāmnāya* is no exception.[37] The master imparted the teaching to the disciple who proved his worth, for it was felt that only in this way could the tradition be preserved and protected from the insincere. It is certainly true, as Abhinavagupta says, that there is a limit to what can be written and learned in books;[38] the master is not, however, merely a source of extra information that cannot be found in the scriptures or simply a man who knows how to decipher their codes or interpret their subtle meanings. He is above all the vehicle through which the hidden power of their teachings is transmitted. He is the one who imparts the initiation which marks his disciple's entry into a new existential condition in which he is on the path to liberation, training himself through the grace of the deity (embodied in the master) to attain the enlightened state his master reached before him and thus perpetuate the transmission of the teachings. His constant companions and supports along his journey are the Mantras he was taught when, during his initiation, he made this transition. Full of the vital, living power of consciousness, Mantras can only be effective if imparted directly, properly intoned by one who has activated their hidden energy in his own consciousness. Written Mantras are powerless;[39] they are as ineffective as lines drawn on water.[40] Equally useless is any other spiritual practice learned from the dead letter of the written word. Thus the *Paścimāmnāya* lays particular stress on the importance of the master. He is the sole essential element[41] of this, the "Tradition of the Master" (*gurvāmnāya*)[42], also known as that of the "Mouth of the Master."[43] It is here that spiritual knowledge and Mantra reside, by virtue of which he is the Lord of the *Paścimāmnāya*.[44]

In the *Paścimāmnāya*, as in all Kaula traditions in general, women are thought to have a special role to play as the transmitters of Kaula doctrine for, as the saying goes, "one should place wisdom in the mouth of a woman and take it again from her lips."[45] She is the master's Tantric consort (*dūtī*) who, like the master, instructs the disciple and so is to be respected as his equal in every way.[46] She can also be the unattached yoginī encountered by the adept (*siddha*) who, in search of yogic accomplishment, wanders on pilgrimage to the sacred places of the Kaulas where meetings take place.[47] It is from her that the wisdom of the tradition is learned and how the rituals should be performed. The *Manthānabhairava* of the *Paścimāmnāya* insists that there is no difference between the teacher and the yoginī.[48] The secret of all the scripture, the supreme essence of the oral tradition, is on the lips of the yoginī.[49] Thus she is venerated as the Supreme Power which bestows the bliss of the innate nature of all things (*sahajānanda*) and is the embodiment of Bhairava's will.[50] The yoginī is the womb from which the enlightened yogi is born and her mouth, from which issues the tradition, is the sacred matrix (*yoni*), the triangle consisting of the powers of consciousness to will, know and act.[51] As the womb (*yoni*) of creation, it is the Lower Mouth (*adhovaktra*) which is the essence of Kaula doctrine.[52] This lower face is that of the yoginī equated in the Trika with the Primary Wheel (*mukhyacakra*), namely, that of consciousness into which all the Secondary Wheels (*anucakra*) of consciousness—those of the senses, both physical and mental—dissolve away and from which they emerge.[53] It is the Circle of Bliss (*ānandacakra*) from which the energy of emission (*visargaśakti*) flows forth as *Kuṇḍalinī*, that is, as *Kaulikiśakti*, who in the *Paścimāmnāya* is represented as Kubjikā, the presiding goddess.

The 'Lower Mouth', which is the Mouth of the Yoginī, is generally considered by the Kaula tradition as a whole to be the source of Kaula doctrine. From it flows the sixth current below the five currents of the Śaivāgama. The Lower Current is hidden there, below the faces of Sadāśiva, symbolizing its esoteric character.[54] By virtue of the monism of its doctrines, it is said to rise through, and permeate, the other Śaiva traditions, leading them ultimately to the undivided bliss of consciousness which is the experience of Śiva in His highest state (*paraśiva*).[55] The *Paścimāmnāya*, like other Kaula traditions, calls this face *"Picuvaktra,"* i.e., the face of the yoginī called Picu.[56] It is the Face of the Nether Region (*pātālavaktra*) from which creation streams forth.[57] According to a system of classification outlined in the *Ṣaṭsāhasrasaṃhitā* of the *Paścimāmnāya*, the Āgamas are divided into seven groups corresponding to the seven psychic centres in the body (*cakra*). The lowest centre is the Wheel of the Foundation (*ādhāracakra*), which is that of the Nether Region, followed by the five currents of the Śaivāgama spoken by the five faces of Sadāśiva. Above these is the Wheel of the Uncreated (*ajacakra*). Schoterman explains that in the first—the highest—mouth resides Śiva as Ādideva together with the Ādiśakti, while in the seventh—the lowest—mouth resides the goddess as *Guhyaśakti:* the union of these two mouths is the goal.[58] One of the points, it seems, that is being made here is that the *Paścimāmnāya* is the highest of the Āgamic schools and contains them all by combining within itself both the highest Kaula and the highest Śaiva doctrines.

The tradition which emerges from the yoginī's mouth is called in the *Paścimāmnāya*, a *Śaivasrotas.*[59] The *Siddhāntāgamas* also consider the Kaula tradition to be represented by two of eight subsidiary currents (*anusrotas*) associated with the five principal currents of the Śaivāgama. These two are called *Yoginīkaula* and *Siddhakaula.* The *Yoginīkaula* is so called because the yoginīs heard it from Śiva's mouth and kept it within their own line of transmission. The *Siddhakaula* is similarly originally derived from Śaiva doctrine but is transmitted by *Siddhas*, the male counterparts of the yoginīs.[60] These two categories are well known in the *Kaulatantras* and are vitally connected with each other. In the *Kaulajñānanirṇaya*, Matsyendranātha figures as the founder of the *Yoginīkula* tradition which is especially associated with the fabulous land of *Kāmarūpa*,[61] although he himself seems to have belonged to the *Siddha*, or *Siddhāmṛtakaula.*[62] That *Kaulatantras* did, in fact, reflect on themselves as belonging to one or other of these two broad categories transpires from the characterization of the *Ūrmikaulatantra* as belonging to the *Siddhasantāna* transmitted through one of its branches.[63] The *Yoginīkula* is mentioned in a work quoted by Jayaratha.[64] The typifying characterization of these two classes by the KMT of the *Paścimāmnāya* is essentially the same as that found in the *Siddhāntāgama* referred to above.[65] The *Paścimāmnāya*, consistent with its characterization of Kula doctrine as the tradition which expounds the essence of the teachings of the Yoginī,[66] considered itself to be the tradition of the yoginīs (*yoginīkrama*)[67] and the secret of their oral transmission.[68] Even so, *Paścima* doctrine is considered to be that of Siddhas of the *Paścimāmnāya*[69] and is not to be revealed to those who do not belong to the *Siddhakaula* school.[70] There are places, however, where the *Yoginīkula* is made to appear to be a part of the *Paścimāmnāya.*[71] Again, Kubjikā, the presiding deity, is *Kuṇḍalinī*, which is the essential teaching of the *Yoginīkula.* Thus amongst the Kaula traditions originating from the sacred places (*pīṭhas*), the *Paścimāmnāya* presents the most vital doctrine of all the Kaula tradition[72]—including the *Yoginīkaula.* At its highest level, however, the *Paścimāmnāya* agrees with the *Yoginīkula* that the ultimate object of devotion is Śiva (here called Śambhu). He is the abode of the *Śāmbhava* state and as such the Supreme Place that, although beyond all characterization, bestows infinite qualities. It is where all practice ceases and all things appear immediately present directly before the yogi.[73]

The Āmnāya Classification

"Srotas" is the term generally used to refer to the major groupings of the scriptures of the Śaivāgamas when fitted into a pattern of directional contrasts. Similarly, the term *"āmnāya"* is used to denote distinct groups of scriptures within the *Kulāgama*, each consisting of Tantras that share a common affiliation to a single tradition and said to have originated from a fixed direction. Our best example is the *Paścimāmnāya* itself—the 'Western Tradition'. The *āmnāya* system of classification did not include all the *Kaulatantras.* We are told in the texts of the existence of many Kula *'āmnāyas'* in the sense of 'traditions' or 'schools' without this implying that they belong to any systematic classification. It is in this broad, generic sense that we occasionally come across this term in the *Siddhāntāgama.*[74] Indeed *"Kulāmnāya"* is a common way of referring to the *Kulatantras* as a whole; it is synonymous, in other words, with *"Kulaśāstra"* or *"Kula-śāsana"* in general.[75]

The *āmnāya* system of classification is nowhere discussed by Abhinavagupta. This fact seems, at first sight, to indicate that the classification of *Kulatantras* (or at least of a part of them) as groups belonging to fixed directions (on the analogy of the Siddhānta classification) was a late development. Thus Tantras such as the *Bhairavakula* or *Niśisaṃcāra* which thought of themselves as being Trika,[76] divided the Śaivāgama into three main groups: *Siddhānta, Vāma* and *Dakṣiṇa* while distinguishing these from *Kula* and *Kaula* of which Trika was considered to be the culmination. They do not refer to the *āmnāya* classification and so, presumably following their lead, neither does Abhinavagupta. Perhaps, therefore, we should not immediately assume that the *āmnāya* classification postdates Abhinavagupta. Indeed, there is positive evidence which leads one to suppose that it did not. The KMT, which is generally considered to be the oldest recovered work of the *Paścimāmnāya*[77], postdates the *Siddhayogeśvarīmata* to which it refers specifically as the Tantra where the goddess Siddhayogeśvarī is exalted.[78] Even so, as one of the sixty-four Tantras listed in the NSA, it can certainly be claimed to be prior to the ninth century (see above p. 48). Moreover, as noted above, Abhinavagupta himself refers to the KMT[79] while it specifically considers itself to be "the Path of the *Paścimāmnāya*"[80] and also knows of the *Uttara-* and *Dakṣiṇa-āmnāyas* which it respects as teaching valid doctrines.[81] It seems also, in one place at least, to refer to the *Pūrvāmnāya.*[82] Nor is it justifiable to suppose that this classification is peculiar to the Tantras of the Kubjikā school as we shall see in the following exposition of the *āmnāyas.*

The Āmnāyas of the Kaulatantras

The division into *āmnāyas* seems to have been originally into four, with each *āmnāya* symbolically set in one of the four directions. We have seen that the KMT knows only of four. The *Yogakhaṇḍa* of the MBT also refers to only four *āmnāyas* where they have a more tangible identity.[83] They are represented as corresponding to the four Ages (*yuga*), with the *Paścimāmnāya* as that which is most fit for the present *Kali* Age.[84] In the ṢaṭSS the *āmnāyas* are said in various places to be either five, six or even seven. The five-*āmnāya* division is equated with the five vital breaths in such a way that the *Paścimāmnāya* corresponds to the Pervasive Breath (*vyāna*), the experience of which is the universal pervasion of consciousness to which the teaching leads.[85] The division into five *āmnāyas* (formed by adding an upper one to the original four) is at times represented as spoken by the five faces of Sadāśiva, following the basic Siddhānta pattern. The six-fold scheme can be formed by adding a sixth upper current "beyond the upper" (*ūrdhvordhva*), although a division into six is also possible by adding a lower current, an example of which we have already noted in relation to the five-fold Siddhānta pattern with Kula as the sixth.[86] The former alternative is found in *Trikatantras* like the *Bhargaśikhā* where Trika is located above the Upper Face which is that of *Īśāna*.[87]

The four-fold division appears to be the oldest. This supposition is confirmed by the *Kulārṇavatantra* which characterizes the secret of the "secrets more secret than secret" (*rahasyātirahasya*) of its own Kaula doctrines as an upper-*āmnāya*[88] situated above the four *āmnāyas* to which the many Kaula traditions belong that are "known to many."[89] These five are here said to be spoken by Śiva. The *Saṃketapaddhati*, an early Kaula text,[90] refers to just four *āmnāyas*.[91] A four-fold division which, as in the *Saṃketapaddhati*, is equated with four metaphysical moments in the dynamics of ultimate reality, represented as aspects of the power Speech (*bhāratīśakti*) which issues from the four faces of the "beginningless Mother"—Mahāvidyā, is found in Amṛtānanda's *Saubhāgyasudhodaya* which he quotes in his commentary on the *Yoginīhṛdaya*.[92]

An account of the spirituality and history of the four *āmnāyas*, from the *Paścimāmnāya* point of view, is recorded in a short but interesting work called the *Ciñcinīmatasārasamuccaya*. All the manuscripts of this text located up to now are found in Nepal.[93] The CMSS claims that it belongs to the *Divyaugha* and is a compendium or essence of the Supreme Kaula doctrine of the Siddha tradition.[94] It also implicitly identifies itself with a type of Tantric work common in the earlier period (i.e., prior to the eleventh century), namely, a *Sāraśāstra*, by referring to a number of other Tantras of this type in its introductory section,[95] while affirming that it presents the essence (*sāra*) of the *Kubjikāmata*. The four *āmnāyas* (here variously called *veśman gṛha* or *ghara*)[96] are presented as originating from the *Paścimāmnāya* which is the "Source Tradition" (*janmāmnāya*) that possesses them all.[97] Similarly, the MBT also says of it that it clearly manifests the four *āmnāyas*, the knowledge of which gives rise to the Divine Tradition (*divyāmnāya*) and so is the highest of them.[98] The *Paścimāmnāya* is where all the sequences of inner mystical states of the other three *āmnāyas*, once abandoned and transcended, ultimately merge.[99] As such, it is equated with the pure thought-free consciousness of the *Śāmbhava* state—Śiva's inner experience of himself which pervades all the Kaula traditions. Thus, because it is also essentially Śaiva,[100] it is their ultimate goal, embracing as it does both Kula and Akula—Śakti and Śiva.[101] So, pure in all respects, and free of both virtue and vice (*dharma* and *adharma*), the *Paścimāmnāya* is above all the other *āmnāyas*.[102]

Let us see then what the CMSS has to say about the *Pūrva, Dakṣiṇa* and *Uttara āmnāya*, after which we shall present our analysis of its views, to conclude with a short account of the *Paścimāmnāya*.

The Āmnāya Classification and the Four Āmnāyas According to the Ciñcinīmatasārasamuccaya

Pūrvāmnāya

This *āmnāya* is described as the *Yoginīmatasāra* present in both Kula and Kaula. The goddess manifests here in the form of the bliss of one's own consciousness. This tradition teaches the best *Kulācāra*, namely, the manner in which Kula emerges in the womb of Kula. Thus, the goddess of this *āmnāya* is Kuleśvarī who "devours the *Kumārīkula*." This tradition transmits the consciousness which pervades the Sky of transcendental reality and through it Trika was brought into this world. Trika doctrine is here embodied as Trikā the goddess of three-fold form who is the Mistress of the Three Worlds (*Tribhuvaneśvarī*). *Trikamaṭhikā* is divided into three lines of transmission, each associated with a *Kulaguru* to which is added a fourth—*Khagendranātha*—who belongs to *Vyomārdhamaṭhikā*. See Figure 2.

Figure 2. The Transmission of Trikamaṭhikā According to the CMSS.

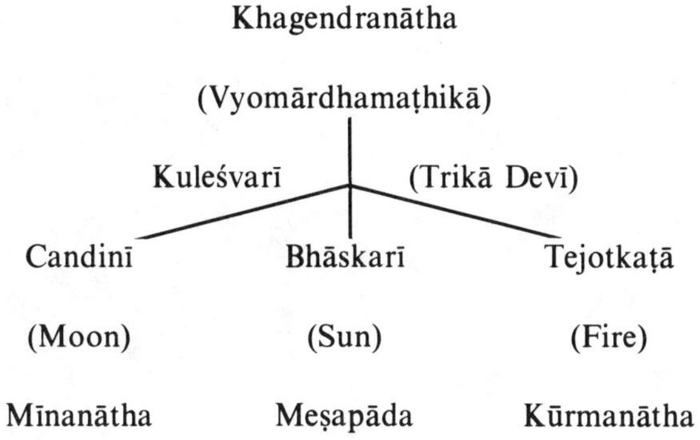

The goddess emerges from the centre of reality along with Paramānandabhairava. The whole universe is instructed by this power which is the paramount knowledge of the Divine Transmission (*divyaugha*). This *maṭhikā* is that of the line of Siddhas known as the Tradition of the Elders (*vṛddhavallī*). It is in this tradition that Siddhanātha incarnated in this world during each of the four Ages (*yuga*) as a Kaula master, as follows:

First Yuga	Khagendranātha and Vijāhutī
Disciples	Vimala, Suśobha
Second Yuga	Kūrmanātha and Maṅgalājyotī
Disciples	Ajita, Vijita
Third Yuga	Meṣanātha and Kāmāṅgā
Disciples	Khakulanātha More than sixty-four Kulas

Fourth Yuga

To this Fourth Yuga belongs the Tradition of Oṃ (*Oṃvallī*) founded by Mīnanātha, also called Piṅgalanātha, who obtained the knowledge of the *Kulaśāstra* which was thrown into the ocean by Kārttikeya. His

Prince	*Master*	*Ovallī*	*Pīṭha*	*Town*	*Direction in relation to Śrīśaila*	*Grove*	*Duration of Vows*
1. (Amara)	Siddhanātha	Bodha	Tripurottara	Ḍohāla	South	Kambilī	12 years
2. Varadeva	Vidyānanda	Prabhu	Kamada	Kuṇḍī	West	?	?
3. Citra-nātha	Kaula-siṃhamuni	Pāda	Aṭṭahāsa	Daṇḍa-ratna	North	Bilvākṣa	12 years
4. Olinātha*	Sṛṅgālamuni	Ānanda	Devīkoṭa	Bālahoma	East	Pāyavṛkṣa	7 years
5. Vṛddha-nātha	Śāṇḍilya-muni	Yoga	Dakṣiṇādi	Piṇḍa	South-West	Khairavṛkṣa	25 years
6. Guḍika-nātha	Candra-bimba	Oṃ	Kaulagiri	Gauḍikā	North-West	Nārikela-phala	8 years

* Olinātha travelled to Kāmaru, to the south of which was a place called Trikhaṇḍinī. There he performed austerities according to the instructions of Candrabimbamuni.

consort was the princess Kuṃkumā from whom were born twelve princes; six of these were: Bhadra, Amarapāda, Mahendra, Khagendra, Mahīdhara and Guṇḍikanātha. These princes were said to have no authority to teach, while the six others, listed below, did teach and were the founders of six traditions (*ovallī*). They are each associated with a *pīṭha*, a town and a forest where they practiced austerities for a varying number of years according to the instructions of a master. This data is listed schematically opposite page:

Dakṣiṇāmnāya

Kāmeśvarī descends into this *āmnāya*. She arises from the three *pīṭhas* and resides in their centre, pleasing to behold as the early morning sun and yet brilliant like a hundred million lightning flashes. She is the Passionate One, full of the passion (*Kāma*) which devours *Kumārīkula* desirous of herself. Kāmeśvarī descends into the world in the form of a young virgin (*kumārī*). She melts the Circle of Birth of her own nature by her energy, and by the intent of her own vitality fills it. She is Kulayoginī of divine form, peaceful and pure as translucent crystal. She has two arms, one face and three eyes and her waist is thin. She resides on the northern side of the Mālinī Mountain behind which is a bower (*gahvara*) called the Place of the Nightingale. It is filled with wild ganders, ducks and other birds of all sorts. Khecarī, Bhūcarī, Siddha and Śākinī reside there absorbed in meditation.

There, in the Divine Circle of the Triangle, is located the cave called the Face of the Moon in which resides the goddess, the virgin who is the flow of vitality (*śukravāhinī*). Siddhas, munis (including Krodhamuni) and ascetics practiced austerities there for thousands of years, until they became aged and emaciated. Their gaze was averted upwards, to the Inner Face until they saw the goddess Śukrā and thus attained the state of divine inebriation (*ghūrmyāvasthā*) by virtue of her divine splendour. Once the goddess had transmitted this divine knowledge to them, Kāmadeva appeared before her in divine form and 'melted' by the power of Kāmeśvarī. Thus the two became one and gave rise to the Rudra Couple. The son born of this union was Kauleśa who taught this divine knowledge.

In this *āmnāya*, Kāmeśvarī is described as the twelve-lettered *Vidyā*, surrounded by twelve goddesses. Then come *Vāgeśvarī, Tripurā, Vāgabhāva* and *Bhagamālinī* who are Kāmeśvarī's powers (*prabhava*). The *Dakṣiṇāmnāya* is where all the Nityās come from.

Uttarāmnāya

The energy which devours *Kālīkaulika* manifests in this *āmnāya*. She is Kāleśvarī and practices *Kaulācāra*, contains Kaula (*kaulagarbha*), is the arising of Kaula and is Trikaula. She resides in the Centre of Birth (*janmādhāra*). This is the Supreme Tradition (*paramāmnāya*), *Divyaugha* transmitted "from ear to ear." It is *Kālikākulakrama* and is twelve-fold taught by Krodharāja and called Actionless Knowledge (*niṣkriyājñāna*). From the centre of the sun (*sūrya*) emerges another Sun (*ravi*) which is the inner light that illumines the entire universe. It is surrounded by the rays of the Sun-goddess, Bhānavīkaulinī, also known as Kauleśvarī and Kulagahvarī. She is the rays of the Sun which shines in the centre of the sacrificial hearth of the Great Sky of the Ocean of Śiva. The Great Mantra consisting of the sixty-four Bhairava wombs (*yoni*) arises and dissolves here. In the centre of the Hearth of the Sun (*bhānavīkuṇḍa*) is the Wheel of Dissolution which is one's own true nature (*svasvabhāva*). Destroying both Being and Non-being, it is the Fire of Consciousness personified as the goddess Kulakṛṣodarī. All this is the Supreme Brahman which is one's own nature (*svasvabhāva*).

We are then told that Niṣkriyānanda "made manifest in the world this nectar of Kula spoken by the yoginī" and so revealed the *Mahākālīkrama*. The text goes on to describe its transmission to Vidyānanda. Vidyānanda practised yoga in the guise of a *Siddhaśābara*. His residence was a cremation ground where he practised yoga at night and delighted in Kaula practice in the company of *Siddhas* and *Vīras*. He worshipped the deity in a cave to the north of the *Śivapīṭha* known as Śrīśaila, wishing to attain Actionless Knowledge (*niṣkriyājñāna*). His devotion was so intense that Niṣkriyānandanātha finally transmitted to him by word of mouth the secret of the *Kālikākrama*. This is called the Knowledge of the Left (*vāmajñāna*) and the Sequence of Sixty-five Stages. It is the dawning of the Twelve-fold Kālī of Light (*Prabhākālī*) in the Sky of Consciousness which arises there in the Sequence which Annihilates Destruction (*saṃhārasaṃhārakrama*), so called because the goddess devours all things. This, the *Kālīkrama*, is the flux of Kula and yet is beyond it. It is the Divine Upper *Maṇḍala* that, fully risen, transcends the mind as the emergence of consciousness that penetrates beyond every level of consciousness and the cosmic flux which it melts away with its rays. Thus the yogi drinks the incomparable nectar of immortality in the Supreme Sky of consciousness which unfolds spontaneously within him. This is the Supreme Exuberance (*parollāsa*), the expansion (*vikāsa*) of consciousness which unfolds as *Kaulinī*, the *Kālī* of twelve aspects.

This is the expansion of the Wheel of Kālī (*Kālīcakra*), which is the Sun of Kula and its Twelve Rays. This, the Sequence of the Sun (*bhānavīkrama*), is the life of every living being and illumines the mind as it rises in the Sky beyond the Sky, intensely aflame and burning up the Three Worlds. As this tradition teaches in this way the secret of both immanent Kula and transcendent Akula, it is called *Kulākulāmnāya.* The twelve-fold goddess of this tradition is identified with the powers symbolized by the twelve vowels and is called Mālinī of the Sequence of Exertion (*udyogakramamālinī*). The yogi who is truly established in his own nature contemplates this Great Supreme (*mahākrama*), the *Kālīkrama* taught by Niṣkriyānandanātha.

The names of the Twelve Suns which dawn as aspects of the Kālī of Light (*Prabhākālī*) are said to be the secret of the *Kaulikāgama.* They are: the Kālī of Creation (*Sṛṣṭikālī*), the Kālī of Persistence (*Sthitikālī*), the Kālī of Destruction (*Saṃhārakālī*), the Kālī of Passion (*Raktakālī*), the Good Kālī (*Sukālī*), the Kālī of Control (*Yamakālī*), the Kālī of Death (*Mṛtyukālī*), the Auspicious Kālī (*Bhadrakālī*), the Kālī of the Supreme Sun (*Paramārkakālī*), the Kālī of the Great Sun (*Mahāmārtaṇḍakālī*), the Terrible Kālī (*Rudrakālī*) and the Great Kālī (*Mahākālī*). Kumārī is worshipped in the centre of the circle of these twelve powers.

Analysis

This account of the *āmnāyas* is striking both for the richness of its expression and the heights of the yogic experiences it conveys through the imposing visionary symbolism of the Kaula traditions it presents. The CMSS is later than the KMT and differs from its doctrinal position in many respects due largely to the development of *Paścima* doctrine (see below). Even so, this account is of value to the historian of Kaula Tantra and the *Paścimāmnāya* because of what it tells us about the character of these traditions and their relationship to the *Paścimāmnāya.* Particularly interesting from the latter point of view is the assignment of Trika to the *Pūrvāmnāya* because of the close relationship that the Trika has with the *Paścimāmnāya*—a point we shall deal with later when discussing how *Paścima* doctrine is built up and its historical antecedents. We shall therefore refer to it last after discussing the *Dakṣiṇa-* and *Uttara āmnāyas.*

Dakṣiṇāmnāya

It is clear from this account that the CMSS identifies the Śrīvidyā tradition with the *Dakṣiṇāmnāya.* The presiding goddess of this *āmnāya* is Kāmeśvarī who, initially alone, unites with Kāmadeva. This broadly corresponds to the union of Kāmeśvarī and *Kāmeśvara* in the centre of *Śrīcakra* locked in the sexual embrace of *Kāmakalā.* Kāmadeva is the god of the seed-syllable known as *'Kāmarāja'* in the Śrīvidyā school. Amṛtānanda, a major early exponent of Śrīvidyā doctrine, clearly links this seed-syllable with the *Dakṣiṇāmnāya* in just the same way as does the CMSS. In his *Saubhāgyasudhodaya,* he characterizes the four *āmnāyas,* along with their attendant features, as symbolic aspects of one of the most important Mantras of this school, namely, the Mantrarāja. Each *āmnāya* contributes to the construction of this Mantra by supplying one of its seed-syllables. The seed-syllable *'Kāmarāja'* belongs to the *Dakṣiṇāmnāya* and is in the form of Rudra in union with his power, Rudrāṇī. Together they form a couple (*yāmala*). This seed-syllable is also linked to the *Paścimāmnāya* as its protector.[103] The CMSS also refers to the other three seed-syllables along with Tripurā, as energies of the goddess Kāmeśvarī. In the Śrīvidyā tradition they are indeed found together in the innermost triangle of *Śrīcakra* with Tripurā in the centre and Vāgeśvarī, Vāgbhāva and Bhagamālinī in the corners around her.[104]

Nor can there be any doubt about the Kaula character of the Śrīvidyā school. The NSA describes the form of Śrīvidyā and her Mantra as rising in waves out of the infinite ocean of Kula[105] as if to express her Kaula origins. Indeed, she is expressly said to be "Kulavidyā" which is the Great Vidyā of the yoginīs.[106] Accordingly, the *Yoginīhṛdaya* enjoins that she should be worshipped only by those who practice *Kulācāra.*[107] The Goddess Tripurā is young and comely. Her eyes slightly red with wine—the perfect archetype of the Kaula female partner.[108] Tripurā is considered to be the greatest of the goddesses that preside over the phases of the cosmic cycles of time. These are the Nityās which the CMSS says originated in the *Dakṣiṇāmnāya.* As Nityā, Tripurā is Kula, the Supreme deity's sovereign power.[109]

The NSA and YHṛ, the original Tantras of this school, never refer to the *āmnāya* system of classification. They do, however, talk about their own tradition as divided into four currents which issue from four sacred centres (*mahāpīṭha*), namely, *Kāmarūpa, Jālandhara, Pūrṇagiri* and *Oḍiyāna.*[110] However, the commentators, supported by early sources, equate these with the four *āmnāyas.*[111] They also associate the four *Yuganāthas* with the *āmnāyas* in a manner reminiscent of the *Paścima* characterization of the *āmnāyas* as each belonging to one of the four Ages. This connection also brings into the Śrīvidyā tradition an essential element of all Kaula ritual, namely, the worship of the *Yuganāthas.* Thus, Śrīvidyā is said by Vidyānanda in his commentary on the NSA to be common to all the *āmnāyas*. He also says that it is particularly important in the *Dakṣiṇāmnāya*,[112] thus confirming that the allocation of Śrīvidyā to this quarter is not peculiar to the CMSS. In fact, the presence of Śrīvidyā is apparent in the *Kubjikātantras*. Thus, of Kubjikā's three forms as a child, young and old woman, her young form is appropriately identified with the young and beautiful Tripurāsundarī.[113]

Uttarāmnāya

The way in which this *āmnāya* is described in the CMSS is of interest not only to the historian of Kaula Tantra but also to the student of Kashmiri Śaivism, particularly of that part of it which modern scholars call the Krama system, otherwise known as the *Kramaśāsana, Kramadarśana* or *Kramanaya* in Kashmiri sources as well as in the original Tantras themselves.[114] The focal point of the spirituality of the *Uttarāmnāya* is here presented as the experience of the Arising of the Sequence of Kālīs (*Kālīkramodaya*).[115] The manner of their arising, as well as the order and names of the Kālīs in this account, is virtually the same as we find in the Āgamic passages quoted by Jayaratha in his commentary on Abhinava's exposition of the sequence of Kālīs (*kālīkrama*) in *Anākhyacakra*.[116] Abhinava considered this to be the central teaching of the Krama system, which he syncretizes with the *Anuttaratrikakulakrama* (generally simply called "Trika") of which his *Tantrāloka* is a comprehensive manual dealing with the liturgy of this Kaula-cum-Tantric school.[117]

Modern scholars of non-dualist Kashmiri Śaivism generally distinguish between Kula and Krama as if they were two separate schools or, to use the current expression 'systems'. In the light of the evidence both from the recently recovered Āgamic sources, as well as that afforded by the Kashmiri authors themselves and their references from the original scriptures, this distinction can be said to be clearly false. The Krama system is a Kaula tradition in every respect. The evidence is enormous in support of this view. We will only refer to a small part of it here, just enough to prove our point.

In the *Kramastotra*, the first of the twelve Kālīs is described as a wave of dense bliss which rises from the ocean of Kula[118] and then merges again in the abyss of Kula. Ultimately, the last Kālī in the series merges in Akula,[119] which is represented generically as the Supreme Abode of the Goddess.[120] In this way, Śakti as Kula merges into Śiva as Akula, having emerged out of her infinite potentiality and traversed through the entire cycle of manifestation, which is nothing but the expression of her own nature.[121] Thus the two, Kula and Akula, constituting the Supreme Kaula reality (*paramakaula*), encompass all of manifestation as an inscrutable union of immanence leading to transcendence and transcendence to immanence. This is pure Kaula doctrine.

Similarly Krama ritual, like Krama doctrine, is Kaula. That Krama ritual at times required the offering and consumption of meat and wine as well as ritual sex is well known to scholars of Kashmiri Śaivism.[122] In Abhinava's exposition of Kaula ritual in chapter 29 of the *Tantrāloka*, he refers to a number of Krama works,[123] as does his commentator Jayaratha. These include the *Kramapūjana*,[124] *Kramarahasya*,[125] *Devīpañcaśatikā*,[126] *Kālīkula*,[127] *Mādhavakula*,[128] *Śrīkulakramodaya*[129] and *Tantrarāja-bhaṭṭāraka*.[130] The *Mādhavakula*, which is a part of the *Tantrarāja-bhaṭṭāraka* that Kashmiris considered to be a major authority on Krama, refers to the type of ritual it expounds as *Kulapūjana*.[131] Abhinava refers to the *Kramapūjana*[132] as an authoritative Tantra in which the Supreme Lord explains the secret essentials of Kula ritual, namely, the worship of the *Yuganāthas* and their consorts, which is a standard necessary preliminary of all Kaula ritual. Thus Abhinava refers to a Krama text as his authority right at the beginning of his exposition of Kaula ritual. Similarly, in the CMSS the *Yuganāthas* and their consorts are worshipped in the *Pūrvāmnāya* which in the course of practice comes first, located as it is in the East.[133] Jñānanetranātha (alias Śivānanda) is venerated by Kashmiri Krama authors as the founder of the Krama tradition of which they are direct descendants.[134] He "brought down to earth" a Krama work called the *Yonigahvaratantra*[135] in which he lists the names of the *Yuganāthas* and their associates, proclaiming that they taught the secret of the Kula path (*kulamārga*).[136] It is not surprising, therefore, that Krama is also known as the *Kālīkula*[137] or *Kramakula*[138] in the Āgamic sources to which Kashmiri authors refer. In short, it appears that although Krama is an independent school (with many subdivisions of its own) it cannot be distinguished from Kula but is, in fact, one of its branches.[139]

We turn now to the next point, namely, the Kālīkula's identity as *Uttarāmnāya*. In Maheśvarānanda's time (thirteenth century) the Krama system he adhered to and which he traces back to Śivānanda (so aligning himself unequivocally to the Kashmiri Krama tradition) was considered to be *Uttarāmnāya*. Maheśvarānanda refers to it as *"Auttarāmnāya"* twice and as the "non-dual principle of *Uttara*",[140] which was originally taught by Bhairava to Bhairavī[141] and ultimately transmitted to him as the Krama doctrine he expounds in his *Mahārthamañjarī*.[142] By extension he also calls this doctrine that of the *"anuttarāmnāya"*[143] as "the philosophy of absolute (*anuttara*) non-dual consciousness"[144] which leads to liberation in this life in which freedom and enjoyment (*mokṣa* and *bhoga*) are united. Although, as we have already had occasion to remark, neither Abhinava nor the Kashmiri authors before him refer to the Krama system as *Uttarāmnāya*, there is evidence to suggest that it was known as such to some, at least, of the earlier Tantras, although this may not have been its original identity in the earliest sources.[145] Thus the colophons of the *Yonigahvara* by Jñānanetranātha state that this Tantra belongs to the *Oṅkārapīṭha* of the *Uttarāmnāya*[146] and says of itself in the body of the text that it is "the tradition of the Great Teaching," and "the essence of the Northern Kula."[147] Similarly, the colophons of the *Devīpañcaśatikā* declare that this Tantra, which deals with the *Kālīkakrama*, belongs to the Northern Tradition.[148]

It transpires from this evidence that, although we can talk of a "Kula system" as a doctrinal standpoint in the context of Kashmiri Śaivism as well as Hindu Tantricism in general, the generic meaning of the term "Kula," when it is used to refer to the entire Kaula tradition with its many schools, is not to be confused with the former sense. Similarly, it appears that the term "Krama," like "Kula," also conveys a broad generic meaning. It refers, in one sense, to the sequence of actions in Kaula ritual, the order of recitation of Mantras, deposition (*nyāsa*) of letters or the seed-syllables of Mantras on the body or on a *maṇḍala*, image or other representation of the deity and its surrounding entourage such as a pitcher or the sacrificial firepit.[149] "Krama" can also mean the liturgy or ritual itself and so is virtually synonymous with the term *"prakriyā."*[150] Again the term "Krama," variously qualified, can serve as the appellation of a Kaula school. Thus the Kashmiri Krama system as a whole is at times called "Kālīkrama" although the term also refers to the order of the sequence of Kālīs worshipped in the course of certain rituals or as a series of states of consciousness. Similarly, the Kubjikā school or *Paścimāmnāya* is also sometimes called "Śrīkrama."[151] "Krama" and "Kula" are in this sense, to all intents and purposes, virtual synonyms: the expressions "Kālīkula" and "Kālīkrama" are interchangeable, as are the terms "Śrīkrama" and "Śrīkula." The term "Krama" lays emphasis on the typical ritual form a particular Kaula school exhibits, while the term "Kula" stresses its doctrinal affiliations and individual identity as a specific Kaula tradition. Thus the combination of the two terms, as in the expressions "Kālīkula-krama" or "Śrīkulakrama", although hardly different from "Kālīkula" or "Kālīkrama", etc., focus primarily on the character of these schools as possessing distinct liturgies of their own. Again, there appears to be a distinction between Kaula schools which were "Kramakulas" (or equally one could say "Kulakramas") and those that were not, in the sense that the Tantras of these schools do not align themselves with any Krama. This is true generally of independent Kaula traditions which had no place in the *āmnāya* system of classification.

Although the *Paścimāmnāya* is a substantial Tantric tradition with a clearly defined identity of its own, and its Tantras contain much that is original, it is, at the same time, built up of diverse elements which it draws from various sources, particularly other Kaula schools. This is a feature common to all these schools in general.[152] Thus, a way in which we can better understand the *Paścimāmnāya* in the broader context of the many Tantric schools which constitute the Āgamic tradition as a whole is through a careful analysis of its constituent elements. By pursuing this approach, we can study the *Paścimāmnāya* as a living tradition whose growth is marked both by the development of its own new ideas and the accretion of others. From this point of view, the integration of Kālī worship into the Kubjikā cult is significant. In the CMSS the mysticism of the Kālīkula is assigned to a high level. Of the Four Doors of Kula (*Kuladvāra*), which constitute *Kaulācāra*, the highest is the experience of the Immaculate (*nirañjana*) attained through the Arising of the Sequence of the Cycle of Kālīs (*Kālīcakrakramodaya*), that is, the Wheel of Time. The yogi who contemplates its successive phases assimilates through it into his own consciousness the one Ultimate Reality which is both the multiplicity of diversity and unity of oneness.[153] This sequence is that of *Anākhya* (the Inexpressible), which is a well-known feature of the Krama system.[154]

According to the KMT, Kālī (as Kālasaṃkarṣinī or Guhyeśvarī) is merely a minor manifestation of Kubjikā.[155] In the KNT, which postdates the KMT, Kubjikā is occasionally considered to be a form of Kālī called "Kākālī", which is probably an abbreviated form of "Kubjikākālī."[156] The MBT, which is later than the KMT, but probably earlier than both the CMSS[157] and KNT, identifies Kālī with Kubjikā, the Supreme Goddess.[158] Moreover, the Śrīkrama of the Kubjikā school and the Kālīkrama are juxtaposed as two Kramas, one belonging to the Western Tradition *Paścimāmnāya* and the other to the Northern—*Uttarāmnāya*.[159] By the time we reach the CMSS, the Kālīkrama is fully integrated into *Paścima* doctrine and they are vitally linked together by their common esoteric Kaula character.

Before we conclude this section and proceed to discuss the *Pūrvāmnāya* and its relationship to the Kubjikā school, we should take note of an important historical reference in the CMSS's treatment of this *āmnāya*, namely that the cycle of Kālīs here described was taught by Niṣkriyānandanātha to Vidyānanda. The CMSS agrees here with other sources, according to which the line of transmission of the Kālīkrama teachings is as follows: Niṣkriyānandanātha (consort Jñānadīptī) →

Vidyānanda (consort Raktā) → Śaktyānanda (consort Mahānandā) → Śivānanda (consort Samayā). We are told by Jayaratha that these teachers and consorts are worshipped as a standard part of the preliminaries to *Kaulapūjā* in works such as the *Devīpañcaśatikā* and the *Kālīkula*.[160] The *Yonigahvara* refers to this line of teachers directly after the standard group of *Yuganāthas* and entourage,[161] and so integrates the two groups as those of Kaula masters who are all equally worthy of veneration.[162] There seems to be little reason to doubt that the Niṣkriyānanda and the Vidyānanda of the CMSS are the same as the teachers mentioned in these sources. However, although the fact that Niṣkriyānanda figures in the CMSS as the revealer of an original transmission is significant, this is not in itself enough evidence to prove that he was the founder of the Krama system as a whole. Perhaps we may attribute to him the distinction of having been the first to have realized this particular sequence of Kālīs.[163] But before saying anything definite about this, we must first examine the earlier Āgamic sources to understand the historical antecedents of the Krama system as a distinct school.

The Pūrvāmnāya

The CMSS clearly identifies Trika with the *Pūrvāmnāya* through which the original Kaula teachings were transmitted by the *Yuganāthas*. Thus the masters which every Kaula, whatever school he may belong to, should venerate as the founders of Kaulism as a whole are here all made to belong to the *Trikamaṭhikā*. We do not possess enough of the early sources to be able to compare directly what the original Āgamic Trika tradition has had to say about this. Fortunately, however, Abhinavagupta explains in his *Tantrāloka* how Kaula ritual should be performed by Kashmiri Trika Śaivites. The way in which Abhinava conceives the relationship between the *Yuganāthas* and the Trika principle (and hence, by implication, their relationship with Trika Śaivism) agrees well enough with the CMSS for us to be reasonably sure that Abhinava must have based his account on Āgamic sources. Moreover, although he deals with several Kaula rites described in different Tantras, he is not solely concerned with them alone but seeks, in broader terms, to explain the method (*prakriyā*) that underlies all Kaula ritual. In other words, what he has to say is, from his point of view, universally applicable by all Kaula Śaivites. This is particularly true of the worship of the *Yuganāthas*, which he describes at the beginning of his account, to which we now turn.

As a prelude to the rite proper, the officiant must first purify himself.

He does so in this case by projecting the *Parā* and *Mālinī* Mantras onto his body in the prescribed manner and, once filled with their cosmic power, then identifying himself with Bhairava. He now offers libations to Bhairava and the circles of his energies that surround him, which are identified with the officiant's own sensory and mental powers. This is done by drinking a mixture of male and female sexual fluid (*kuṇḍagolaka*) from a sacrificial jar previously filled for this purpose. According to Abhinava, the officiant attains in this way a vision of the fullness of his universal nature which has been rendered brilliantly manifest by the energy of the sacrificial offering. He has, therefore, no need to do anything else unless he wishes to see this same fullness manifest also in the outer world through the outpouring of his sensory energies, in which case he proceeds to perform the outer ritual.[164] This begins, as usual, with the worship of the Kaula teachers in a sacred circle (*maṇḍala*) drawn on the ground with coloured powders. The form of this *maṇḍala*, called *"siddhacakra"*, is basically as we have illustrated it here. See Figure 3. The *Yuganāthas* with their consorts and disciples are worshipped in the inner square. Their names are as shown in Table 7.

Table 7. The Yuganāthas, their Consorts and Disciples According to the Tantrāloka.

Direction	*Yuganātha*	*Consort*	*Disciple*	*Consort*
East	Khagendra-nātha	Vijjambā	Viktaṣṭi Vimala	Illāīambā Anantamekhalā
South	Kūrmanātha	Maṅgalā	Jaitra Avijita	Illāīambā Ānandamekhalā
West	Meṣanātha	Kāmamaṅgalā	Vindhya Ajita	Kullāīambā Ajaramekhalā
North	Macchanda-nātha	Kuṅkumāmbā	(*Six Princes*) Amaranātha Varadeva-nātha Citranātha Alinātha Vindhya-nātha Guḍikānātha	(*Consort*) Sillāī Eruṇā Kumārī Bodhāī Mahālacchī Aparamekhalā

Figure 3. Siddhacakra.

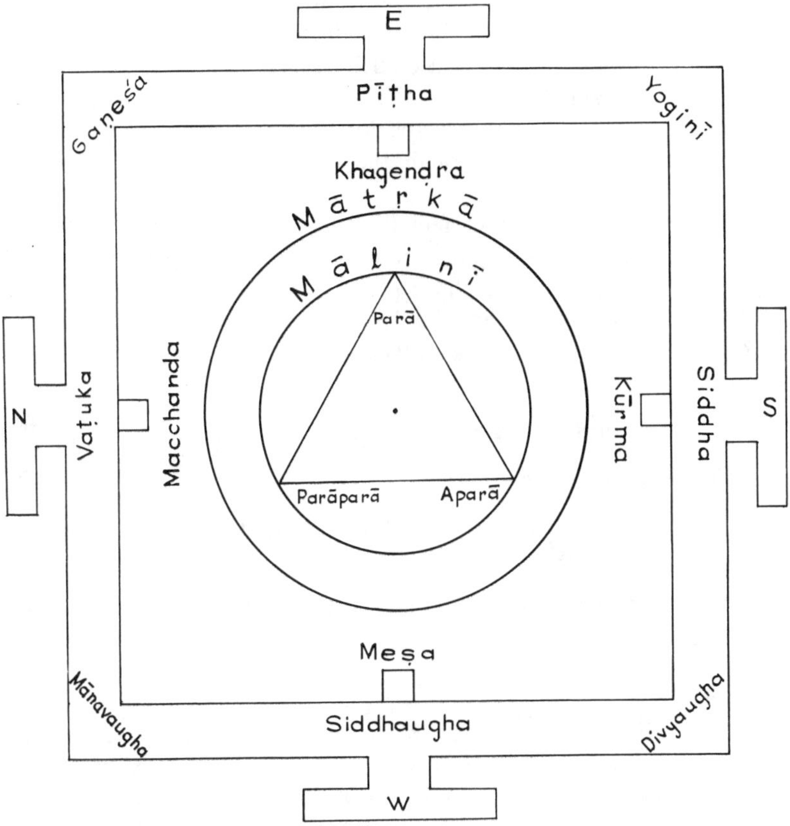

The names of these teachers as well as those of their consorts and disciples are substantially the same as those recorded in the CMSS. Moreover the names of the *ovallīs* and *pīṭhas* associated with the Six Princes, according to the CMSS, agree exactly with Abhinava's account and the *Kulakriḍāvatāra*, which Jayaratha quotes in his commentary.[166] Note, incidentally, that the names of the *ovallīs* in these accounts do not quite agree with the KRU (see above p. 62). Abhinava does not record the town (*nagara*) associated with the Six Princes but lists instead their *ghara* (literally "house") and *pallī* (literally "village").

More interesting than the coincidence of these details is the formation and identity of the triangle in the centre of the *maṇḍala*. Abhinava explains the form of this triangle and the way in which it is worshipped in his *Parātriṃśikāvivaraṇa*.[167] The triangle represents the divine matrix (*yoni*), in the centre of which resides Kuleśvarī, in her aroused state, in union with Parānandabhairava from whom flows Kula, the blissful power of emission (*visargaśakti*), through which the cosmic order is generated. The triangle (whose microcosmic equivalent is the female sexual organ) is worshipped by contemplating this creative flow of bliss in the unity of universal consciousness. This can be done either directly in elevated states of consciousness and/or through the ecstatic experience of physical orgasm.

It seems that the CMSS refers to this distinctly Trika practice when it remarks that the goddess emerges from the centre of its energies along with Paramānandabhairava (see above p. 69). In this way "Kula emerges in the womb of Kula" (ibid.) and the worship of the *Yuganāthas* bears fruit. The *maṇḍala* in which the *Yuganāthas* are worshipped is divided into five sections, namely:

1) the Mantras of the Trika goddess,

2) the Kaula masters,

3) the sphere of the flux of the Wheel of Mālinī which corresponds to the vital breath,

4) the sphere of the Wheel of *Mātṛkā* corresponding to the activity of consciousness, and

5) the outer square representing the senses.

These together constitute Kula, the micro- and macro-cosmic Totality. In the centre resides Kuleśvarī who can be worshipped in the form of any of the three Trika goddesses, either alone or with Kuleśvara, her consort.[168] We can conclude, therefore, that the CMSS records, in broad terms, the manner in which the *Yuganāthas* are worshipped in the Trikakula. Associated with the *Pūrvāmnāya*, they are the first to be worshipped in the order of the *āmnāyas* and so accorded a peculiarly high status, which at the same time sets them apart from the *Paścimāmnāya* and its own line of transmission, while integrating them into it.

We move on now to our next object of enquiry, namely, the relationship between these *āmnāyas* and Trika. The *Kularatnoddyota* repeatedly associates the *Pūrvāmnāya* with the *Paścimāmnāya*. The Kaula tradition with which this Tantra is associated develops, it says, in these two forms.[169] Thus the KRU at times combines both together. For example, the fire ritual, *maṇḍala* and initiation is said to be explained in accord with the ritual procedures of both traditions.[170] At the same time, however, the two traditions are also distinguished. Thus it is clearly stated in places that the rituals and doctrines of this Tantra are basically those of the *Paścimāmnāya*, which has incorporated elements of the *Pūrvāmnāya*. For example, in a sequence of sixty-four energies divided in the usual pattern of eight times eight (which in this case are eight energies associated with eight sacred places), the eight powers (*mātṛ*) belonging to Prayāga are said to originate from the *Pūrva* tradition.[171] But even though the KRU admits that it has borrowed from the *Pūrvāmnāya*, it maintains that the *Pūrvāmnāya* as a whole is derived from the *Paścimāmnāya* and that this is why they are essentially similar. The *Pūrvāmnāya* is a direct offshoot of the Kubjikā tradition and is similar to it in every respect, just as a reflection is a reproduction of the reflected object.[172]

The KRU's account of the origin of the *Pūrvāmnāya* associates it with Mitranātha, a well-known *Paścima* master. Mitranātha was a direct disciple of Vṛkṣanātha who, as an incarnation of the goddess Kubjikā, brought the *Paścima* teachings down into the world during this Era.[173] Accordingly, insofar as the *Pūrvāmnāya* is derived from *Paścimāmnāya* in this way, the goddess enquires how the *Pūrvāmnāya* arose from it.[174] The account of its origin which follows is basically a variant of many similar myths which explain how Matsyendranātha received the Kaula teachings.[175] Here the story goes that Pārvatī taught the *Pūrvāmnāya* to her son, Skanda, secretly from a book. For some unexplained reason Skanda became angry and in a fit of rage threw the book into the sea where it was swallowed by a fish (*mīnaka*). In the belly of this fish resided a great Siddha who read the book and practiced the yoga it taught and so grew powerful and full of splendour. From the belly of this fish emerged Ādinātha in the form of Matsyendranātha.

A connection is here clearly being made between the first Kaula teacher of this era, Matsyendranātha, and the *Pūrvāmnāya*, as it is in the CMSS. However, the KRU does not equate the *Pūrvāmnāya* with Trika, although it knows of the *Trikatantra* as an independent group which it mentions along with the *Siddhānta, Vāma, Bhūta* and *Gāruḍa* Tantras as well as the Kāpālika Somasiddhānta, amongst others.[176] In a long list of Tantras[177] at the beginning of this work, the *Siddhādevīmahātantra* is mentioned which is clearly none other than the *Siddhayogeśvarīmata*. We have already noted that both CMSS and KMT refer to this, the root *Trikatantra*.

Indeed, there can be little doubt that Trika is an important element of the *Paścimāmnāya*. Thus the worship of the three goddesses, Parā, Parāparā and Aparā, which is a distinguishing characteristic of Trika, is an important feature of the Kubjikā cult as well.[178] Their Mantras are the same as those of the Trika,[179] as are those of the male consorts associated with them, namely, *Bhairavasadbhāva, Ratiśekhara* and *Navātmā*.[180] Triads in general are a prominent feature of the *Paścimāmnāya;* we often find groups of three related to one another.[181] The goddess Kubjikā herself is three-fold in the form of a young girl, maiden and old woman.[182] Moreover, she is explicitly said to be three-fold as the union of the goddesses *Parā, Parāparā* and *Aparā.* An important triad is here, just as it is for the Kashmiri Trika, that of *Śāmbhava, Śākta* and *Āṇava,* which are three basic ritual patterns at one level, and at the inner level of consciousness correspond—as in the Trika—to will, knowledge and action. Cosmic counterparts are attributed to them in the form of the Three Worlds into which the universe is divided.[183] The whole of the teaching is similarly divided into these three types,[184] which is why there are three types of initiation (*devīdīkṣā*) through which the Śrīkramá becomes manifest.[185] Even more vital and fundamental than these similarities are the basic forms of the Mantric codes adopted by the Kubjikā cult, namely, those of *Śabdarāśi* and *Mālinī.*[186] They are the very backbone of the entire Mantric system of this tradition, just as they are of that of Trika, so much so that the god tells the goddess in the KRU that:

> The *Trikatantra* will be constructed by the conjunction of the parts primary and secondary, of the three Vidyās along with *Mālinī* and *Śabdarāśi.*[187]

Although the use of the future here implies that the god is going to make *Trikatantra* after the revelation of the Kubjikā cult, there can be little doubt that Trika precedes the *Kubjikātantra* and it is the latter which has borrowed from the former, not the other way around. Indeed, in places these Tantras themselves inform us that they have drawn elements from *Trikatantras.*[188] Moreover, the oldest known *Paścimatantra,* the *Kubjikāmata,* must be later than the first *Trikatantra,* the *Siddhayogeśvarīmata,* because it refers to it. Again, the MBT and KRU both know Trika as Trika. This means that they were redacted when Āgamic Trika had reached an advanced stage of development because the earliest Tantras that taught Trika doctrine and ritual, such as the SYM, did not consider themselves to be *Trikatantras* as such.[189] Thus the KMT, which is earlier than the MBT and KRU, does not refer to Trika as a school, possibly because it precedes this phase of Trika's development. Whether this is the case or not, it it a significant fact that the later *Paścimatantras* know of Trika's existence especially because reference to Trika is rare in the primary sources. Moreover, that the CMSS knows the *Trikasāra,* an extensive *Trikatantra* frequently referred to by the Kashmiris, shows that the followers of the Kubjikā cult continued to consult Trika sources throughout its development.[190] It is significant, from this point of view, that it is in Nepal, where the Kubjikā cult flourished, that the *Siddha-*

yogeśvarīmata has been recovered. This is probably because it was felt to be related to the Kubjikā cult and so was copied and preserved.

The Kulatantras and Śaivāgama

Before we move on to discuss the *Paścimāmnāya*, we take this opportunity to sum up what we have said up to now about the development of these Kaula traditions. Firstly, we should emphasize that the essential features of Kaula doctrine and ritual are by no means exclusive to Tantric works which call themselves Kaula. Practically all that is generally considered to be the ritual, yogic practice and life style of a Kaula (whether itinerant ascetic or householder) can be found prescribed in the *Bhairavatantras*. The JY, SYM, BY and *Bhairavatantras* of this sort all seem at first sight highly Kaula in character. They themselves, however, do not consider themselves to be such, even though they do sometimes describe rituals that they specifically state are Kaula. Indeed, this fact only serves to make the contrast between them and the *Kaulatantras* even more striking, despite much that they seemingly share in common. How then are we to distinguish a *Kaulatantra* from other Tantric works? The reply to this question lies essentially in what a given Tantra says about itself and its relationship to other Tantras and Tantric traditions. A *Kaulatantra* will itself tell us that its dominant concern is with Kaula doctrine which it labels as such in its own terms. This is a simple principle of general application in trying to assess to what type a Tantra belongs.

As we have already noted, the earliest Tantras which Kashmiri Śaivites refer to as original sources of Trika doctrine are not, in this sense, Kaula. It makes sense, therefore, that according to Abhinavagupta the *Mālinīvijayottaratantra* which he considers, along with the SYM, to be the most important *Trikatantra*, refutes Kaula doctrine. Although he says that it goes beyond Kula doctrine, in fact it belongs to the strata of *Trikatantra* which had not yet become Kaula (or a 'higher' Kaula) in the way that it is for example, in the *Bhairavakulatantra* or *Kularatnamālā*. The same is true of the Kālīkrama. The *Tantrarājabhaṭṭāraka* (alias *Śiraścheda* or *Jayadrathayāmala*), to which the Kashmiris refer as an authority for certain points of Krama doctrine, is a sophisticated Tantra which typologically can be said to be highly Kaula in character; it does not, however, define itself as such even though it does deal with Kaula ritual in places.[191] Therefore, we cannot say that this Tantra belongs to the Kālīkrama in the specific sense of the term, although it is certainly concerned in parts with the worship of Kālī in many forms and is full of typically Kālīkrama notions. Other, probably later, Tantras of the Kālī cult were, however, Kaula and conscious of themselves as Kālīkrama Tantras. One could say that the Kālīkrama, like Trika, acquired a specific independent identity as a Tantric tradition when it became conscious of itself as Kaula. Moreover, at this stage of its development we can begin to identify figures in the line of the Āgamic Kālī cults who brought Tantras 'down to earth' or transmitted the oral tradition of the Kālīkrama which finally emerged in Kashmir, fashioned at the hands of the Kashmiri authors, as a fully fledged system, not just a mass of ritual details or scattered visions in chaotic scriptural sources.

We can trace a continuity from the virtually total anonymity of the earliest scriptural sources of the proto-Krama and proto-Trika, namely, the *Bhairava* and *Vāma* Tantras, to the more distinctly sectarian *Kaula-tantras* of the Trika and Krama, right up to the extra-canonical exegetical works of monist Kashmiri Śaiva authors. In this way, by the middle of the ninth century, they emerged out of the world of the Śaiva Āgamas into that of the *śāstras.* For at least two centuries these two worlds of discourse remained vitally linked through the Tantric adepts who belonged to the line of transmission of the Āgamic teachings and served as living sources of their hidden meaning. Although we have taken a leap outside the ambit of Śaiva scripture into a different dimension of discourse, the line of transmission is linked to that of the canonical works themselves. In other words, the Trika and Krama schools matured to this level following the pace of a progressively more refined hermeneutics of the Tantras' esoteric meaning, which developed in the oral traditions. It was Śambhunātha—Abhinavagupta's Trika master—who gave him the basic exegetical Trika-based model upon which the culminating work of the Trika tradition—the *Tantrāloka*—is based. Again it appears that it was largely due to him that Trika was taken to be the apogee of monist Kashmiri Śaivism, for there can be no doubt that Trika is far from the central focus of monist Kashmiri Śaivism before Abhinavagupta.

To get back to the point: when the Krama emerged as a self-conscious Kaula cult, it seems that it also became conscious of itself as one of a group of *āmnāyas.* Whether these two events are concomitant or not, that is, whether the Kālīkrama as an independent Kaula tradition knew itself right from its inception as the *Uttarāmnāya* or not, it certainly did so at some stage of its development. The Trikakula on the other hand, it seems, never thought of itself as belonging to an *āmnāya* even though the CMSS refers to Trika as the *pūrvāmnāya.* This is probably why the Kashmiri Śaiva authors ignored the *āmnāya* system and preferred to relate the Trika—as a 'higher' Kaula tradition—to the Śaivāgama as a whole, just as the Āgamic Trika itself did.

The Tantras of the Kubjikā cult were, however, it seems, Kaula right from the start and thought of themselves as belonging specifically to the *Paścimāmnāya*. We know that the KMT is older than the JY—a proto-Krama Tantra—which refers to it (see appendix C) and that it is also older than the NSA. The JY is well aware of an independent current of Kaula scripture although it does not say specifically that the KMT belongs to it. Are we therefore to assume that the Kālīkula already existed at the time and that it represented an *Uttarāmnāya* in relation to the Kubjikātantras? Or is the KMT the oldest extant type of *āmnāya*-oriented Tantra? We have already noted that it nowhere clearly defines the *āmnāyas* of the other directions, although it refers to them. Could this be because they were simply empty categories? In other words, did they have no more than an ideal existence as mere logical complements to an existent *Paścimāmnāya*? If we accept this hypothesis, we are led to consider the possibility that the Kālīkrama accommodated itself later to this pattern, as did the Śrīvidyā tradition in a less certain manner. Perhaps, on the other hand, it would be better to think of them as developing together with their roots firmly embedded in the Śaivāgama, drawing life from it and growing out of it, as well as alongside it.

The Paścimāmnāya—The Cult of Kubjikā

Some scholars have assumed that the cult of Kubjikā is of Nepalese origin largely because virtually all the manuscripts of the Tantras of this school are Nepalese.[192] This assumption is not, however, supported by the texts themselves. They do say that this school originated in a mountainous region, probably the Himalayas (see below), and make the point that it spread throughout India. Even so, Nepal is hardly mentioned as a place sacred to the goddess,[193] while the Nine Nāthas who are said to have propagated the doctrine of Kubjikā in our times, although all of North Indian origin,[194] are not Nepalese. However, wherever it may have originated, the cult of Kubjikā was known in Nepal by the first half of the twelfth century A.D.—the date of the oldest manuscript of the KMT.[195] The great abundance of manuscripts of Tantras and related works belonging to this school copied from this time up to the seventeenth century testify to its popularity there during this period. Judging from the number of manuscripts copied from this period onwards, the Kubjikā cult seems to have waned in importance although it must have continued to command a small following up to quite recent times because a few manuscripts did continue to be copied right up to the present century. I was informed during a recent visit to Nepal that Kubjikā is still worshipped on certain occasions in the Kathmandu valley although her cult is now hardly known to anybody.

Scholars have pointed out that references to Kubjikā and her school are rare,[196] nor are images of her common whether drawn or sculptured.[197] This is true of another goddess associated with her worship and whose cult has similarly been popular in Nepal since the inception of the cult of Kubjikā, namely, Guhyakālī.[198] The reason for this seems to be that such cults either disappeared along with countless others or else managed to survive only at the regional level. A prime example of this phenomena is Trika Śaivism which, but for its following in Kashmir and the genius of those who applied themselves to it there, would probably be unknown. It is not quite right, therefore, to think of the Kubjikā cult as a school which "remained very independent and stood aloof from other Tantrik schools."[199] In fact, one of the aims of future research into this school could be to identify, as far as the available sources permit, the various elements of other Tantric traditions which have contributed to its formation and to distinguish them from its own original contributions.

Kubjikā, the 'Crooked One'

"Kubjikā" is the feminine form of the Sanskrit word *"Kubja"* which literally means "humped-back" or "crooked." Even so, although the Tantras of the Kubjikā school describe many forms in which the goddess can be visualized, she is not commonly represented as bent over. It has been suggested, in order to account for this fact, that *"Kubjā"* is a word of Muṇḍā origin[200] that does not originally mean "crooked." The Tantras do not, however, support this contention. Thus we find that Kubjikā is also called *"Vakreśvarī,"* Vakrikā or Vakrā because, as the Tantras explain, her limbs are crooked (*vakra*).[201] Of her three principal forms as a girl (*Bālā*), young woman (*Kumārī*) and old woman (*Vṛddhā*), it is the last which, as one would expect, is associated with her crooked form.[202] Perhaps this image of her as old and deformed is the reason why she is also called "Khañjanī" which means literally "she who walks with a limp."[203] A myth recorded in the KRU that explains why she is bent over does not, however, relate this to her age.[204] The story goes that Kubjikā once sat with devotion to worship the union of the god with the goddess. The god then appeared to her and took hold of her hand as a prelude to union but she, overcome with apprehension and bashfulness, contracted her body, and so became 'Kubjikā'. As such, she is equated with *Kuṇḍalinī* who, when awakened, becomes bent over with 'shame'.[205] Again, Kubjikā's crooked form relates to her nature as *Kuṇḍalinī* who is the matrix (*yoni*) or Triangle (*sṛgāta*) from which creation pours forth and in which it resides. As such, she is bent over, not when awakening but when she is dormant, and the power of consciousness (*cicchakti*) is contracted, which is as one would expect, and is in fact usually the case in representations of *Kuṇḍalinī*. From this point of view, consciousness is 'straight', i.e., unconditioned when it is free of 'crooked' obscuring thought-constructs.[206] From another point of view, Kubjikā is said to be crooked because she must contract her limbs to reside in the body of Kuleśvara just as someone whose body is large must stoop down when moving about in a small hut.[207] While according to the *Parātantra*, she is bent over because she initially 'churns' her navel with her tongue to give birth to the universe within her womb.[208] This is because, as the CMSS explains, the navel is the Great Matrix (*mahāyoni*) from which *Kuṇḍalinī* rises. Thus in this account Kubjikā is bent over in order to stimulate her cosmic power which, rising through the body, leads the yogi to liberation.[209]

Kubjikā is the Supreme Goddess (*Parā devī*) where form is the divine light of consciousness that shines in the centre of the brilliant radiance enlightened yogis perceive.[210] As such, she is the Great Mother they experience within themselves.[211] As *Kuṇḍalinī* she is pure bliss, the power of the Light which resides in all the six centres in the body (*cakra*) and so is of six forms.[212] As the power of consciousness she is the source of all Mantras and as such has three aspects: Supreme (*Parā*), Middling (*Parāparā*) and Inferior (*Aparā*). In this three-fold form she is, just as in Trika doctrine, *Mālinī*[213] consisting of the fifty letters of the alphabet in a state of disorder, symbolizing the rising of *Kuṇḍalinī* and the disruption of the cosmic order that takes place when it is reabsorbed into the Supreme Matrix (*parayoni*)—the goddess Kubjikā—from whence it was originally emitted. At this level the goddess resides in the state which is Beyond Mind (*unmanābhāvātītā*) as Śiva's divine power (*śāṃbhavaśakti*) to will, know and act. She has thus three forms (*trirūpā*) and travels along the three paths (*tripathagā*)[214] of the sides of the triangle of the organ of generation (*bhaga*) which is both the source and ultimate end of all creation.[215] At the corners of this triangle are located the *Mahāpīṭhas:* Pūrṇagiri, Jālandhara and Kāmarūpa. In the centre is Oḍiyānapīṭha where the goddess resides in union with the divine *liṅga* whose nature is bliss itself and whose seed (*bindu*) is the Sky of Consciousness.[216] In the centre Akula and Kula unite, while the goddess, as Rudra's power (*rudraśakti*), pervades each part of the triangle and lords over it as the Mistress of Kula (*Kuleśvarī*) who is also called Mahākaulikā and Bhairavī.[217]

According to the CMSS, the form in which Kubjikā resides in the centre of this triangle is as a tamarind tree: *Ciñcinī.* Thus it refers to the doctrine of the *Kubjikātantras* as *Ciñcinīśāstra.*[218] The abode of this doctrine is the Circle of the Divine Transmission (*divyaughamaṇḍala*), higher than that of the Transmission of the Perfected Ones and of Men (*Siddha* and *Mānavaugha*).[219] It is under this Tamarind Tree that Ciñcinīnātha (alias *Vṛkṣanātha*) attained, by divine command, the highest state.[220] This tree is the tree of the light of consciousness (*ciñcinīcit-prakāśa*) brought into this world by Siddhanātha[221] who planted it on the Island of the Moon (*candradvīpa*) which is in the Great Ocean of Kula. The roots of this Tree and its branches are extensive and it bears the fruits of the Divine Transmission. It is Kaula rooted in Kula and flourishes in Śiva's Circle. The juice of this tree is one's own nature (*svasvabhāva*); its young sprouts are the Vedas and Vedāṅgas; its flowers are the senses, and the divine fount which waters it is the delight of consciousness, its inner glory.[222] To lie in its shade is to experience the highest state of rest (*viśrānti*) in which one is free of the opposites of pleasure and pain.

The Origins of the Kubjikā Cult

The founder of the Kubjikā cult is said to be Śiva who is venerated as Ādinātha,[223] the primordial teacher. It is Ādinātha who imparts the doctrine to the goddess Kubjikā in the KRU. He, the first Master, is, according to one myth, the source of the goddess[224] even though he declares that both he and his consort are beginningless and with no end. It is he, not the goddess, who is the essence of the *Paścima* tradition which draws its life from him, because he is the authentic identity of those who worship him and the goddess.[225] His body is the source of the sacraments offered to him and the goddess with whom he unites to emit the 'sequences' (*krama*) of the liturgy and the sacred circles (*maṇḍala*) in which he is worshipped with the sacrificial formulas he himself has taught.[226] Ādinātha is also called Śrīnātha[227] who is identified with Mahābhairava, the Lord of Kula and Kubjikā's consort, Kubjeśvara.[228] He receives the doctrine from the goddess but at the same time is praised by her as the source of all Kula doctrine.[229] Śrīnātha is also identified with Śrīkaṇṭha, said to be the original propagator of the Śaivāgama[230] who is worshipped at times even before Śaṅkara.[231] Although Śrīnātha is extolled as the highest God, there are reasons to believe that he was an historical person. He is listed as the last of eighteen teachers in the line of the Divine Tradition (*divyāmnāyānukrama*) and was said to be the only teacher in the town of Candrapura who belonged to the Western Tradition. He was helped at the beginning of the present Age of Darkness to propagate the doctrine by Oḍīśanātha, Śrīṣaṣṭhanātha and Śrīcaryendranātha who lived in the land of Koṅkoṇa where where Candrapura was situated.[232] As the founder of a line of teachers, he is called "Olinātha".[233] A Siddhanātha is also referred to as the original propagator of this tradition but he may be none other than Śrīnātha if we take "Siddhanātha" to be a way of referring to an accomplished adept rather than a proper name.[234]

As we have noted above, Siddhanātha was said to have brought the teachings to earth on the Island of the Moon (*candradvīpa*), also called the "City of the Moon" (*candrapura*), the "City of the Island of the Moon,"[235] or the "City of the Sacred Place of the Moon" (*candrapīṭhapura*).[236] It symbolizes the Innate Nature (*svabhāva*) of all things where the divine body of the goddess Kubjikā resides in the form of *Kuṇḍalinī.* It is probable that Candrapura did exist although the Tantras overlayed it, as they did other places sacred to the goddess, with a symbolism which interiorized it into an inner sacred geography, thus making it difficult for us to locate the site of this town. The land of Koṅkoṇa, where Candrapura was situated, is said to have been in the Himalayas. Schoterman, however, does not believe that this is likely but thinks instead that: "Koṅkoṇa denotes the whole strip of land between the Western Ghats and the Arabian Sea."[237] It seems more likely, however, that Candrapura was located somewhere in the Himalayan region in view of the many associations that the goddess and her place of origin has with mountains. Thus in the KMT the Mountain of the Moon (*candraparvata*) is said to lie to the west of mount Meru near Gandhamālya[238] which is where the Island of the Moon is located according to the ṢaṭSS.[239] Indeed, this is probably one of the reasons (if not the main one) why the cult of Kubjikā is associated with the western quarter.

Between the three peaks of Himavat is the site of the Land or Town of the Tradition (*santānabhuvana/pura*) which is equated with the Western Tradition, also called (as is common practice in these Tantras), the Abode of the Moon (*candragṛha*).[240] According to the mystical physiology of these Tantras, Himavat symbolizes the mind (*manas*) found at the end of the Twelve-finger Space above the head (*dvādaśānta*) where *Kuṇḍalinī* abides in her most risen state.[241] Thus Kubjikā is said to descend onto the peak of the Snow Mountain (*himagiri*) in the land of India. This peak is located at the end of the stream of divine sound (*nāda*)[242] which resounds throughout the micro/macrocosm until it merges into the Silence of the Transcendent at the highest level of being at the End of Sound (*nādānta*) in the Twelve-finger Space. The goddess is therefore said to reside on the peak of mount Kailāsa and, as such, is the Goddess of the Peak (*śikhādevī*) and the Mistress of the Wheels of Energy which revolve in the cosmic body.[243] Her body is pure consciousness and bestows the bliss of the 'churning' or arousal of the power of enlightened consciousness.[244] As the power of consciousness, she is also Speech and as such is adorned with the fifty letters of the alphabet and resides in this form within the divine triangle of the Three Peaks once she descends into it along the Path of Meru.[245] The MBT, according to the colophons, has also emerged along the Path of Meru in the Primordial Sacred Abode (*ādyapīṭha*).[246] The KRU explains that the Path of Meru means, according to Kula doctrine, the Tradition (*santāna*). The Lord of the Tradition is the Great Meru, the Supreme Sky of Consciousness which knows its own nature completely. It is from here that the beginningless sequence of the progressive unfolding of consciousness and the transmission of the doctrine originates and so is called the Primordial Abode (*ādipīṭha*) located in the Centre between Kailāsa and Malaya. The Lord resides here with his power that pervades all things.[247]

Although it is not possible on the basis of the evidence so far available to say anything definite about where the Kubjikā cult originated, if we assume that the Tantras of these schools invest with symbolic meaning the environment and localities in which the Kubjikā cult originally developed, it seems likely that we would be right to seek its origins somewhere in the western Himalayas. That this cult was known in the mountains of the North of India during the earliest period of its development seems to find support by a reference in the KMT to birch bark as the material on which a Mantra is to be written.[248] The MBT also refers to it as a writing material[249] and the GS prescribes that a sacred diagram be drawn on it with sexual fluids mixed with poison.[250]

The study of the cult of Kubjikā and the Tantras of the Western Kaula Tradition is barely in its infancy. We hope that some of the more important of these texts will be edited and studied in the near future. There can be no doubt that this is an early Kaula tradition which is of great interest not only for the richness of its doctrines and the beauty of its symbolism but also because it can tell us something important about a part, at least, of the history of Hindu Tantra.

PART THREE

Appendices

APPENDIX A

A History of the Study of the Kubjikā Cult

Scholars first heard of the existence of the literature of the Kubjikā school at the turn of the century when Haraprasāda Śāstrī and C. Bendall published their catalogue of manuscripts belonging to the Darbar Library in Kathmandu.[1] In 1934, P. C. Bagchi published an edition of the *Kaulajñānanirṇaya* along with a number of short tracts attributed to Matsyendranātha. In his introduction he quoted extensively from the *Kubjikānityāhnikatilaka*, which was correctly identified by Śāstrī in the Nepal catalogue as belonging to the *Paścimāmnāya.* Bagchi however failed to grasp the distinctive character of the *Paścimāmnāya* and so simply identified it wholesale with the Kaula school.[2]

The next brief reference to the existence of this corpus of literature appeared in an article by Chintaharan Chakravarti published in 1937 in the *Yearbook of the Asiatic Society of Bengal.* This brief article dealt with the Nepalese manuscripts of the works of this school deposited in the library of the Society.[3] One manuscript of the KMT, which was thought at that time to have been written in late Gupta script (but has since been proved to be an early form of Śāradā[4]), aroused particular interest due to its presumed antiquity. Chakravarti also wrote short notices of these manuscripts in his catalogue of Tantra manuscripts belonging to the Society which came out in two volumes in 1939 and 1940 respectively.[5]

In 1947 a series of articles written by the Nepalese major-general Dhana Saṃśer Jaṅgabahādur Rāṇā came out in the Hindī magazine *Caṇḍī.* They were published every two months and each gave a brief account of the *āmnāyas* amongst which was the *Paścimāmnāya.*[6] In 1963 De Mallmann published a book on the iconography of the *Agnipurāṇa* in which she briefly discussed the form of Kubjikā described there.[7]

This was the state of affairs up to the beginning of the 1970s when a group of scholars at the University of Utrecht in Holland decided to edit the KMT which resulted in 1972 in a preliminary article by Dr. K. R. Van Kooj on the problems involved.[8] In 1976, an edition of the *Gorakṣa-*

saṃhitā was published by Janārdana Pāṇḍeya from Sampūrṇānanda Sanskrit University, Benares. This edition was prepared on the basis of two manuscripts, one the scholar noticed in 1963 in the manuscript library of the said university and another he found in the collection of the All-India Kashiraj Trust in Ramnagar near Benares.[9] This was the first edition of a Tantra belonging to the Kubjikā school made, as it happens, without the editor knowing that this was the school of Tantra to which this text belongs.

In 1977, Schoterman published a short article on the KMT[10] and in 1980 an article on the worship of Kubjikā in the *Agnipurāṇa*.[11] In 1982, he published an edition of the first five chapters of the *Ṣaṭsāhasrasaṃhitā* along with an English translation and extensive notes.[12] This text is an expanded form of the 3500 verse KMT and so Schoterman's work is the first major study of a Tantra of this school. At the University of Utrecht an edition of the *Kularatnamūlapañcakāvatāra* has been prepared for a research degree. Dr. Schoterman is also preparing an edition of the *Kubjikānityāhnikatilaka* by Muktaka (alias Mañjuka) which is a manual for the worship of Kubjikā written before the twelfth century (the date of the manuscript). Dr. T. Goudriaan and Dr. Schoterman have completed the edition of the KMT and will hopefully manage to publish it shortly with an English introduction.

Appendix B

The Manthānabhairavatantra

The *Manthānabhairava* is a lengthy Tantra belonging to the *Paścimāmnāya.* It also calls itself *caturviṃśatisāhasra,*[1] that is, a "book of 24,000 verses" and is in fact not much short of this size. The oldest dated manuscript traced so far was copied during the reign of Someśvara and is dated N.S. 300, i.e., 1180 A.D.[2] The most recent was copied during the reign of Vīravikrama Sāha and is dated Sam. 1897, i.e., A.D. 1841. Forty-one manuscripts, many of which are more than 150 folios long, are listed in Appendix C. One manuscript of a part of this Tantra is preserved in the Asiatic Society of Bengal. It is in Bengali script and was copied from a manuscript belonging to a monk in Bodhagaya dated N.S. 761, i.e., 1641 A.D.. It contains chapters 74-89 and is written on 199 folios of foolscap paper.[3] Apart from this one, no manuscript of this Tantra has so far been found that is not Nepalese.

The MBT is divided into four sections, three of which are called *"khaṇḍa."* Although a colophon of one of these sections states that this Tantra is divided into three parts,[4] in actual fact it appears, on the basis of the descriptions in the catalogues, that they are not three but four. These are listed below along with their approximate length:

Yogakhaṇḍa	4,500 verses
Kumārikākhaṇḍa	6,000 verses
Siddhakhaṇḍa	2,900 verses
Navanityāyāgādhikāra	4,300 verses
Total	17,700 verses

In the *Parātantra,* the MBT is referred to as the *"mahāmanthāna-ṣaṭkaka"*[5] which may be translated to mean the "Great *Manthāna* (*bhairavatantra*) consisting of a group of six [thousand verses]" or also as "consisting of groups of six [thousand verses]." If the first meaning is intended, then perhaps the *Parātantra* is referring to just a part of it. Perhaps, however, the work is conceived to be divided into four parts of six thousand verses, as is the *Jayarathayāmala*. This is perhaps not the case because, as we have already noted, only three out of the four sections refer to themselves as a *"khaṇḍa,"* while the MBT describes itself (in the *Kumārikākhaṇḍa* at least) as divided into three parts. Does this mean then that the *Navanityāhnikādhikāra* is a later addition? Or is it, in fact, a part of one of the three original sections? This is just one of the many preliminary problems that need to be solved. Indeed, without carefully examining all the MSs it is not possible even to make out which parts of the MBT they contain. Certainly there is no single MS that contains it all. Moreover, the order of the sections also needs to be assessed. From the notices we have of these MSs there appears to be a commentary on this Tantra called *"Vidhāna"* written by a certain Rūpaśiva. Again, without examining the MSs it is impossible to say whether the commentary extends to cover the entire Tantra or just a part and if so, which part.

The MBT is also called *Khañjinīmata* indicating its close connection to the KMT for, as the reader will recall, Khañjinī is another name for Kubjikā. It was brought down to earth by Kalaṅkanātha (see below) while the *Kulālikāmata* of 3,500 verses, i.e., the KMT, which the MBT also calls the *"Ratnasūtra,"* was brought down to earth by Tumbura. The reference here to the KMT of 3,500 verses proves that the MBT is a later work.[6] This is further confirmed by another passage where the presiding god of this school is described as sitting in the *maṇḍala* of the *Vidyāpīṭha* holding in one hand the *Śrīmata*, i.e., the KMT.[7] That the MBT is probably not the original Tantra of the Kubjikā school is also indirectly confirmed by the highe regard that the Tantras of this school have for the KMT, rather than the MBT, and that it is the former, not the latter, which figures as one of the sixty-four Tantras listed in the NSA. The *Kumārikākhaṇḍa* of this Tantra is particularly interesting from this point of view as it seems to be closely related to the KMT. Perhaps, indeed, it is an expanded version of it, like the *Ṣaṭsāhasrasaṃhitā* referred to above. Nor can it be the ṢaṭSS because this Tantra is divided into fifty chapters whereas the *Kumārikākhaṇḍa* is in sixty-six chapters.

It is not possible at present to date the MBT with any degree of accuracy. It cannot be earlier than the seventh century Buddhist logician, Dharmakīrti, to whom it refers.[8] Probably, however, Dharmakīrti much precedes the reduction of this portion of this Tantra. A reference to an invasion by foreigners who conquered the entire country after crossing the Indus[9] is apparently a reference to the full-scale invasion of India by Muslims in the early eleventh century. It appears, therefore, that the MBT cannot be older than this nor is it younger than 1180 A.D. which is the date of the oldest Nepalese manuscript.

To conclude, we shall say a few words about the traditional accounts of the revelation of the MBT. Up to now, I have managed to trace two. One is found in the *Yogakhaṇḍa*[10] of the MBT, and the other in the concluding portion of the *Kumārikākhaṇḍa.*[11] According to the latter account, the original form of this Tantra (here called *"Pārameśvaramata"*) was a fabulous million, million verses long (*lakṣakoṭi*). The essence of the doctrine of this Tantra was transmitted in another seventy million verses from which another version was supposed to have been derived consisting of one hundred and twenty-five thousand verses. The most essential doctrines of this Tantra were then recorded in a twenty-four thousand verse version which is the present MBT. This was transmitted by Kujeśī to Mitranātha in three sections.

The *Yogakhaṇḍa*'s account is more complex than that of the *Kumārikākhaṇḍa* and differs from it in certain details. Here the Divine Transmission of the *Khañjinīmata* is said to have passed originally from Ādinātha to Mitranātha, who then transmitted it to Ṣaṣṭinātha, who gave one half to Caryānātha. Caryānātha in his turn passed on half of what he had learned. Unfortunately, a break occurs in the text here so we do not know whom Caryānātha taught; possibly this was Oḍiyāṇanātha who is usually associated with the three other teachers. Whoever this teacher was, he transmitted half to Bṛhatkaṇṭha, who gave one half to Gaṇāvekṣa. The remaining portion of the *Khañjinīmata* was transmitted by Akulanātha. The text now goes on to explain that the version consisting of one hundred twenty-five thousand verses was brought to earth by Ciñca(nātha) and that all the rest of the teaching was transmitted by the community of Siddhas on the Island Free of Thought-Constructs (*nirvikalpadvīpa*) from whence it spread to India. We are also told that the Tantra of twenty-four thousand verses was brought to earth by Kalaṅkanātha. These two accounts are illustrated graphically in Table 8.

Table 8. The Transmission of the Manthānabhairavatantra.

1) *Pārameśvaramata* of 1 million, million verses

|

Version of 70 million verses

|

Version of 125,000 verses

|

MBT revealed to Mitranātha in three *khaṇḍas* together consisting of 24,000 verses.

2) Ādinātha
Mitranātha
Ṣaṣṭinātha - Caryānātha - ? - Bṛhatkaṇṭha -
Gaṇāvekṣa - Akulanātha
Ciñcanātha (also called Ciñcinīnātha) revealed
the 125,000 verse version.
Kalaṅkanātha revealed the 24,000 verse version.

Appendix C

The Canon of the Jayadrathayāmala

After completing this monograph, it was my good fortune to have been given a copy of a manuscript of the first *ṣaṭka* of the *Jayadratha-yāmala* by Mr. G. S. Sanderson who is at present lecturer in Sanskrit at Oxford University. Several chapters of this text are dedicated to the Śaiva canon.[1] P. C. Bagchi examined this section of this Tantra in the 1930s[2] but did not publish an extensive report of its contents, although he did point out its importance. It does, in fact, contain a great deal of interesting information relevant to the study of the Śaiva canon and its history. We have, therefore, thought it best to present it as a single unit largely as it stands in the original. The numbers in the margin refer to the folio numbers of the manuscript.

Bhairava, prompted by the goddess, sets out to give an account of the 165b
śāstras. He starts by explaining that a *śāstra* is so-called because it teaches (*śāsanāt*) those who are frightened, suffering or wicked the way to salvation (*trāṇa*) from their sins and worldly troubles.[3] All *śāstras* belong to four basic categories:[4]

Common (*sāmānya*)
Common-cum-particular (*sādhāraṇaviśeṣa*)
Particular (*viśeṣa*)
Specially particular (*viśeṣatara*)

Once Bhairava has enumerated these categories, he tells the goddess that this progressive development from less to more specialized knowledge through these four stages is inevitable because it is impossible to teach everything at once. Even so, however broad or focalized the terms of reference may be, all human and divinely revealed knowledge refers to the same reality. Bhairava also implies here that there is a temporal as well as a logical progression between these categories and, indeed, the last three do follow each other in roughly chronological order. Thus these are:

Common (sāmānya). The *śāstras* belonging to this category enjoy extensive popular support and are not criticized as improper by anyone. Thus, because everyone is fit to study and hear them and because their scope is very extensive, they are said to be 'common' as well as 'worldly' (*laukika*). They include the *Purāṇas*, literary works (*kāvya*) and those dealing with history (*itihāsa*), mathematics (*gaṇita*), dramaturgy (*nāṭaka*), metrics (*chandas*) and grammar (*śabda*).

Common-cum-particular (sādhāraṇaviśeṣa). Only Brahmins are competent to study these texts and so they are said to be 'particular'; while because those who study them do not need to affiliate themselves to any cult, they are also said to be common. To this category belongs the *Śruti*, here reckoned to be the three Vedas, namely, *Ṛk, Sāma* and *Yajus*—not the *Atharvaveda*. They are the most important in this group. Then comes *Smṛti*, the *Upaniṣads*, *Mantrasūtra*, the *Kalpasūtra* and logic (*anvīkṣā*).

Particular (viśeṣa). The texts belonging to this category are said to be 'particular' because they belong to specific traditions (*samaya*). These include the Saura, Śaiva, Pāñcarātra, Pramāṇa, Vaimala,[5] Ātharva, Sāṃkhya, Yoga, Bauddha and Ārhata.

"Śaiva" here means specifically the Śaivasiddhānta scriptures which are of two types according to whether they belong to the Śiva or Rudra group.

Specially Particular (viśeṣatara). These texts are more 'particular' than those belonging to the previous group because they are meant for the followers of specific cults within the various traditions. Amongst them are the scriptures of the Vajrayāna, including the *Guhyasamājatantra*.[6] To this category also belong the *Bhairava, Bhūta* and *Gāruḍa* Tantras.

The exposition of the canon which follows is concerned with this last category and more particularly with the Tantras of the Bhairava cult which encompass, from the JY's point of view, virtually the entire Śaiva canon apart from the Siddhānta. Thus this category of 'specially particular' texts is said to be divided variously into three, four and five currents (*srotas*) as well as into four *pīṭhas*.

166b Before going into the details of these divisions extensively, the discussion digresses to deal with the origin of the Śaiva scriptures in general. The goddess wants to know how the scriptures originated. She wants to know about the nature of the relationship (*saṃbandha*) between those who transmitted and received the scriptures because unless this relationship is established, the scriptures cannot serve as a source of insight (*pratipatti*).

Bhairava explains that Maheśvara is the sole cause of liberation in this beginningless, confined world of transmigratory existence. It is Maheśvara's nature to seek to grace mankind, while the latter is the object of his grace because every man is a victim of his own faults. Moreover, in his omniscience, Śiva knows how to grace humanity and liberate man from his state of bondage. The most direct means to this end is scripture which, like a powerful medicine, heals man's suffering and, through the revelation of its meaning, extinguishes the lamp of pain. It is through scripture that Śiva's divine vitality (*vīrya*) is made to fall into the wombs of liberation, fertilizing them to issue forth into the new life of the liberated state. Scripture is ultimately the instrumental cause (*nimitta*) of liberation and immediately that through which the relationship (*saṃbandha*) to the teachers of its purport is established and hence with its original source which is Śiva himself.

The Lord's body is pure consciousness; thus when he wishes to generate this relationship through the production of scripture, a movement (*pravṛtti*) arises within him that issues out of his transcendental, unmanifest state. *Kuṇḍalinī*, the power of consciousness and speech latent within him, is aroused by the fullness of the growing intensity of this movement and so straightens to become a manifest resonance (*svara*) within consciousness.[7] Śiva is in this way filled with the energy of speech and so assumes the form of the aggregate of all words (*śabdarāśi*), here identified with Sadāśiva who, eternal, (*sadā*) and endowed with Śiva's nature, is ever at the upper level (*ūrdhvasthāna*). Sadāśiva reflects upon the manifest universe as consisting essentially of two categories, namely, the 'listener' and 'speaker'. This is the one relationship (*saṃbandha*) through which the meaning of scripture is communicated. Therefore, although these are two aspects of a single reality and the relationship between them is undivided, it is of various types according to the level of its manifestation, namely:

Great (*mahat*): that between consciousness and its power.
Subsequent (*ānantara*): that between Sadāśiva and the Vīras.
Intermediate (*avāntara*): that between he who awakens and he who is awakened.
Divine (*divya*): The relationship between Sadāśiva as he who awakens and divine beings below him up to the level of Māyā.
Mixed (*miśra*): that between divine beings and sages.
Other than divine (*adivya*): that between sages and ordinary men.[8]

Sadāśiva as the source of Śaiva scripture is in his supreme (*para*) form. At the intermediate (*parāpara*) level he is said to be the vitality of yoga and his body consists of the five Mantras associated with his five faces which are the sources of the five currents (*srotas*) of Śaiva scripture.[9] In his lower (*apara*) form, Sadāśiva is the lord of the *Mantrapīṭha* and is here said to have four faces. Now, although the JY itself belongs to the *Vidyāpīṭha*, it also considers the *Mantrapīṭha* to be very important and deals with this class extensively. Accordingly, the *Mantrapīṭha* is said to be the divine *pīṭha* (*divyapīṭha*) of the *Mudrā-* and *Maṇḍala- pīṭhas* of which Sadāśiva is also the Lord. From Sadāśiva's five faces issues the pure knowledge (*śuddhavijñāna*) through which the divine Sound (*nāda*) and Drop (*bindu*) emerge. When these combine with the metres, they generate through their rhythm all the *śāstras.* The gods first revealed reality (*artha*) through the Vedic metres (*chandas*); even so all the scriptures are forms in which Sadāśiva embodies himself. Consciousness has no form in itself but is said in this way to possess a body made of Mantras. As such, Sadāśiva is full of divine powers and has a form (*vigraha*). Through the four instruments (*karaṇa*) of mind, ego, intellect and speech, he assumes the identity of the teacher who instructs; while when the fourth instrument—speech—is substituted by the power of hearing, he becomes the disciple who listens. He who knows the four instruments is said to be a "Mahākāruṇika".[10] Within these gross bodies is the subtle body (*ātivāhikaliṅga*) governed by the vital breath which moves through the right and left currents of vitality. In this way the right and left currents of scripture descend into the world along with a 'mixed' current formed by their conjunction to which the *Yāmalas* belong.

1. The Pīṭha Division

The JY deals with Āgamic Śaivism from two points of view. Firstly it enumerates the Tantras which belong to the *pīṭhas;* then it enumerates the lines of transmission of the scriptures from master to disciple (*santāna*) and the schools (*maṭhikā*) belonging to the currents (*srotas*) of the scriptures.[11] Thus the JY seeks to present a picture of Āgamic Śaivism and its many different branches from the point of view of both systems of classification. It reserves, however, pride of place for the *pīṭha* system as the most fundamental classification of scripture while the *srotas* system is, in a sense, devolved to a classification of groups of Śaiva traditions and lines of transmission of doctrines, each peculiar to its own parent current. The ideal Śaiva master (here the term *"guru"* is generally used rather than *"ācārya"*) is one who is conversant with the teaching of all the currents.[12]

The relationship between the *pīṭha* and *srotas* classifications is peculiar and somewhat strained. It appears, as we have already had occasion to remark, that it is a system which developed after the classification into five currents, at a time when they were reduced to three (see above p. 42 ff), namely into 'right', 'left' and 'mixed' currents and takes over from it as a system of classification of scriptures as a whole (and as a set of groups to which the Tantras affiliated themselves), cutting across the distinctions made within it. We have already noted that this is happening in the BY's account of the Śaiva canon while the following remark in the JY seems to echo the view of the BY which, as we shall see, is considered by the JY to be a particularly important Tantra: "The four *pīṭhas* are together said to reside in the right, left and mixed currents as if they were the principal branch in a subsidiary branch (of the teachings)."[13]

Before dealing with the *pīṭhas* extensively, Bhairava talks about them in general and deals with their contents summarially. Bhairava starts by listing a number of synonyms for the word *"pīṭha"*, all of which mean a "group" or "collection".[14] The *Mantrapīṭha* is associated with masculine words while the *Vidyāpīṭha* is associated with feminine ones. Perhaps by this is implied that the Tantras of the *Mantrapīṭha* deal more extensively with male deities while those of the *Vidyāpīṭha* with female ones, as the *Svacchandabhairavatantra* and the SYM, which belong to these two *pīṭhas* respectively, exemplify. The *Mudrāpīṭha* is of three forms related to mind, speech and body. It is called "terrible" (*ghora*). The *Maṇḍalapīṭha* is where all three unite and is said to be undivided. This does not mean that the Tantras of this *pīṭha* are monistic but rather that it has, according to the JY's account, no subdivisions. Again, the preference the JY has for the *Mantrapīṭha* is evidenced by the way it characterizes it as the repository of the supreme brilliance (*paramaṃ tejas*) which symbolizes the state of the enjoying subject (*bhoktṛ*), while the *Vidyāpīṭha* is the object of his enjoyment (*bhogya*). Mudrā includes both of these while Maṇḍala is present in them all.[15]

To the *Mantrapīṭha* ("beyond which there is nothing") are said to belong twelve thousand Mantras. It consists essentially of eight *Bhairavatantras*, namely, the *Svacchanda, Unmatta, Asitāṅga, Ruru, Caṇḍa, Krodha, Jhaṅkāra* and *Kapālīśa*[16] with which secondary Tantras are associated. The JY appears to quote a verse from the *Sarvavīratantra* recorded by Kṣemarāja in his commentary on the SvT which states that the Tantras of this *pīṭha* are four, namely, the *Svacchanda, Caṇḍa, Krodha* and *Unmatta-bhairavatantras.*[17] The apparent contradiction is reconciled if we understand that what is meant here is that these are the four major Tantras of the *Mantrapīṭha*, each of which is linked with one of the four remaining *Bhairavatantras.* Consequently the *Mantrapīṭha* is said to be two-fold.[18]

The *Vidyāpīṭha* is also extensive.[19] The major Tantras listed as belonging to this *pīṭha* are the following: *Sarvavīra, Samāyoga, Siddhayogeśvarīmata, Pañcāmṛta, Viśvādya, Yoginījālaśaṃbara, Vidyābheda, Śiraścheda, Mahāsaṃmohana, Nayottara* and *Mahāraudra*. Then comes a list of *Yāmalas* (it appears that all the *Yāmalas* belong to the *Vidyāpīṭha*); these are: *Rudra, Brahmā, Viṣṇu, Skanda, Auma* (i.e., *Umā*), *Rudrabheda, Hari* and *Gautamī yāmalas*.

Firstly, it is interesting to note that the JY itself does not figure amongst the *Yāmalas* but is separately listed as the *Śiraścheda*. Although eight *Yāmalas* are listed here, in the detailed exposition which follows (see p. 114 ff.) only the first five of them are discussed, of which the BY is considered to be the most important. Eighteen subsidiary *Yāmalas* are said to be associated with them, namely, seven *Mātṛkāyāmalas*, six *Yoginīyāmalas* (beginning with *Jayā*) and five *Mātṛyāmalas*. According to the detailed account of the five *Yāmalas*, four of them are said to generate four others as follows: Brahmā → Vetāla, Viṣṇu → Īśāna, Rudra → Atharva and Skanda → Sarasvatī.[20] The standard complement of eight *Yāmalas* is thus complete, although these eight are not the ones listed above. Nor are they quite the same as those listed amongst the sixty-four *Bhairavatantras* (see p. 121 ff.) which are: *Brahmā, Rudra, Viṣṇu, Skanda, Gautamīya, Atharva, Vetāla* and *Ruruyāmala*. However, if we identify the *Ruruyāmala* with the *Rurubheda*, only the *Umā* and *Hari-yāmalas* are missing in this list.

The *Mudrāpīṭha* consists of eighteen thousand Mantras and one hundred and eight *Kalpas*. It has three principal divisions associated with the following root Tantras (*sūtra*): *Hṛdbheda, Mātṛbheda* and *Kubjikāmata*.

The *Maṇḍalapīṭha* has only one division belonging to its root *sūtra* and is said to be sealed by a hundred (i.e., countless) *maṇḍalas*. It appears from the JY's account that the *Maṇḍalapīṭha* had little substance of its own (at least at the time of the redaction of the JY). Essentially, it is considered to be a part of the other *pīṭhas*, enjoying little autonomous existence of its own as a separate category.

Finally, the JY refers to another important classification of the scripture, one we have already discussed at length (see above p. 43 ff.) namely, that into eight groups of eight (*aṣṭāṣṭaka*) which, as we shall see, is essentially the same as we find in the *Śrīkaṇṭhīyasaṃhitā*.

After this brief exposition Bhairava goes on to give a detailed description of the contents of these *pīṭhas* along with the lines of their transmission.

2. Mantrapīṭha

This is basically divided into the Tantras associated with four root 169b
Tantras or *mūlasūtras*, namely, *Svacchanda-*, *Caṇḍa-*, *Krodha-*, and *Unmatta-bhairavasūtras*.

Svacchandabhairavasūtra. This is divided into two branches, namely, those of *Svacchanda* and *Asitāṅga*. The *Svacchanda* branch was made manifest at the command of Svacchandabhairava. It consists of eight sections, each taught by a Bhairava starting with Kaṅkālabhairava and ending with Sitabhairava. The first to hear these teachings was Ananta who received it through the power of yoga (*yogaśakti*) operating on the Pure Path. They were then adopted by Śrīkaṇṭha and Lakulīśa. Lakulapāṇi expounded the teachings extensively to sages like Gautama who knew the Veda. His best disciple was Musalendra to whom he transmitted the essence of the teachings.[21]

Asitāṅga, the second branch, was revealed by eight Bhairavas including Asitāṅga and Kapāla to the Anantavīras manifested through them. The teaching was then transmitted through the ages in various Tantras considered to be schools or branches (*śākhā*) of the *Asitāṅgon-mattasūtra*. These include *Asitāṅga, Mahānāda, Ekapāda, Mahodaya,* 170a
Bindukapāla, Nādendu, Śekhara, Caryāmṛta, Kalājāla, Kālakūṭa, Mahāmṛta, Mahāghaṅghala, Bhairavaghaṅghala, Mahānirvāṇayoga, Vicitrabhairava, Bhīma, Mahābīja and *Parampada*.[22]

Caṇḍabhairavasūtra. This *sūtra* is also divided into two sections, namely those belonging to Caṇḍa- and Ruru-Bhairavas. The *Caṇḍabhairava-sūtra*, which has twelve *Kalpas*, was originally revealed to Vikarāla, Siṃhakeśa and to one other(?) along with eight Vīras by Caṇḍanātha. These sages founded several schools. This Great Knowledge (*mahājñāna*) was then transmitted by Caṇḍanātha's will along the following line of teachers.

From Siṃhakesara to Manohara → Viṣṇu → Kauśika → Śrīvatsa → 170b
Śrīvināśa → Śrīgarbha → Viśvavaiśrava → Saura → Midhāswāmi → Subhadra → Muñjakeśin → Adhokṣaja → Medhasas. It was also given to Agastya's circle of masters by Vigraheśa and, by the will of the Śrīkaṇṭha-sūris, was transmitted by Bhairava who gave it to the gods. It was then transmitted to Śākaṭāyana → Pippalāda → Uddālaka → son of Nāciketas who brought it into this world with its many branches (*śākhā*).

The Tantras belonging to this *sūtra* are twenty-one in number, namely *Daṇḍatantra, Vīratantra, Mahāpīṭha, Supīṭha, Caṇḍapīṭha, Suśrāvaṇa, Purākalpa, Caṇḍogra, Caṇḍamaṇḍala, Caṇḍāsidhāra, Bhūtogra* (?),

Bhūtanigraha, Vijaya, Tripāda, Karṇa, Amogha, Ardhalocana, Pātālavijaya, Trailokyavijaya, Mahāḍāmara and *Ghoraḍāmaratantra*.[23]

171a **Krodhabhairavasūtra.** This *sūtra* is divided into two main groups—the superior (*para*) and inferior (*apara*), taught by Krodhabhairava and Jhaṅkāra respectively. The Krodhabhairava group has eight branches. The Tantras of these branches were taught by eight Bhairavas, including Kāntibhairava, Śikhāśekhara and Rodhina (?). The branch associated with Saṃghātabhairava is also divided into eight branches taught by eight Bhairavas starting with Śaśāṅkaśekhara up to Virūpākṣa. All these branches again have many subdivisions so that the *Krodhatantra* group is said to have been transmitted along innumerable lines. Kāntabhairava spoke it to Rudroṅkāra and Maheśa while the *Krodhograsaṃhitā* belonging to this Tantra was taught by Krodhabhairava himself to Kamaleśvara who transmitted it to Bhīma who gave it to Jñānabhṛt and Aṃśumati. Again Vimalabhairava gave the *Vimalātantra* to Candrāpīḍa, while Krodheśa gave it to Surāpīḍa and Tārāpīḍa. (Śikhā?) śekhara-
171b bhairava gave the *Krodhamālinīsaṃhitā* (said to describe many *mudrās*) to Amaleśa, while Mahāvīraśikhara transmitted it to his disciples on the lower level. The *Krodhānalasaṃhitā* of one hundred seventy-five thousand verses was taught by Māyāpiṇḍa and Amaleśa; the hundred thousand verse recension was taught by Bhairava, while Nandin taught the version of twenty million verses. At his command Bhairava and the goddess taught it to the Bālakhilyas. The one thousand eight hundred verse version was taught by Nandinātha, that of seventeen (hundred?) verses by Krodhin(?) and that of eight (hundred?) by Dattātreya, while the third group of eight Vīras gave it to Śītāṃsuśekhara. The *Nānājhaṅkāramālinīsaṃhitā* was received by Viśālāja from Jhaṅkāra while Krūrabhairava taught a section of this Tantra called *Krodhakaraṅkiṇīsaṃhitā* to Kandarpa. The *Binduvijayatantra* was imparted to Śaśibhūṣaṇa. *Bindukīṭīratantra* (?) was taught by Kalikāhlādadeva. Sāmanta received the *Yogamālinīsaṃhitā* from Krakaca and Śaśikānti gave the *Krodhasamvarttakā* to Mahāsāmantadeva. Tāra received the *Mahānādatantra* while the *Viṣamakṣodhāmalītantra*(?) belongs to Mahātārāpati. The *Krodhatantra* was transmitted from Tārāpati → Sutārāpavana → Dhāmalīla → Jitalāvaṇyaka → Hāṭakanātha and was finally received
172a by Kālānala.

Bhairava concludes this section by defining the term *"krodha"* (meaning literally "anger"): "Anger is said to be that by virtue of which one becomes genuinely one-pointedly intent on removing whatever obstacle there may be to liberation."[24]

Unmattasūtra. Bhairava starts by saying that this root Tantra and its ramifications are but a drop from the infinite ocean of Sadāśiva. The *Unmattapaddhati* is divided into two lines, each of which is of eight divisions corresponding to eight Bhairavas. Unmattabhairava taught the *Unmattatantra* to which belong twenty-one Saṃhitās, while Kapālīśa presides over the second line of which there are eight principal Saṃhitās, namely: *Anantabhairava, Anantavijaya, Bhairava, Para, Vīṇāśikhā, Acaloḍḍīśa, Mārtaṇḍasaṃhitā* and *Caṇḍograbhairava.* These Saṃhitās were brought to earth by eight sages amongst which only Viśālalocana, Tārāpati and Sutāra are named, the latter being the revealer of the *Mārtaṇḍasaṃhitā.* These Saṃhitās are linked to each other and to other Tantras as follows:

Śikhā - Amṛta, Ānanda, Pramoda, Anantavijaya[25]
Anācala and *Amṛtānanda - Ānanda, Gambhīra, Jīvānanda, Śirottara, Sunanda.*
Mārtaṇḍa - Mantharā, Vijayānanda, Surānanda
Caṇḍogra - Sadānanda, Aśritānanda, Maṅgalānanda, Maṅgalā.
(Bhairava) - Lelihānā, Mahājvāla, Caṇḍamālinī, Karaṅkinī, Karālā, Karṇamūla, Kalevarā, Mahāphetkārabījā

Each of the Tantras associated with the *Unmattabhairavasaṃhitā* have other Tantras associated with them. These are:

Lelihānā	*Nityānityā, Anityā, Nityā.*	
Mahājvālā	*Umādeha, Nīlakaṇṭha, Yoganidra*	
Caṇḍamālinī	*Pūjodaya, Kuraṅgākṣī, Padākṣī, Citrakandharā.*	173a
Karaṅkinī	Two extensive Saṃhitās - not named.	
Karāla	*Nigraha, Dhvastavighnā*	
Karṇamūla	*Vighnā, Sudīptabhāva.*	
Kalevarā	*Samayā, Kṣudrā.*	
Phetkāra	*Vimalā, Śivā.*	

The *Unmattatantra* of the first line was transmitted by *Unmattabhairava* (?) to the gods starting with the five Śivas (*Śivapañcaka*). From *Śuddhavidyā* it was transmitted in a version of three hundred and fifty (chapters?) to Dhyānāhāra who taught it to Prapañca, then to Kuṇḍabhadra and Śikheśa who gave it to Bhīra (?).

Bhairava then explains that he assumed the form of Unmattabhairava when he became mad with passion at the sight of Dākṣāyaṇīkālī. A seed-syllable issued from him in this state from which Bhairava was generated in his terrible (*ghora*) form. The goddess, his consort (*jāyā*), saw him then and after coupling with him asked him for the knowledge whose awesome

power assumes the 'extremely terrible' (*mahāghora*) form of Unmatta-
173b bhairava. Pleased with her, Bhairava spoke the *Jāyātantra* of twelve thousand verses. This Tantra has five versions (*kalpa*) of six thousand, three thousand, one thousand eight hundred, eight hundred and seventy-five, and five (or five hundred?) verses.

Before concluding this section on the *Mantrapīṭha* with the affirmation that it is very extensive, Bhairava states that the *Bhairavatantra* was brought down to earth by the eight sages: Durvāsas, Sanaka, Jiṣṇu, Kapila, Kāśyapa, Kuru, Saṃvarta and Śaṅkhapāla.

3. The Vidyāpīṭha

The *Vidyāpīṭha* is said to be closely connected to the *Mantrapīṭha*. The account of its contents is basically divided into three sections. Firstly, a brief outline of these sections and their contents:

The Śaktitantras belonging to the Middle Current. These are the *Sarvavīra, Triśūla* (i.e., the SYM), *Śrīcakra, Viśvādya, Yoginījālaśambara, Vidyābheda* and *Śirohṛta* (i.e., *Śiraścheda*).[26]

The Tantras belonging to the Left Current. *Nayottara, Mahāraudra, Mahāsaṃmohana.*[27]

The Tantras belonging to the Right Current. These are basically the *Yāmalas* of which five are the root texts. Of these, four are in a group of
174a their own, namely *Raudra-, Auma-, Vaiṣṇava-* and *Skanda-yāmalas.*

The fifth is the *Brahmayāmala* which is said to expound "the conduct which involves the use of rotten flesh" (*kravyācāra*) whereas the others do not. It is also called *"Picumata," "Dvayakṣara"* or just *"Mata."* Seven other root Tantras (*sūtra*) are associated with it, namely *Ucchuṣma, Nirācāra, Mahācāra, Sarvatobhadra,*[28] *Dvika, Sarvātmaka* and *Mahādakṣiṇa.* The last Tantra is divided into two sections. Thus there are eight Tantras altogether and as these are all *Matatantras* they are called the "Eight Matas" (*matāṣṭaka*).

After concluding that there are fifteen root Tantras (*mūlasūtra*) in the *Vidyāpīṭha*, the JY moves on to a more detailed treatment of each of them.

The Sarvavīratantra. This Tantra was revealed by Mahādeva and transmitted along the following line: Dakṣiṇa → Mahāvīra → Pracaṇḍa → Kaṅkala → Nīlakaṇṭha → Bhairava → consort → Garutmat → Daśakhaṇḍara → Rāvaṇa and Vibhīṣaṇa → Pataṅga → Bhavapāpin who then transmitted it to men.

The basic form of this Tantra (*mūlasūtra*) is said to be of three hundred and fifty (chapters?), its concise (*saṃgraha*) version is called *"sāhasra"* which presumably means that it is one thousand verses long. Other versions consist of sixteen thousand, twelve thousand and twenty-four thousand verses. Altogether this Tantra is said to be over one hundred thousand verses long and has been heard, spoken and transmitted many times.

The Siddhayogeśvarīmata. This Tantra has three (sections/versions?) taught by three different teachers, namely: *Para* by Mahendra, *Parāpara* by Bhīṣma and *Apara* by Siddhayogin. 174b

A number of Tantras, all of which are said to be two hundred and fifty (chapters?) long, are associated with the SYM and transmitted by various teachers. These are:

	Teacher	Tantra
	Mālādhara	*Mālinī* (?)
	Karālin	— (?)
	Ajakarṇa	*Khecarīvijaya*
	Śaṅkhadhārin	*Mahāśaṅkhatantra*
	Marmaphetkāra	*Phetkāraikākṣara*
	Vidyādhipati	*Vidyālakṣa*
	Vidyolka	*Vidyāprasūti*
	Aghora	*Sitāghora*
	Ghoreśvara	*Raktāghoreśvarī*
	Vidyā	*Kṛṣṇaka*
	Kīṭacakṣus	*Kṛṣṇaghoreśvarī*
	Bhairava's will	*Pītaghorī*
	Padmamudrā	*Mahāmāyā* (?)
Rudras	Nirañjana	*Bhadra*
	Icchā	*Kālī*
	Jnātṛ	*Karaṇkinī*

The *Siddhayogeśvarītantra* was transmitted along the following line: Śrīkaṇṭha → Kṣudra → Amṛtabindu (=Binduparāpitṛ) → Vipra → Bhairava → consort → Kṛṣṇa → Umāpati → Vedaśiras → Aṅgiras → Utathya → Ūrdhvaretas who taught it to men.

The Śrīcakratantra. Eight *Cakrasaṃhitās* are associated with this Tantra, namely: *Svaracakra, Varṇacakra, Nāḍīcakra, Guhyacakra, Kālacakra, Sauracakra, Vāhneyacakra* and *Somajacakra.*[29] Śiva 'resounds' (*svarati*) 175a
and is manifest in the *Svaracakratantra* while *Varṇacakra* deals with

Mantra. *Nāḍīcakra* (also called *Sutārā*) and the *Guhyacakra* deal with the nature of *Śakti*. There are two *Kālacakratantras;* both are said to deal with the duration of man's life (*āyus*). One of the two is Saura and said to be auspicious (*śubha*); the other is Buddhist and is considered to be inauspicious (*aśubha*). *Vāhneyacakra* is said to be 'enflamed' (*dīpta*) by Mantra while the teachings of *Somajacakra* (also called *"Caṇḍatantra"*) destroy death.

The Pañcāmṛtatantra. The only information supplied about this root Tantra is the line of its transmission which is: Śakti → yoginīs, gaṇas, gods and snakes → Prahlāda → Auśanasena → Bhārgava → Devala → Kṛṣṇātreya ("who knew the Vedas") → Kuśadhvaja → Sitoda → Patadra (?) → Dantya.

The Viśvādyatantra. This Tantra is named *"Viśvādya"* because it teaches the nature of the group of yoginīs (*yoginījāla*) starting with the one named
175b Viśvā. The line of transmission is as follows: Sadāśiva → Viśvātman → Vimaladṛśa → Kānticchatra → Śauṇḍin → Bhairava → Śakti who hid it. A few of the Mantras of this Tantra were known to Kilaheli who learned them from Śakti and transmitted them to the world of men.

Yoginījālaśambara. There are twelve Tantras associated with this root Tantra: *Mahāsaṃvarttaka, Bhīma, Tilaka, Nakha, Bimba, Candralekha, Caṇḍāśitaka, Śilāda, Bhagamālā, Bhoginī, Sukeśin* and *Sudhāma.*[30]

Associated with these Tantras are twenty Upasaṃhitās: *Tāraka,*
176a *Akṣī, Pāśaghnī, Nandinī, Gāminī, Bhṛguṇī, Satyā, Dākṣāyaṇī, Umā, Māyā, Mahākālī, Caṇḍālī, Acalaśrī, Bhadrakālī, Sumedhā, Tārā, Arkamaṇi, Tārakābharaṇa, Raudrī* and *Jvālāmālāntika.*

The line of transmission of the *Yoginījālaśambara* is as follows: Mahāsaṃvartanātha → Bhīma → Tailaka → Dīrghanakhin → Bimba → Caṇḍavṛddha → Caṇḍāśilātaka → Śilāda → Bhagamālin → Bhaginī → Vīra → Sukeśin → Sudhāma → Jvālāmukhāntika → Bhairava → Śakti → Ūrdhvaretas → Ananta.

The *Yoginījālaśambaratantra* is said to the glory of the *Anantasrotas.*

The Vidyābhedatantra. Seven Saṃhitās are associated with this Tantra taught by as many teachers; these are:

Teacher	*Tantra*
Vidyeśāna	*Siddhārthā*
Pralamba	*Vidyālayā*
Padadru	*Vidyārajñī*
Karāla	*Vidyāmaṇi*
Ajātman	*Vidyārāśi*

Vidyeśāna	*Vidyāprasūti*
Aṃśaphala	*Tridaṇḍī*

Six of these Saṃhitās have not yet been revealed.[31] Bhairava will give them to the world in the last age (*yuga*). 176b

The Śiraśchedatantra. This Tantra is taught by Bhairava himself in the last aeon. It is the last of the seven root Tantras of this Current to come to earth and also belongs equally to the Right and Left Currents. It is expressly said to be a *Yāmalatantra* and is also called *"Jayadratha"* or *"Ṣaṭsāhasra."* It was transmitted from Mīna(?) → Narasiṃha → Yoginī → Daivavatsyaikacakṣus → Śukra. A number of Tantras are associated with it:

Teacher	*Tantra*
Vajrakāya	*Vajramālinīsaṃhitā*
Jvalantākṣa	*Jvālātantra*
Yamāntika	*Yamāntakatantra*
Kālānta	*Kālāntakatantra*
Plavana	*Plavanatantra*
Caṇḍavega	*Caṇḍavegasaṃhitā*
Nidhīśa	*Tārānidhitantra*

The *Śatrughnatantra* was transmitted by Śatrumardana → Ekākṣa → Kāla and Mīna who divided it into two sections (*skandha*). Bhairava received it in the form of the *Kālabhedatantra* (also called *Kālasaṃkarṣaṇa*). He taught it to his consort and to Yātudhānadhipa and Vṛnadārakamuni. It was transmitted through his divine power in countless sections (*skandha*).

The Saṃmohanatantra. Once when the Lord of the Demons, in alliance with the Heroes and the circle of Mothers, was fighting the gods, he drank the sacred nectar and became drunk. In this state he started to dance while the Mothers, headed by Cakrakāralinī, began to devour the circle of the gods along with Bhairava who presides over it. Śiva, aware of the danger, emitted into the ocean of wine a Lotus of Power of four petals on which sat the goddesses Jayā, Vijayā, Jitā and Aparājitā with their brother, Tumburu, seated in the centre. They played upon their *vīṇās* and the terrible circle of Mothers, attracted by the music, desisted from their intent.[32] It was the same Tumburu, skilled both in playing the *vīṇā* and vocal music, who, along with his four sisters, brought the *Mahāsaṃmohanatantra* to earth. 177a

The line of transmission of this Tantra is as follows: Tumburu → 177b

Maheśāna → Saṃmohana → Ananta → Trimūrti → Dundubhi → Nīlakaṇṭha. Nīlarudra was another teacher of this Tantra. He had a large number of disciples who were also conversant with the sixty-four *Bhairavatantras.*[33] These all belonged to the *Bhārgava* branch of the line of transmission.

Associated Tantras. *Māyābījottara, Saṃmohanāmṛta, Jayāmṛta, Vicitra, Tārāmṛta, Mahāmṛta, Guṇāmṛta, Kalāsāra, Parāmṛta, Trottala, Bindusāra, Māyāsāra, Mahodaya, Vidyājāla, Mahājāla, Madana, Madanodaya, Mantrodaya, Pramoda, Rakṣarakṣa, Surakṣa, Traiguṇa, Bhūtaḍāmara, Trailokyavijaya, Vijaya, Nīlaketu,* (*Vasudhārā*?), *Aṅkapraśna, Priyodaya, Mahābala, Vipraghna, Jambhana, Mohana, Prabhā, Śikhā, Cuḍāmaṇī, Kānta, Karkoṭa, Karapūjita, Saṃmohatilaka, Bimbatilaka, Tilaka, Prayojana, Durvāsāmṛta, Sundara, Kandarpa-vijayā, Līla, Lalita, Rativardhana, Bhogineya, Viśāla, Bhrātṛtantra.*[34]

178a ***The Nayottaratantra.*** The sages Śukra and Aṅgiras received this Tantra and brought it down into the world, transmitting it to Candraśekhara. A number of related Tantras are listed: *Trailokyamohana, Bimba, Dānavārivimohana, Tārākābhyudaya, Samgrāmavijaya, Nayasāra, Tilaka, Kolāhala, Amburāśi, Cāpamālī, Mṛgadhvaja, Nārāyaṇa* and *Vaṣaṭkāra.*

The Mahāraudratantra. The deity of this Tantra is called Mahāraudra or Ruru (bhairava). He taught this Tantra to Śarva → Rudra → Saṃvarta → Caṇḍa and Śauṇḍin → Ardhanarīśa who taught a short version to Bhṛṅga.

182b ***The Yāmalas.*** The term "yāmala" which literally means "a couple in union" and commonly refers to the coupling of the god with his consort, is here given a special meaning as the union of Mantra and Vidyā. The implication here is that these works deal with both the ritual formulas corresponding to and embodying the gods (as Mantras) as well as the goddesses (as Vidyās).[35] Again these operate in the domain of another couple, namely, knowledge (*jñāna*), which is both insight into ultimate principles and an understanding of the methods described in the Tantras, together with action (*kriyā*) which is the application of this knowledge. They depend on one another.[36] The goal of spiritual endeavour is achieved by following the teachings of the *Yāmalas*, dealing as they do with these four topics.

179b ***The Brahmayāmala.*** The root of all the *Yāmalas* is considered to be the *Brahmayāmala.* It has three principal divisions called Raurava, Andhaka and Kanaka. The *Viṣṇu, Skanda* and *Rudrayāmalas* belong to these three respectively. The four Vedas are said to originate from them along with

the *Umāyāmala.*[37] The *Brahmayāmala* has many other secondary
divisions and many Tantras are associated with it. It is said to partake of
the character of all five *srotas* and is also called *"Picumata."* The word
"Picu" is said to consist of two units, namely, "Pi" which means "body" 179b
(*piṇḍa*) and "cu" which means "seed" (*bīja*): a true yogin is one who unites
these two elements, that is, his body with the seed of consciousness. Again,
"Pi" denotes menstrual flow (*kāminīpuṣpa*) and "cu" the male seed (*retas*).
The repeated union of these two in conjunction with the performance of
the appropriate ritual (*kriyā*) and recitation of Mantra is considered to be
Picu. "Pi" is also said to denote the female organ (*yoni*) while "cu" is the
male seed. This seed—called *"vindu"*—is the omniscient knower—'vid'.
It is the supreme seed of consciousness.

The BY is the main *Matatantra* and has eight *Matatantras* associated with it. These, along with the teachers who brought them to earth and *anutantras* associated with them, are as follows:[38]

Teacher	*Matatantra*	*Anutantra*
Bindusāra	Raktā°	Utpala°
Kapālin	Pecikā° (Hedāmata)	Karālinīmata
Hetuyāna (?)	Mṛgālinīmata (Vṛkādaya)	Aitreya
Śiva	Śāmbara	Sārasvata
	Utphullaka[39]	Kalāsāra + Mukuṭa
Nīlakeśin	Nīlakeśa	Lampaṭa
Bhāruḍī	Bhāruṇḍa	Kālākhya
Kauśikī	Piṅgalā	Picusāra and Nayodaya

Associated with the eight *anutantras* are eight *pariśiṣṭatantras.* How these 180a
are linked is not always made clear. They are *Pañcālika* (linked with the
Utpalatantra), *Mānava* (associated with the *Vāgāvalitantra*), *Karālīmata*
and its *'sārasaṃgraha'*, *Lakṣmī* (associated with the *Kālākhya*), *Vimala*
(associated with the *Lampaṭatantra*), *Kacchapi* (associated with the
Kampakūhādrūtantra) and *Garbhaprakaraṇa* (associated with the
Nayodayatantra).

From the *pariśiṣṭatantras* originate the *upasūtras.* These are *Aśvapluta, Sāraṅga, Gojika* (?), *Bhedavipluta, Vaibhaṅga, Mātaṅga, Kusumālī* and *Savitraka.*

All these Tantras are the root ancilliaries (*mūlapariśiṣṭa*) of the BY. Along with them are seven *miśrasūtras* which are said to belong to all five currents of scripture. These are *Muṣṭi, Kuśa, Lava, Kālasāra, Ambikā, Tilaka* and *Avadhūta.*

Bhairava now goes on to discuss an interesting matter which concerns both the exegesis of these Tantric texts and how they are conceived to be related to one another. Bhairava explains that there are five types of basic Tantras (*sūtra*) which disclose the different levels of meaning of the teachings.[40] These are as follows:

Mūlasūtra: This is the root Tantra. There are different root Tantras for each *pīṭha*.[41] Each one is supposed to deal extensively with the teachings of a given tradition as a whole. It is the text which indicates (*sūcaka*) the entire extent of the doctrines and ritual procedures of its tradition.

Gūhyasūtra: The Tantras of this type discuss the hidden esoteric meaning of the teachings.

Nayasūtra: These Tantras deal with how the adept is likely to fall from the path and lose the attainments he has already acquired (*siddhi*) and how he can get them back.

Uttarasūtra: This discusses and clarifies the intended sense of the teachings as determined by these *sūtras*.

The Uttarottarasūtra: This elucidates and supplements what remains to be understood or has, inadvertently, not been dealt with fully in the previous four *sūtras*. It is said to teach the ultimate purport of these scriptures just as it is inherently in itself and beyond all thought-constructs (*nirvikalpa*).

It is the teacher's responsibility to expound the meaning of the scriptures clearly. He does this by connecting their sense into a coherent whole through a number of correlates (*sambandha*) he establishes between their contents. He deals with the root Tantras individually at first in order to bring out the underlying coherence between them and their associated Tantras, and to then ideally establish it between all the *sūtras* and their teachings. According to the JY, there are five correlates which, by implication, it juxtaposes with the five types of *sūtras*. These are:

Indication (*sūcana*): The teacher summarizes what has been taught before and on the basis of that indicates what is going to be taught further.

Preliminary Exposition (*abhidhāna*)

Validation (*gamaka*): The teacher now gradually unfolds the meaning of the *sūtra*. In order to make it clear, he makes use of examples and refutes possible objections.

Clarification (*prakāśaka*): This follows from the previous correlate.

Ordering the Disordered (*saṅkīrṇa*): In order to explain the meaning of a Tantra, the teacher must distinguish between the sections of it which deal with particular matters. As he proceeds from one chapter to the next of the Tantra, he points out where one topic begins and another ends. He deals first with each section individually and then indicates how they are related to the others.

Other Āgamas also deal with these correlations in their own way. Abhinava devotes a section of his *Tantrāloka* to an explanation of how the teacher should transmit the meaning of the scriptures to his disciples (*vyākhyāvidhi*).[42] Abhinava bases himself mostly on the *Devyāyāmala* which Jayaratha accordingly quotes extensively in his commentary. Paraphrasing this Tantra, Abhinava starts by saying that there are five kinds of teachers:

Those who know just one *Kalpa*, that is, a version of a given root Tantra or a Tantra associated with it.

Those who know the entire range of *Kalpas* associated with a given Tantra.

Those who know all scriptures belonging to a given class (*śāstra*).

Those who know the meaning of all the Saṃhitās.

Those who know all the classes of scriptures.[43]

The best teacher is, of course, one that belongs to the fifth group. However, if a student cannot find a teacher who knows the scriptures in their entirety, he should seek a teacher who is well conversant with the particular Tantra he wishes to learn and whose teachings he seeks to put into practice.

The *Devyāyāmala*, like the JY, says that there are five correlates through which the teacher can explain the meaning of a Tantra with reasoned argument in order to preserve the doctrines of his own tradition (*svāmnāya*). These are:

The Sections (*pāda*): Theoretically a Tantra of the *Saṃhitā* type is divided into four sections, called *pāda*. The teacher must first explain the overall sense of the Tantra. He does this by dealing with each one of these sections, explaining their contents in general terms in the order in which they appear in the beginning, middle and end of each section.

The Coherence of Each Section (*pādagata*): The teacher should explain how each part of each section fits with every other in a coherent manner and without contradictions.

The Chapters (*paṭala*): The teacher can now explain the contents of the Tantra chapter by chapter and in so doing connect one to the other.

The Meaning of the Words (*padārtha*): The teacher now explains each statement in the Tantra individually.

The Meaning of the Sūtra: The teacher can now deal with the entire root Tantra. He reflects on its overall content, distinguishing it from other *sūtras*, in order to elucidate its unique character in relation to other *sūtras*.[44]

Although the divisions into grades of *sūtras* is more theoretical than real, it is interesting to observe how the Āgamas attempted to find through it coherence in their extensive and diverse literature. Certainly some Tantras were more closely linked to each other than were others; even so we can't help feeling that we have here an ideal scheme. We can compare this scheme with the Buddhist Tantras which do, in fact, tend to develop in this way, at least in part. Perhaps we might hazard to suggest that the Śaiva Tantras took over this scheme as a theoretical possibility which did, in a partial way reflect an aspect of the relationship between the Tantras and their traditions.

The Rudrayāmala. Eleven *Saṃhitās* are associated with the *Rudrayāmala: Arthasāra, Suradharma, Daityaghnī, Vīrārthinā, Vīrāsāra, Raudrī, Mudrāntamālinī, Kālottarā, Kālaghnī, Mahāmṛtuñjaya* and *Caṇḍabhairava*.[45]

180a ***The Viṣṇuyāmala.*** The line of transmission of this Yāmala is as follows: Sadāśiva → Kapālīśa → Svacchanda → Krodha → Ucchuṣma → Ruru → Caṇḍabhairava → Unmatta → Vīrabhairava → Ananta → Bhāskara → Manthāna → Nīlakaṇṭha → Bhīma → Vāmaka → Mahākāla → Viṣṇu → Munīndra → Śāndilya.

Associated with this Yāmala are the following *Saṃhitās: Trimuṇḍinī, Bahurūpa, Ucchuṣma, Caṇḍa, Pronmatta, Vīrabhairava, Anantamata, Anantabhāskara, Tṛṇaka* (?) and *Anantavijaya.* A group of four *Saṃhitās* collectively called *"rūpa"* are said to be derived from the *Anantavijaya.* These are *Bhīmā, Vāmā, Mahākālī* and *Gṛdhrapāṭī.* Along with these scriptures is the *Kālavadanasaṃhitā* of twenty-one thousand verses and the *Viṣṇupasaṃhitā* of six thousand verses. The *Durdarśanasaṃhitā* (also called *Sudarśana*) of three thousand five hundred verses was brought to earth by Śāndilya.

181b ***Skandayāmala.*** This Tantra, also called the *"Senāpatiyāmala"*, was transmitted along the following lineage: Tejodhāman → Pṛthuśiras → Samadṛśa → Viśvabhuk → Viṣavalayagola → Bhairava → Consort → Viśākha → Kuñjāramukha → Sambhadra → Vīrabhadra → Ugracaṇḍa → Mahendra → Candrārkavāyumuni → Manugaṇa.

The Saṃhitās associated with this Yāmala are *Gauhāsphandā, Analakāntha, Viṣacchadā, Śaiśava, Mayūraśikhā, Ramanodbhava, Varadā* and *Līlotpatamālikā.*

Umāyāmala. The line of transmission of this Yāmala is as follows (Bhagarudra) Bhairava → Asitadṛśa (Kṛṣṇākṣa) → Yamāntaka → Piṅgaleśa → Huṃkāra → Śaṅkukarṇa → Piṅgala → Mṛtyuñjaya. 182a

There are eight Saṃhitās associated with this Yāmala and they are said to belong to all four *pīṭhas.* These are *Umā, Rauravī, Bhīma, Gambhīrā, Laṅgalā, Mātryānanda, Surānandā* and *Bhairavānanda.*

The *Umāyāmala* is supposed to have originated from the *Somayāmala* while countless other *yāmalas* are supposed to be derived from the other ones. These include four *Devatāyāmalas,* four *Dūtibhavayāmalas,* four *Kiṅkiṇīyāmalas,* six *Yoginīyāmalas,* eighteen *Bhīmayāmalas,* ten *Ḍākinīyāmalas* and a number of *Mātṛyāmalas.*

4. The Mudrāpīṭha

The *Mudrāpīṭha* is also called the *Kriyāsūtra,* probably because *Mudrā* is a manifestation of the power of action (*Kriyāśakti*) just as Mantra is a manifestation of the power of knowledge. The revealer of the Tantras of this *pīṭha* is Bhairava who also created the sixty-four *Bhairavatantras.* The Mudrā which the Tantras of this *pīṭha* are said to disclose is the Gesture or Seal of Emptiness (*vyomamayī mudrā*). It is one's own authentic nature (*svasvabhāva*) that is self-established and delights in eternal bliss. This seal is 'stamped' onto all the relationships between the categories of existence and melts away all bodily bondage. When it descends onto the level of the empirical world where meditation and its object are distinct, it is variously conceived and so assumes countless forms. Three root Tantras belong to this *pīṭha:*

Hṛdbheda. All the JY tells us about this Tantra is the line of its transmission which is as follows: Phetkārabhairava → Kāntichātra → ? → Prapalambha → Nirañjana → Vyāpin → Vigraheśvara → Bhairava → goddess who revealed a short version to mankind.

Mātṛbheda. Bhairava explains that this Tantra is so-called because it 183b
exalts the mother (*mātṛ*) in whom and by whom all the universe is

measured (*māpita*) and saved (*trāṇita*) and of whom there are many diverse forms (*bheda*).[46] There are five Saṃhitās associated with the *Mātṛbheda*, namely *Aparājitā, Vāstuvidyā, Sarvabimbā, Karoṭinī, Siddhasārārtha, Citrārtha* (?).[47]

184a ***The Kubjikāmata.*** The KMT is said to have originated in the mountains.[48] It is considered to be the most important Tantra of the *Mudrāpīṭha* although it is linked with all the *pīṭhas.* This is the Tantra of the goddess Kubjikā. She is the power Beyond Mind (*manonmanī*) who, in the bliss of loving union (*samplava*), withdraws her limbs to form the divine triangle of the Seed (*bīja*), Drop (*bindu*) and Sound (*nāda*) through which the universe is created. The KMT is said to deal with the Seal of Speech (*vācikā mudrā*). This is of countless forms although it consists essentially of the fifty letters of the alphabet. It denotes the meaning of countless words and indicates the true nature of things leading thus to its realization. The sections (or associated texts) of this Tantra are *Ekākṣara, Dvyākṣara, Padamālā, Śabdamālā, Śabdamālārtha, Mālinī, Vākyamālā* and *Vidyāmālā.*

5. Maṇḍalapīṭha

This *pīṭha* is said to be equally present (*sāmānya*) in the other three *pīṭhas.* Although it has only one *mūlasūtra*, which is not named here, it is divided in many parts (*kalpa*). The line of transmission is as follows: Pañcaśekhara who brought it to earth transmitted it to Ratiśekhara → Saṃhārabhairava → Ḍiṇḍi → Daṇḍeśvara → Ghoreya → Gomati → Trikalā → Śrīkaṇṭha → Bhairava → Brahmā who heard it in each *pīṭha.*

6. The 'Eight Times Eight' Bhairavatantras

After the goddess has been told about the contents of the four *pīṭhas* associated with Bhairava, she then wants to know about the sixty-four *Bhairavatantras* said to constitute the Wheel governed by Sadāśiva. These Tantras are listed below along with the names of their teachers who are considered to be incarnations of Bhairava. The ordering of the eight groups is just as we find it in the ŚKS (see above p. 45 ff.). Moreover, more than half of the Tantras listed in the ŚKS are the same as those listed here. We have therefore recorded their names in a separate column as shown in Table 9.

Table 9. The Sixty-Four Bhairavatantras.

Teacher	*Tantra*	*Group*	*Corresponding Tantras in the ŚKS*[49]	185a
		Bhairava		
Durvāsa	*Svacchanda*		*Svacchanda*	
Sanaka	*Caṇḍa*		*Bhairava*	
Viṣṇu	*Krodha*		*Caṇḍa*	
Kapila	*Unmatta*		*Krodha*	
Kaśyapa	*Asita*		*Unmatta*	
Kuru	*Ruru*		*Asitāṅga*	
Samvartta	*Jhaṅkāra*		*Mahocchuṣma*	
Śaṅkhapāla	*Kapālīśa*		*Kapālīśa*	
		Yāmala		
Bhṛgu	*Brahma*		*Brahma*	
Cetas	*Rudra*		*Viṣṇu*	
Nidhīśa	*Viṣṇu*		*Svacchanda*	
Viśvāmitra	*Skanda*		*Ruru*	
Gautama	*Gautamīyā*		x x x x	
Gālava	*Atharva*		*Ātharvaṇa*	
Yājñavalkya	*Vetāla*		*Rudra*	
Vibhāṇḍa	*Ruru*		*Vetāla*	
		Mata		
Kurcāla	*Raktā*		*Rakta*	
Krandana	*Peṭikā*		*Lampaṭa*	
Kaṅka	*Bhāruṇḍī*		*Lakṣmīmata*	
Kekara	*Iḍā* (*Huhā*)		*Mata*	
Kānana	*Piṅgalā*		*Cālikā*	
Kṣamī	*Nīlakeśī*		*Piṅgala*	
Koṭarākṣa	*Śambarā*		*Utphullaka*	
Samvartta	*Utphullā*		*Viśvādya*	
		Maṅgala		
Bindu	*Bhairavamaṅgalā*		*Picubhairavī*	
Sabindu	*Candragarbhā*		*Tantrabhairavī*	
Śātātapa	*Śāntimaṅgalā*		*Taṭa*	
Parāśara	*Sumaṅgalā* (also called *Brahmā* + *Rudrā*)		*Brāhmīkalā*	
Āpastamba	*Sarvamaṅgalā*		*Vijayā*	
Ambubhuk	*Vijayamaṅgalā*		*Candrā*	

Table 9. The Sixty-Four Bhairavatantras (continued).

Teacher	*Tantra*	*Group*	*Corresponding Tantras in the ŚKS*
Vyāsa	*Viśvāmbā* (also called *Ugra-maṅgalā*)		*Maṅgalā*
Kātyāyana	*Sadbhāvamaṅgalā*		*Sarvamaṅgalā*
		Cakra	
Ulūka	*Svara*		*Mantra*
Sthūlanāḍī	*Varṇa*		*Varṇa*
Haṃsa	*Nāḍī*		*Śakti*
Haṃsarava	*Guhya*		*Kalā*
Śuka	*Kāla*		*Bindu*
Manu	*Saura*		*Nāda*
Pīta	*Vāhneya*		*Guhya*
Akṣaka	*Somaja*		*Kha*
		Śikhā	
Vaśiṣṭha	*Śaukrī*		*Bhairavīśikhā*
Dakṣaśukra	*Maṇḍā*		*Vīṇā*
Kanaka	*Mahocchuṣmā*		*Vīṇāmaṇi*
Kokila	*Bhairavī*		*Saṃmohana*
Śuka	*Śambarī*		*Ḍāmara*
Viśvabhuk	*Prapañcakī*		*Atharvaka*
Kaśyapa	*Mātṛbhedī*		*Kabandha*
Śveta	*Rudrakālī*		*Śiraścheda*
		Bahurūpa	
Bṛhaspati	*Andhakī*		*Andhaka*
Yamoghaṇṭa	*Rurubhedā*		*Rurubheda*
Kaṅkara	*Śaṅkhā*		*Aja*
Śyāmaka	*Śūlinī*		*Mūla*
Śikhī	*Karṇāmoṭī*		*Varṇabhaṇṭa*
Karṇa	*Ṭāṅkī*		*Viḍaṅga*
Jaṭā	*Jvālinī*		*Mātṛrodhana*
Adhīśa	*Mātṛrodhanī*		*Jvālin*
		Vāgīśa	
Haṃsa	*Siddhā*		*Bhairavī*
Soma	*Citrā*		*Citrikā*
Anuloma	*Hṛllekhā*		*Haṃsā*
Viloma	*Bhairavī*		*Kadambikā*
Lomaka	*Kadambikā*		*Hṛllekhā*

Table 9. The Sixty-Four Bhairavatantras (continued).

Teacher	*Tantra*	*Group*	*Corresponding Tantras in the ŚKS*
Śata	*Haṃsinī*		*Candralekhā*
Jaṭa	*Haṃsamālā*		*Vidyullekhā*
Vālmīka	*Candrakoṭī*		*Vidyutmat*

7. The Srotas Division

The JY knows and accepts the standard classification of the Śaivāgama into five currents and even explicitly states that this is the original basic form of the canon.[50] However, it also refers to a sixth Upper Current which we shall discuss later. Each of these six Currents is here analysed in terms of the transmission of the teachings of the Tantras belonging to them. They are, in other words, distinguished from one another on the basis of the teachers (*guru*) and traditions (*santati, santāna*) associated with them.[51] Each of Sadāśiva's five faces (with the sixth Current above them) is accordingly linked with a family of lineages technically called *"gotra"* to which belong various lines of transmission (*santati*). The members of each Current (or *gotra*) undertake vows (*vrata*) and practice their own particular disciplines (*caryā*) which the JY enumerates for each in serial order. Again, each Current has its own monastic centres called *maṭhikās*.

It is not essential to list all these names here; we shall limit ourselves instead to making a few observations. Firstly, it is worth noting that the Āgamas understand themselves as *transmitted* doctrine not just as scripture. It is the living tradition that matters and hence also the teacher who preserves and passes it on to his disciples. Although each Current has its teachers, the ideal teacher according to the *Bhairavāgamas* is one who knows all six Currents. He alone can explain the teachings of each Current along with their esoteric meaning.[52] The personal imparting of the teaching to a small group of disciples entails the existence of numerous monastic centres, each of which is headed by its own teacher who can bequeath it to his successor.[53] Some of these monastic centres came to prominence and acquired an importance in their own right. The Kashmiri tradition, for example, associates the dualist, monist and qualified monistic schools of Śaivism with three *maṭhikās* named after Tryambaka, Āmardaka and Śrīnātha respectively.[54] The word *"maṭhikā"* thus comes ultimately to denote a particular school of thought associated with the founder of the monastic centre from which it was propagated.

The JY, as we have said, accepts the basic Five Current division of the Śaivāgamas. However, although it does classify them in these terms, it does not concern itself to do so in detail. The Śiva and Rudra division of the Siddhāntāgamas are said, as usual, to consist of ten and eighteen Āgamas respectively. The Left Current consists of the Tantras which 'delude'[55] which is clearly an allusion to the *Saṃmohanatantra* that is regularly considered to characterize the scriptures of this Current. The Current of the Right contains, amongst others, the sixty-four *Bhairavatantras* and the *Yāmalas.* To this Current also belong the SvT and the entire *Mantra* and *Mudrāpīṭha.*[56] The *Gāruḍa* and *Bhūtatantras* are characterized in the usual way as concerned with remedies for poison and with exorcism respectively.[57] They are ascribed, as usual, to the Eastern and Western Currents.[58] The Tantras of the Left Current are said to deal with the acquisition of the eight yogic powers (*siddhi*) and power to control others,[59] while the Right Current is the eternal non-dual abode of all the pleasures of this world and every type of liberation.[60]

The Sixth Current is above the others. It belongs particularly to Śiva's power through which all the traditions and their teachings are revealed in this world.[61] Śiva is the root source of all the Āgamas; infinite and full of the knowledge of consciousness he is both omniform and tranquil like a waveless sea. His power is his vitality (*vīrya*) whose field is the delight of the abode of consciousness and is beautiful with its blissful pulsation generated through the diversity of its immanently manifest and transcendentally unmanifest forms.[62] This vitality is Speech at all levels[63] and pours out of universal consciousness in countless extensions (*prasara*) of its power of which the six Currents of scripture are the main streams.[64] Full of this divine power at its very source the Sixth Current leads to realization in an instant with great force (*haṭhāt*) and so the form of Śiva that governs it is Haṭhakeśvara. He is said to know the mysteries of Kula and Kaula and so all the secret teachings originate from here. Consequently this Current is present in those of the Left and Right.[65] Moreover, although it flows in the upper regions (*ūrdhva*) it is also connected with the lower ones as well, that is, with those frequently assigned, as we have seen, to the *Kulāgama.* Thus Haṭhakeśvara's domain is said to be "the abode of the fire of time" which burns in the hells below the world-order. The SvT confirms that Hāṭaka is the name of the Lord of Sauvarṇa which is the eighth and lowest hell[66] while the JY tells us that all the lords of the hells (*pātālanāyaka*) are born from Haṭhakeśvara's mouth.[67] According to a passage quoted by Abhinavagupta from the *Raurāgama,*[68] when Śrīkaṇṭha resides in the hell worlds he assumes the form of Hāṭaka because he bestows yogic powers suddenly and with great force (*haṭhataḥ*) while the JY expressly states that the Upper Current "bestows all yogic powers." The *Ānandādhikāratantra*[69] declares that Hāṭaka is the lord of the hell where souls burn in the "fire of time." This place is destined for those initiates who have broken their pledges and, more especially, for those who, although votaries of the Left-hand Path, censor it. Here, according to this Tantra, go those who have been taught higher doctrine but have, nonetheless, resorted to lower teachings or Mantras of a lower order such as those practised by the devotees of Garuḍa. They can, however, free themselves of their suffering by offering themselves to Lord Hāṭaka and so reach the higher divine principles and then, from there, ultimately merge into Śiva.[70]

8. Conclusion

Accounts such as these not only teach us a great deal about the extent of the Āgamic corpus but also about its history and, consequently, about the history of the development of Āgamic Śaivism. We should, however, treat these accounts with caution. As we have seen, all the major Āgamas have their own peculiar view of the Śaiva canon and, although their accounts are in many ways compatible and even supplement each other, none of them are either complete or unbiased. Moreover, they give rise to many questions which still remain unsettled. Thus, we cannot help asking ourselves whether all these Tantras did, in fact, exist. For example, although the eight Bhairava Tantras are generally considered to form a standard group, it is by no means certain whether they all existed. Certainly the *Svacchandatantra*, at least, does and possibly a number of others but it is hard to believe that all the Tantras said here to have been associated with them did as well. Bhairavas are commonly worshipped in groups of eight while the group which has given its name to these Tantras is particularly well known. It is hard not to suspect that these lists are not entirely genuine when we notice that groups of eight are such recurrent features in them. May it not be the case that some of these titles are purely fictitious additions to fill out ideal schemes? We can only be sure that a Tantra existed when we find additional evidence to corroborate the statements made in accounts such as these. We must, for example, find direct quotations from it, or reference to it in independent sources such as inscriptions. Best of all, of course, would be to find the text itself or fragments of it.

Again, how genuine are the names listed in the lines of transmission of these Tantras? Certainly the gods, divine beings and Upaniṣadic sages who figure in these accounts cannot be considered to be historical figures connected with them. Even so, it is not impossible that the last few members of these lines did, in fact, live at some time and propagated these Tantras; perhaps, indeed, they even wrote them. It is worth noting, however, that the account of the line of transmission given here of the SYM and its own account as presented by Abhinavagupta in the *Tantrāloka* do not agree. This fact should put us on our guard to deal cautiously with what these account tell us because our knowledge of the extent and content of even the extant Tantras is still very superficial. Even so, there can be little doubt that future research will reveal a vast field of inquiry and that these accounts of the Śaivāgamic canon will serve as important guidelines by which we may orient ourselves in the course of work to help us to locate ourselves in this vast body of literature.

Appendix D

Manuscripts of the Kubjikātantras

For almost twenty years German scholars have been directing a project to photograph manuscripts in Nepal. Amongst the many thousands of manuscripts that have been photographed so far, there are many of Tantras and related literature belonging the the Kubjikā school. Unfortunately, no descriptive catalogue of the manuscripts the project has photographed has as yet been prepared and, due to the amount of material collected, it will probably take a great deal of time to produce. In the meantime, in order to make part of this new material more readily accessible, we have listed below some manuscripts relevant to the study of the Kubjikā cult. This list is by no means exhaustive. For one thing, I have had the opportunity to consult only the index cards of the microfilms made of manuscripts belonging to the National Archives in Kathmandu. I have not had the time to see index cards of the numerous manuscripts in private collections the project has photographed and so they could not be listed here. Nor have short tracts with generic titles such as *"Kubjikāpūjā"* been included, both because they are very many and also because it is impossible to assess their content or value without seeing them. For the same reason I have had to list many manuscripts of sections of the MBT as "unidentified." I have also not listed manuscripts of the KMT (also called *Kulālikāmnāya*) because it has already been edited by Goudriaan and Schoterman. A few entries, such as the important *Ṣaṭsāhasra*, are listed without reel numbers. This is because it appears that the project has failed to photograph these manuscripts although they are listed in the catalogues.

Scholars who are interested in acquiring further information should contact the Nepal Research Centre, New Baneshwar, P.O. Box 180, Kathmandu, Nepal or the Staatsbibliothek PK-Orientabteilung, Postfach 1407, 1000 Berlin 30, West Germany.

Title	Reel No.	MS No.	Folio
1) *Aṣṭaviṃśatikarmārcana*	B 176/6	1/1130	54
2) *Kubjikākavacamālāmantra*	B 178/19	1/1539	11
3) *Kubjikākuladevatāpūjā*	B 181/16	5/5032	57
4) *Kubjikākarmārcana*	B 181/11	5/1934	50
	A 232/15	5/5026	39
	B 182/3	5/1882	40
	B 181/15	1/1698/395	41
5) *Kubjikākhyadvādaśasūtra*	A 231/36	1/1696/813	10
6) *Kubjikāgurumaṇḍalapūjā*	A 234/12	1/1696/1642	11
7) *Kubjikāguhyeśvarīpūjāpaddhati*	B 181/17	1/1696/2247	65
8) *Kubjikāgnikubjikāpūjāvidhi*	A 233/6	1/1696/869	13
9) *Kubjikāgnikubjikāpratiṣṭhavidhi*	A 232/31	1/1696/1363	50
10) *Kubjikāgniyajñavidhi*	B 702/5	3/56	63
	A 233/11	1/1696/289	21
	A 233/9	1/1696/1112	15
11) *Kubjikāgnilakṣāhutiyajñavidhi*	B 179/12	1/1696/2200	42
12) *Kubjikāgnividhi*	A 232/35	1/1696/202	59
13) *Kubjikāgnihomavidhi*	B 178/32	1/1696/2186	59
14) *Kubjikādamanārohaṇapavitrārohaṇavidhi*	B 180/19	5/1880	66
	B 179/18	5/1886	31
	B 865/5	5/5023	20
15) *Kubjikānityāhnikatilaka*	A 228/3	1/239	85
	—	3/384	90
	B 26/11	1/1361	93
	B 26/10	1/1320	78
	B 26/12	1/1360	93
	B 26/19	1/1320	68
	A 41/11	3/384vi	90
	B 26/22	5/8541 vi	122
	A 161/21	3/195	57
	A 162/7	5/4995	99
	B 415/22	5/1937	37
16) *Kubjikāpūjāvidhi*	B 865/5	5/5023	20

	Title	*Reel No.*	*MS No.*	*Folio*
17)	*Kubjikāmataṣaṭsāhasraṭippanī*	—	1/1686	100
18)	*Kubjikāmālāmantroddhāra*	B 121/8	5/4818	76
19)	*Kubjikāmūrtisthāpanavidhi*	B 363/42	1/504	7
20)	*Kubjikāyutākṣarī*	A 210/19	1/678	15
21)	*Kubjikārdharātridīpayāgavidhi*	A 231/27	5/5024	25
		B 179/10	1/1696/2211	42
22)	*Kubjikāvidhāna*	A 232/6	1/1030	31
23)	*Kubjikāviṣayakatantra*	—	2/135	24
24)	*Kubjikāṣoḍhanyāsa*	B 180/7	1/1696/181	15
25)	*Kubjikāṣṭaviṃśatikarmārcana*	B 181/18	5/1891	85
26)	*Kubjikāsaṃdhyāvidhi*	A 232/20	1/109	3
27)	*Kubjikāsahasranāmastotra*	A 629/16	5/4999	10
28)	*Kubjikāsahasrākṣarī*	A 229/2	1/62	2
		B 174/15	1/356	6
29)	*Kubjikāsiddhāgniyajñavidhi*	B 179/22	5/5000	140
30)	*Kubjikāsiddhilakṣmīpūjā*	B 363/43	5/2483	3
31)	*Kubjikāstotra*	B 393/76	1/1696/397	3
32)	*Kubjikopaniṣad*	B 180/8	1/1696/929	55
33)	*Kulamūlaratnapañcakāvatāra*	A 150/26	5/6571	3
		A 40/7	5/425	50
		B 158/3	1/1499	54
		B 121/3	5/5185	37
		B 117/5	1/45	40
		B 112/3	1/1552	71
34)	*Kularatnoddyota*	A 147/10	5/5142	19
		B 119/3	1/1653	138
		B 118/2	5/4807	100
		A 149/1	5/5151	64
		A 206/10	1/16	96
		A 40/21	5/427vi	72
		A 146/6	4/2454	93
35)	*Kulālikāmnāyaṭippaṇīṣaṭ-*	B 25/20	1/285	80

Title	Reel No.	MS No.	Folio
sāhasrikā	B 174/20	1/1686	51
36) *Kramakallolinī*	A 146/9	5/1933	86
37) *Kramasaṃgraha*	A 148/6	4/1602	18
38) *Kramasūtrādhikāra*	B 157/26	1/1653	25
39) *Gorakṣasaṃhitā*	B 39/4	1/1268	13
	A 213/21	5/3978	118
40) *Ciñcinīmatasārasamuccaya*	B 123/8	—	34
	B 157/19	1/767	38
	B 123/5	1/199	69
	B 121/9	1/145	36
41) *Parāpūjākrama*	A 242/7	5/4908	14
	A 165/6	5/4911	26
42) *Paścimakarmārcana*	A 242/14	1/1696/290	34
43) *Paścimacaruvidhāna*	A 49/13	1/1559 vi	4
44) *Paścimajyeṣṭhakarmastava*	B 535/13	1/679	4
45) *Paścimajyeṣṭhanityakarmadevārcana*	A 242/40	1/1696/2280	26
46) *Paścimajyeṣṭhanityakarmārcana*	B 525/10	1/220	8
47) *Paścimajyeṣṭhalakṣaṇa*	A 242/22	1/1696/1206	24
48) *Paścimajyeṣṭhaṣaḍviṃśatikarmārcana*	A 242/15	4/2254	40
49) *Paścimajyeṣṭhājyeṣṭhamahāmāyākubjikākarmavidhi*	B 190/37	1/1696/880	—
50) *Paścimajyeṣṭhānujyeṣṭhāmnāyasamayadīkṣāvidhi*	A 242/21	1/1696/2175	30
51) *Paścimajyeṣṭhānujyeṣṭhāmnāyāṣṭaviṃśatikarmārcana*	A 242/27	1/1696/1255	32
52) *Paścimajyeṣṭhāmnāyakarmārcanapaddhati*	B 191/1	4/214	144
53) *Paścimajyeṣṭhāmnāyakubjikākarmārcana*	B 191/4	5/1879	—

	Title	Reel No.	MS No.	Folio
54)	*Paścimajyeṣṭhāmnāya-caturdaśīmahāparvavidhi*	A 242/30	1/1692/679	14
55)	*Paścimajyeṣṭhāmnāya-pavitralakṣaṇa*	A 242/17	1/1696/1206	24
56)	*Paścimajyeṣṭhāmnāya-pavitrārohanavidhi*	A 242/22	1/1696/2136	36
57)	*Paścimadevārcanapaddhati*	A 242/28	1/1696/1406	10
		A 242/25	1/1696/495	10
		A 242/16	1/1696/392	34
58)	*Paścimanityārcana*	A 242/38	1/1696/5038	10
59)	*Paścimamūlasthānavidhi*	A 243/12	5/2486	10
60)	*Paścimāmnāyakarmārcana-pūjāvidhi*	A 242/20	5/1883	32
		A 248/39	4/214	29
61)	*Paścimāmnāyakubjikā-karmārcana*	B 190/36	3/56	45
62)	*Paścimāmnāyagurumaṇḍala-pūjāvidhi*	B 191/7	1/1696/1016	32
63)	*Paścimāmnāyapavitralakṣaṇa*	A 242/19	1/1696/2077	8
64)	*Paścimāmnāyapavitrārohaṇa-vidhi*	A 242/22	1/1696/2136	36
65)	*Paścimāmnāyapūjāvidhi*	A 242/24	1/1696/405	32
66)	*Paścimāmnāyasamayadīkṣā*	A 243/11	4/214	16
67)	*Paścimāmnāyasarvādhikāra-nirvāṇadīkṣā*	A 242/37	1/1696/749	46
68)	*Paścimāmnāyasahasrākṣarī*	A 243/31	1/1538	2
69)	*Paścimāmnāyāṣṭaviṃśati-karmārcana*	B 190/38	1/1696/961	55
	Manthānabhairavatantra:			
70)	*Kumārikākhaṇḍa*	A 172/3	5/4822	245
		A 171/11	5/4630	216
		A 175/3	4/980	238
		H 330/4	H 5530	236

Title	Reel No.	MS No.	Folio
	A 173/1	1/811	243
	A 173/3	2/212	239
	A 209/14	1/230	9
	B 135/42	1/1697-28/7	20
	A 180/3	4/83	169
	A 170/2	2/278	81
	H 366/4	H 6563	92
71) *Ṭīkā*	A 176/4	5/4878	186
	B 27/9	3/383	151
	A 179/4	1/228	152
72) *Navanityādhikāra*	B 27/7	2/118	89
	B 135/50	2/298	4
73) *Yogakhaṇḍa*	A 173/5-	5/4654	204
	A 174/1		
	A 176/3	3/164	150
	A 180/4	2/165	156
	B 27/8	1/1151	154
	B 27/19	2/118	203
	B 157/10	2/86	4
74) *Siddhakhaṇḍa*	A 172/4	5/4877	91
	A 178/2	1/228	93
	B 27/12	1/1697-7/5	21
75) (Unidentified sections)	A 179/6	5/1928	251
	B 27/23-	1/1151	222
	B 28/1		
	B 139/15-	1/227	215
	B 140/1		
	A 170/3	1/1127	58
	E 653/31	E 13836	84
	C 24/2	217a	185
	C 55/9-	592	210
	C 56/1		
	A 42/7	3/788	214
	A 168/7	2/105	86
	A 176/2	3/164	73
	A 169/3	1/1119	120

Title	*Reel No.*	*MS No.*	*Folio*
	B 180/8	1/228	40
	B 27/14	1/787	115
	B 136/9	2/298	9
76) *Śaktisūtra*	B 28/9	1/619 vi	50
77) *Śrīmatasāra*	A 177/13	5/4956	28
	B 135/29	1/1697-21/2	11
	A 168/11	5/4853	72
	A 192/2	5/4849	114
	A 194/4	3/275	85
78) *Śrīmatottaratantra*	A 193/3	2/214	339
	B 197/3	1/218	32
	B 148/6	1/261	263
	A 190/5-	1/261	585
	A 191/1		
	B 28/35	1/1697/7/4vi	25
	A 194/2	2/220	333
	A 196/6	2/279	263
	B 150/5	4/331	207
	A 194/6	4/2506	362
	B 149/7	5/5150	13
	B 28/21	3/191vi	55
	B 28/17	2/226vi	189
	B 146/3	5/4628	223
	B 148/5	4/2114	229
	A 228/2	1/186	346
	A 195/8	1/1278	36
	B 146/7	5/7941	35
	B 154/1	1/218	1
79) *Ṣaṭsāhasra*	A 44/6	1/1363	78
	A 200/4	2/219	38
80) *Samvartamaṇḍalasūtravyākhyā*	B 28/22	5/879vi	5
81) *Samvartārthaprakāśa*	B 156/6	4/1060	19
82) *Siddhapañcāśikā*	B 2/2	C 1147	—
	B 28/15	1/1473	9
	B 155/10	5/5149	6

ABBREVIATIONS

ASB	Asiatic Society of Bengal
U.Ka.	Uttarakāmikā
EI	Epigraphica Indica
KSTS	Kashmir Series of Texts and Studies
KNT	Kubjikānityāhnikatilaka
KMT	Kubjikāmatatantra
KRU	Kularatnoddyota
KĀ	Kulārṇavatantra
KJN	Kaulajñānanirṇaya
G.P.	Garuḍapurāṇa
G.S.	Gorakṣasaṃhitā
CMSS	Ciñcinīmatasārasamuccaya
JY	Jayadrathayāmala
TĀ	Tantrāloka
Ta.Sā.	Tāntrikasāhitya
DB	Devībhagavata
NGMPP	Nepal German Manuscript Preservation Project
NA	Nepal National Archives
NT	Netratantra
NTu	Netratantroddyota
NSA	Nityāṣodaśikārṇavatantra
Parāt.	Parātantra
PTv	Parātriṃśikāvivaraṇa
Pāśu.Sū.	Pāśupatasūtra
P.Kā.	Pūrvakāmikā
PLSS	Pratiṣṭhalakṣaṇasārasamuccaya
BEFEO	Bulletin de L'École Française d'Extrême Orient
BSOAS	Bulletin of the School of Oriental and African Studies
BSP	Bṛhatsūcīpatra
BY	Brahmayāmala
Br.Sū.	Brahmasūtra
MS	Manuscript
MBT	Manthānabhairavatantra

MBT(Y)	Manthānabhairavatantra (yogakhaṇḍa)
MhB	Mahābhārata
MP	Mahānayaprakāśa
MM	Mahārthamañjarī
Mat.P.	Mataṅgapārameśvarāgama
MV	Mālinīvijayatantra
MVV	Mālinīvijayavārtika
Mr.T.	Mṛgendratantra
Mr.vṛ.	Mṛgendratantravṛtti
YHṛ	Yoginīhṛdaya
RASB	Royal Asiatic Society of Bengal
RASB Tantra Cat.	Royal Asiatic Society of Bengal Tantra Catalogue
RT	Rājataraṅginī
LAS	Luptāgamasaṃgraha
VMT	Vāmakeśvarīmatatantra
VŚT	Vīṇāśikhatantra
Ś.R.S.	Śataratnasaṃgraha
Ś.Dṛ.	Śivadṛṣṭi
Ś.Sū.vi.	Śivasūtravimarśinī
ŚKS	Śrīkaṇṭhīyasaṃhitā
ṢaṭSS	Ṣaṭsāhasrikasaṃhitā
SYM	Siddhayogeśvarīmata
SŚP	Somaśambhupaddhati
Sp.Pra.	Spandapradīpikā
SvT	Svacchandabhairavatantra
ZDMG	Zeitschrift der Deutschen Morgenländischen Gesellschaft

Notes

PART ONE

1. I have borrowed this expression from the title of Agehananda Bharati's book *The Tantric Tradition*, Rider and Co., London, 1969.

2. See for example, Bose and Halder, *Tantras: Their Philosophy and Occult Secrets*, Firma K. L. Mukhopadhyay, Calcutta 1973; or Kulacarya Srimat Virananda Giri (alias Dr. Nando Lal Kundu) *Constructive Philosophy of India*, volume II (Tantra), Firma K. L. Mukhopadhyay, Calcutta, 1973.

3. *Principles of Tantra* (*Tantra-tattva*). *The Tantratattva* of Siva Chandra Vidyarnava Bhattacharya with an introduction by Arthur Avalon and Baroda Kanta Majumdar, edited by Arthur Avalon, 3rd edition, Madras, 1960.

4. I am thinking here particularly of the *Somaśambhupaddhati*, Traduction, Introduction et Notes par Hélène Brunner-Lachaux, Institut Français d' Indologie, Pondicherry, vol. I 1963; vol. II 1968 and vol. III, 1977.

5. *Mahābhāṣya* under *sūtra* 5/2/76.

6. Introduction to the *Pāśupata Sūtram with Pañcārtha-Bhāṣya of Kauṇḍinya*, translated by Haripada Chakraborti, Academic Publishers, Calcutta, p. 7.

7. Bāṇa's *Kādambarī* part II, edited by P. V. Kane, Nirnaya Sagar Press, Bombay, 1913 pp. 68-9.

8. TĀ., vol. I, p. 236.

9. *The Yaśastilaka and Indian Culture* by K. K. Handiqui, Sholapur, 1949, p. 204.

10. Ibid.

11. KMT fl. 7a, Asiatic Society of Bengal (Government collection) MS. no. 4733.

12. *The Kaulajñānanirṇaya*, edited by P. C. Bagchi, Calcutta, 1932, Introduction pp. 68-72.

13. For Maheśvarānanda's date see *The Krama Tantricism of Kashmir* by Navajivan Rastogi, Motilal Banarsidass, Delhi 1979, p. 215.

14. M.M., p. 4.

15. Ibid. p. 108, 126.

16. The manuscript is palm leaf and the script is Malyālam no. C 2319C.

17. TĀ, 37/38.

18. We shall discuss what we mean by the term 'Kulaśāstra' in the second part

of this monograph.

19. TĀ, 29/60.

20. YHṛ, 3/37.

21. vārāṇasyāṃ śmaśānantu etat sarvaṃ samālikhet |
BY, NA, MS no. 3/370 fl. 6b.

22. See K. N. Sukul *Vārāṇasī Vaibhava* Bihār Rāṣṭrabhāṣā Pariṣad, Patna 1977, p. 406.

23. That the *Paścimāmnāya* was known in Kashmir is established by a number of references. Thus Abhinavagupta quotes from the *Kubjikāmata* in PTv, p. 184. Unfortunately, this reference has not been traced in the 3500 verse recension edited, but as yet unpublished, by T. Goudriaan and J. A. Schoterman. Jayaratha quotes an unknown Āgama which refers to the *Thohakāsamata* of the *Paścimāmnāya:*

madyariktāstu ye devi na te siddhyanti paścime |
thohakāsamate nityaṃ kulabhraṣṭāḥ svayaṃbhuvaḥ ||
(TĀ, vol. XIb, p. 13).

In the following verse, quoted by Jayaratha in his commentary on the *Vāmakeśvarīmata* from an older commentary by the Kashmiri Allaṭa, Kubjikā, the goddess of the *Paścimāmnāya*, is mentioned:

ūrmiriti bhoginītyapi kubjeti kuleśvarīti jagaduryām |
śrīkālakarṣaṇītyapi kuṇḍalinītyapi ca naumi tāṃ devīm ||
(VMT, p. 28).

Another reference is found in the following passage which Jayaratha quotes without naming his source: "The triangle is called the female organ (*bhaga*), the secret circle in the Sky. Its corners are will, knowledge and action and in its centre is the sequence (*krama*) of Ciñcinī." (TĀ, vol. II, p. 104).

The worship of the absolute viewed as the source of cosmic manifestation symbolized by the female organ from whence arises the power of *Kuṇḍalinī* is an important feature of the Tantras of the *Paścimāmnāya.* Kubjikā, the Supreme Goddess, is frequently called Ciñcinī (see below p. 90). In a hymn to *Bhaga* in the *Ciñcinīmatasārasamuccaya* we find the same verse. Thus, the first line of Jayaratha's quote reads:

trikoṇaṃ bhagam ityuktaṃ viyatsthaṃ guptamaṇḍalam |

In the CMSS (fl. 10b, line 1):

bhagaṃ trikoṇavikhyātaṃ dhiyasthaṃ guptamaṇḍalam |

The second line is identical.

We cannot be sure that Jayaratha quoted this verse from the CMSS, but there can be little doubt that he drew it from a Tantra of the same school.

Also, in the KNT a śūdra named Śrasehila, whose initiatory name was Rāmānandanātha, is listed as being a follower of the *Paścimāmnāya* who lived in Kashmir. Bagchi KJN, p. 69.

24. Although the SvT is a *Bhairavatantra* and not a *Siddhāntāgama*, the initiations and other ritual procedures it describes are similar to those of the Siddhānta. Consequently, Somaśambhu (eleventh century) incorporates a great deal of material from the SvT in his compendium of Siddhānta ritual, the *Kramakāṇḍakramāvalī*, better known as the *Somaśambhupaddhati.* Composed in South India, this manual is the oldest one still extant. Although no longer in use, Aghoraśivācārya's *Kriyākramadyotikā* (written in 1158 A.D.), which is still popular in South India, follows the SŚP very closely. Brunner in her notes on the SŚP frequently refers to the SvT without thereby contravening her principle not to quote from Āgamas whose rituals differ radically from these of the SŚP. The SvT, which she describes as a revealed text of Kashmiri Śaivism (ŚSP, vol. III, intro. p. liv), evidently inspired Somaśambhu. Brunner notes that a number of cosmological concepts and forms of yoga the Siddhānta does not know about have passed from the Northern to the Southern Āgamic schools through this text (ibid). But even though the SvT adds something new to Siddhānta ritual, it is clearly compatible with it and shares much in common with it, even in matters of detail. Indeed, old South Indian authorities on Siddhānta ritual refer to it frequently as does, for example, Nirmalamaṇi in his commentary on Aghoraśiva's manual. Viśvanātha in his *Siddhāntaśekhara* and Īśānaśivagurudeva in his *paddhati* go so far as to prefer, at times, to follow the SvT in matters of detail concerning ritual and cosmography rather than the *Siddhāntāgamas* (SŚP, vol. III, p. 185).

25. Jayaratha more than once refers his reader to a teacher for information about matters he feels that he cannot elaborate, particularly the secret details of Kaula ritual. Thus when dealing with how the sacrificial vessel should be filled in the course of a Kaula rite he says:

> yaśca atra etat pūraṇe sampradāyaḥ sa rahasyatvāt samayabhaṅga-bhayāc ca na iha asmābhiḥ pradarśita iti | etad gurumukhād eva boddhavyam |
>
> (TĀ, vol. XIb, p.19).

Such passages indicate that differences of opinion prevailed about practice in his day (see also TĀ, vol. XIb, pp. 40-1), clearly proving that these rituals were actively performed in Kashmir at that time. There is ample evidence that Kashmir was a society where Kaula ritual was an active concern of an appreciable, although probably small, part of the populace. This, as one would expect, charmed and pleased sincere Śaivites of Abhinavagupta's stamp who wrote enthusiastically about Kaula ritual in Kashmir. Thus, in a poetic vein, he praises the wine Kaulas drink:

> [This is] the wine which imparts boldness to the words of lovers and frees them from fear while making love; the wine in which all the deities [of consciousness] who reside in the shade of the tree of the Kali age and practice mystic union (*cakracaryā*) gladly abide; the wine which here [in Kashmir] bestows first pleasure then liberation. (TĀ, 37/44).

But not all thought so highly of these practices. We know that bans were imposed and practising Kaulas ostracized. Some, such as the satirist Kṣemendra, who lived in Kashmir at the time, considered Kaula ritual and practice to be merely a source of moral corruption and an excuse for licence. See my *Doctrine of Vibration*, vol. I SUNY Press, Albany, 1987, chapter 1.

26. For definitions of the word "Tantra" see *Tantra in Bengal: A Study in Its Origins, Development and Influence* by S. C. Banerji, Naya Prakash, Calcutta 1978, pp. 1-3.

27. Renou remarks that the later Tantric texts Woodroffe studied that "describe the worship of the great Goddess" are called "Tantras" rather than "Āgamas" (preface to SŚP, vol. I, p. 1). Brunner notes, however, that in the early Siddhāntāgamic context the terms "Āgama" and "Tantra" are synonymous (ibid., intro. p. iv.). Thus we find the following definition of Tantra, which has been repeated frequently throughout the centuries in a wide variety of Tantric scriptures, in the *Kāmikāgama* also. This must be one of the earliest citations of this definition:

tanoti vipulān arthāṃs tattvamantrasamāśritān |
trāṇaṃ ca kurute yasmāt tantram ityabhidhīyate ||

(P.Kā., 1/29).

28. Thus, Abhinavagupta, in the course of discussing one of the basic principles of Kaula doctrine, namely, that purity or impurity is not an inherent quality of things but a mental projection which must be overcome along with all other thought-constructs to achieve the pure conscious state of liberation says that: "such was also (the insight of) the ancient sages (*muni*) by virtue of their state free of thought-constructs but who, in order not to disrupt the order of the world, concealed it." (TĀ, 4/243b-4a).

29. R. C. Hazra writes: "At the time the chapters on vows, worship etc. first began to be included in the Purāṇas, the Tantric elements were eliminated as far as possible." *Studies in the Purāṇic Records on Hindu Rites and Customs*, Motilal Banarsidass, 2nd edition, Delhi, 1975, p. 260. According to Hazra the additions made to the Purāṇas prior to the ninth century were largely free of Tantric influence. From about the beginning of the ninth century the authority of the Tantras came to be gradually recognized by the Purāṇas and so Tantric rituals were increasingly incorporated into them (ibid., pp. 260-2).

30. See, for example, Hazra p. 119.

31. Schoterman has published a study of these chapters in an article entitled: *A Link between Purāṇa and Tantra: Agnipurāṇa 143-147* in ZDMG Supplement IV, Wiesbaden, 1980.

32. TĀ., 28/407a.

33. Bhairava addresses the goddess in this way in the *Niśisañcāratantra*. Copies of this text are indeed rare; I know only of one MS, namely, NA, no. 1/1606 (incomplete).

34. TĀ., 37/10-12a.

35. We see in the following quotation from *Kūrmapurāṇa* (1/11/272-3) that the Yāmala and Vāmatantras which belonged to this lost corpus are as

objectionable as Bauddha scripture:

> yāni śāstrāṇi dṛśyante loke'smin vividhāni tu |
> śrutismṛtiviruddhāni niṣṭhā teṣāṃ hi tāmasī ||
> kāpālaṃ pāñcarātraṃ ca yāmalaṃ vāmam ārhatam |
> evaṃ vidhāni cānyāni mohanārthāni tāni tu ||

36. "There is no other scripture apart from the Veda which explains Dharma. Brahmins should not converse with those who find delight elsewhere (in other scriptures)." (Ibid. 1/11/271; also ibid. 1/50/23-4).

37. Kūrma 1/15/112-115; 2/16/15-6; 2/21/34-5; 2/37/144-6.

38. Varāha 71/58.

39. Ibid. 70/41; Kūrma 1/15/104.

40. *Devībhāgavata* 7/39/26-31 quoted by Hazra p. 226. Cf. also ibid. 9/1/21-32.

41. Mādhava's *Śaṅkaradigvijaya* with Dhanapatisūri's *Ḍinḍima* commentary. Ānandāśrama Sanskrit Series no. 22, Ānandāśrama Press, Poona, 1915, 15/1-7.

42. RT, 6/108.

43. Translation by E. C. Sachau in *Alberuni's India* 1, 22.

44. *Daśāvatāracarita* quoted by Hazra p. 89. Translation mine.

45. Rohana A. Dunuwila *Śaiva Siddhānta Theology*, Motilal Banarsidass, Delhi, 1985, p. 44.

46. For this reference see Appendix B, fn. 21.

47. ṢaṭSS, 3/79b.

48. Thus the Ṛṣis in the *Kāmikāgama* were, "intent on Śiva and Śakti desirous of understanding the Supreme Knowledge." They praise Śiva saying of Him:

> [You] are of the nature of the flow of innate bliss whose characteristic is one's own consciousness, [You Who are] united with the Supreme Power whose nature is supreme consciousness.
>
> (P.Kā., 1/7a-8b).

49. There are a number of later Tantras whose names are the same as Tantras of the older group; examples of these are the *Kulacūḍāmaṇī*, *Kulārṇava*, *Tantrarāja*, *Guptatantra*, *Jayadrathayāmala*, *Saṃmohanatantra* and a medieval work not at all associated with the *Paścimāmnāya* called *Kubjikātantra*. Schrader writes: "That occasionally the same name has been given to two or even more different works is nothing unusual in Āgamic literature. For instance, among the Śākta Tantras there are, . . . three Prapañca tantras, two Harigaurī tantras, three Kubjikā tantras, two Yoginī tantras and two Mṛdani (?) tantras." *Introduction to the Pāñcarātra and Ahirbudhnya Saṃhitā* by F. Otto Schrader, Adyar Library Series, Adyar, 2nd edition 1973, pp. 14-5.

In the later period Śāktatantras are distinguished from Śaivatantras and called "Nigama" and "Āgama" respectively. The characterizing distinction between them is stated to be that the former are spoken by the goddess and the latter by the god. Originally the Tantras were generally spoken by the male partner to his companion, however much they may have been concerned with female divinities and their rituals. Thus the NSA, which belongs to the early period but was in the later period considered (quite justifiably in terms of its content) to be an exemplary *Śāktatantra*, is taught by *Īśvara* to the goddess. The goddess herself remarks that the god had taught all the preceding Tantras including those which the goddess defines as the "Tantras of the Mothers" although the ones that are listed are of many types including Siddhāntāgamas. The passage reads:

bhagavan sarvamantrāśca bhavatā me prakāśitāḥ ||
catuṣṣaṣtiśca tantrāṇi mātṝṇām uttamāni tu |

(NSA, 1/13).

evam etāni śāstrāṇi tathānyānyapi koṭiśaḥ ||
bhavatoktāni me deva sarvajñānamayāni tu |

(Ibid., 1/21b-22a).

The *mātṛtantra* figure as a separate group along with the *Yāmalas* in the Siddhāntāgamas (see P.Kā., 1/122) while a reference from an unknown source in Jayaratha's commentary on the TĀ shows that a distinction was made between the *Śaṅkaratantra* and the *Devītantra* (see TĀ, vol. XIb, p. 12). Even so, we do not find that a clearcut distinction exists between Śākta and Śaiva Tantra in the early sources, even in the *Kulatantras* which were in practice Śākta in most respects. By the middle of the ninth century, when Somānanda wrote the *Śivadṛṣṭi*, the Śāktas figure as a distinct group (see ibid., chapter 3) but in this case they could arguably be said to be connected to the tradition only indirectly as its commentators and exegetes. The Siddhāntins during this period also applied this distinction. Nārāyaṇabhaṭṭa does so in his commentary on the *Mṛgendrāgama*, although it is not found in the Āgama itself. Thus he says:

śaivānām eva deśikādīnām iha lakṣaṇam | śāktādayastu te anyādṛśā eveti vijñāpayituṃ śaivapadopādānam |

(Mṛ.T. (*caryāpāda*), 1/2).

50. yena tantreṇa cārabdhaṃ karṣaṇādyarcanāntakam |
tena sarvaṃ prakartavyaṃ na kuryād anyatantrataḥ ||

(P.Kā., vol. I/106).

Also:

tantrasaṃkaradoṣeṇa rājā rāṣṭraṃ ca naśyati |

(Ibid., 1/114).

51. TĀ, 28/400-2.
52. P.Kā., 1/14-16.
53. Ibid.
54. tatrāpi śaivasiddhāntas sarvebho'hy uttamottamaḥ

(U.Kā.24/81b).

55. SŚP, vol. III., p. 548.
56. Brunner has discussed this point in her article: *Differentes conceptions du term 'Śaiva' dans la litterature āgamique du Sud de l'Inde* presented at the

30th Congress on Human Sciences in Asia and North Africa, Mexico 1976. See also the *Pūrvakāraṇāgama*, 26/38b-9a.

57. *Bhāmatī* on Bṛ.Sū.2/2/37. *Brahmasūtrabhāṣya*. Published together with Vācaspati Miśra's *Bhāmatī*, Āmalānanda Sarasvatī's *Kalpataru* and Appayadīkṣita's *Parimala*, 2nd edition edited by Bhārgava Śāstrī, Nirṇaya Sāgar Press, Bombay, 2nd edition, 1938.

58. See K. K. Handiqui's translation of the *Naiṣadhacarita*, footnote on p. 644.

59. *Śrībhāṣya* on Br.Sū.2/2/37. Monistic Kashmiri Śaivites knew of this view and emphatically rejected it. Bhagavatotpala quotes a verse from the *Āgamarahasya* which says: "There are those who teach that even God is [merely] an instrumental cause [of creation] although they offer sesame seed and water with folded hands to the Lord. Yet what can they say about the Lord's [miserable] state [once] He has come under [another's] control by approaching other aspects [of reality in order to create]." Sp.Pra., p. 100; also quoted in SvT, vol. II, p.4.

60. R. G. Bhandarkar, *Vaiṣṇavism, Śaivism and Minor Religious Systems*, Indological Book House, reprint Benares, 1965, p. 119.

61. Ibid.

62. David N. Lorenzen, *The Kāpālikas and Kālāmukhas: Two Lost Śaiva Sects*, University of California Press, Berkeley and Los Angeles 1972, pp. 7-10.

63. *Kūrma*, 1/15/113.

64. *Kūrmapurāṇa* edited by Nīlamaṇi Mukhopadhyaya, Bibliotheca Indica, Girīśa Vidyāratna Press, Calcutta, 1980, ii, 121 p. 740.

65. Kūrma, 2/37/146.

66. *Uttarakhaṇḍa* cited by A. P. Karmakar, *The Vratya or Dravidian Systems*, p. 220.

67. *Śivapurāṇa*, *Vāyavīyasaṃhitā* edited by Mallikārjunaśāstrī, 2/24/177.

68. *Aruṇācalamāhātmya*, 10/65 cited by Karmakar, p. 220.

69. *Yajñavaibhavakhaṇḍa*, 22/3.

70. Quoted in *Īśānaśivagurudevapaddhati*, vol. III, Kriyāpāda, chap. I, cited by V. S. Pathak, *History of Śaiva Cults in Northern India from Inscriptions*, p. 3.

71. Veṅkaṭeśvara Press edition 6/87.

72. Ibid., 67/10-12.

73. In a verse attributed to these two *Purāṇas* by the *Tantrādhikāranirṇaya* cited by C. Chakravarti in *Tantras: Studies on their Religion and Literature*, p. 51.

74. *Śaṅkaravijaya*, cited by Pathak, p. 4.

75. *Ṣaḍdarśanasamuccaya*, cited by Pathak, p. 21.

76. *Śaktisaṅgamatantra*, edited by B. Bhattacharya, 1/5/92-3.

77. Cited by Pathak, p. 26.

78. Cited by Pathak, p. 3.

79. See above p. 16.

80. Lorenzen, p. 102.

81. Ibid., p. 104, 105.

82. Ibid., p. 107.

83. MhB, 12/350/64. Quoted in *The Great Epic of India* by E. W. Hopkins

reprint by Punthi Pustak, Calcutta, 1978 p. 96.

84. Ibid., 12/285/194-5, quoted by Hopkins pp. 114-5.

85. umāpatir bhūtapatiḥ śrīkaṇṭha brāhmaṇaḥ sutaḥ |
uktavān idam avyagro jñānam pāśupataṃ śivaḥ ||
(MhB, Śāntiparvan, 349/64).

86. Pathak, pp. 4-6.

87. Lorenzen rejects the view that Pāśupata orders existed before Lakulīśa and declares that "Lakulīśa was in all likelihood the founder of the Pāśupata order." (Lorenzen p. 175). This was also R. G. Bhandarkar's view. He remarks: "Lakula was the general name by which the Śaiva sects were called. This general name has for its basis the historical fact that a person of the name Lakulin or Lakulīśa founded a Śaiva system corresponding to the Pāñcarātra system, which the Vāyu and Liṅga Purāṇas consider to be contemporaneous with it. The other general name, Pāśupata, arose by dropping the name of the individual Lakulin and substituting that of the god Paśupati, whose incarnation he was believed to be." Quoted by Chakraborti in his introduction to the *Pāsupata Sūtram with Pañcārthabhāṣya by Kauṇḍinya*, Academic Publishers, Calcutta, 1970, p. 9.

88. Lakulīśa's date is uncertain. Much controversy centres on an inscription published in 1931 by D. R. Bhandarkar found on a pillar near Mathura dated 380 A.D. (EI XXl 11-9). It records a donation by the Māheśvara teacher, Uditācārya, of two *liṅgas* named after his teacher, Bhagavat Kapila and grand-teacher, Bhagavat Upamita. Uditācārya is described as tenth in descent from Kuśika and fourth from Parāśara. Bhandarkar identified this Kuśika with Kuśika the disciple of Lakulīśa. Thus he assigned Lakulīśa to the first half of the second century A.D. (Lorenzen pp. 179-80). We cannot be sure, however, that these Śaivites were indeed Lākulīśa Pāśupatas. A figure is sculpted on the pillar with a trident; the base shows a pot-bellied standing figure, nude with two hands, leaning on a staff and with a third eye (*Lakulīśa: Śaivite Saint* by U. P. Shah in *Discourses on Śiva* edited with an introduction by Michael W. Meister, Vakils, Feffer and Simons Ltd., Bombay, 1984, p. 96). There is no mention in the inscription of the Pāśupatas nor of Lakulīśa; nor does the figure on the pillar bear the standard attributes of Lakulīśa. Even so, Kuśika is well known as one of Lakulīśa's disciples who heads a lineage of Lākulīśa Pāśupatas. That this name is found associated with a Śaivite ascetic has seemed to most scholars grounds enough to accept this identification. But whether this date is correct or not, a fairly regular iconography of Lakulīśa as a Śaivite saint begins to emerge by about the sixth century (Shah p. 97) and so must belong to at least the fifth century.

89. *The Development of Hindu Iconography* by J. N. Banerjee, Munshiram Manoharlal, 3rd edition, Delhi, 1974, pp. 448-52.

90. Chakraborti, p. 12.

91. Lorenzen, p. 181; R. G. Bhandarkar, p. 116.

92. See *purāṇavarṇitaḥ pāśupatayogācāryāḥ* in Purāṇam XXIV no. 2, July 1982. In this article Dvivedi has collated the names of the twenty-eight teachers and their disciples as found in the *Skanda*, *Śiva*, *Vāyu*, *Liṅga*, and *Kūrma* Purāṇas.

93. TĀ, 37/13b-17.

94. See Hazra (p. 101) who refers to chapters 70-1 of the *Varāhapurāṇa*.

The *Vāyavīyasaṃhitā* of the *Śivapurāṇa* (7/1/32/13) declares that the scriptures which describe the Pāśupata vow are "hundreds of millions" of verses long.

95. *Bṛhatsaṃhitā*, 59/19, quoted with Bhaṭṭotpala's commentary by Banerjee, p. 230.

96. Chakraborti, p. 14.

97. For references to editors of these texts, other translations and studies on Pāśupata Śaivism in general, see Lorenzen, p. 173 ff.

98. See LĀS, II, p. 116, fn. 1.

99. Shah, pp. 95-6.

100. See commentary on Pāśu., Sū.1/9.

101. Ibid.

102. Pāśu.Sū., 1/13.

103. Kauṇḍinya writes: "patience lies in celibacy, penance lies in celibacy and those brāhmaṇas who live celibate lives go to heaven. Those brāhmaṇas who practice celibacy drink milk, honey and Soma juice mixed with ambrosia and become immortal after death." Pāśu., Sū.1/9.

104. Kauṇḍinya on Pāśu., Sū.1/9.

105. Lorenzen, p. 176.

106. Comm. on Pāśu.Sū., 1/1.

107. See Bühler EI 1, 274.

108. *Śivapurāṇa*, *Śatarudrasaṃhitā*, 5/45-8.

109. Kūrma, 1/51/10.

110. Ibid., 1/51/28.

111. Chakraborti, p. 19.

112. Pāśu.Sū., 4/20 and commentary.

113. Ibid., 1/13.

114. Ibid., 1/17.

115. Lorenzen, p. 114-5.

116. Ibid., p. 103-4.

117. Chakraborti, intro. p. 31.

118. Dvivedi, p. 4 fn. 3 with reference to MhB *ādiparvaṇa*, 1/225-238.

119. Vāmana, 6/86-91. This passage states that Bharadvaja who was a Mahāpāśupata taught king Somakeśvara through whose influence the sect gained strength. The Kāladamana (i.e., Kālāmukha) sect is there said to have been founded by Ṛṣi Āpastamba whose disciple was Krātheśvara, the ruler of Vidarbha, then known as the Kratha-Kaiśika country. See V. S. Agrawal *Vāmana Purāṇa—A Study*, Prithivi Prakashana, Varanasi 1983, p. 6, 30.

120. Pāśu.Sū., 1/12. Abhinava refers to such practices in his *Tantrāloka*. According to him, consciousness is the one reality and so can never be contaminated. The distinction made between 'pure' and 'impure' is no more than a thought-construct generated by an inner, personal conflict which, like all other conflicts, is binding and so must be overcome. This is why the *Vīrāvalītantra* declares that "the ancient ṛṣis ate both beef and human flesh" (TĀ, III, p. 268). Again (the same) Tantra enjoins that "Tantric adepts of a higher order (*vīra*) should eat that which the common man detests and, being revolting, is censorable and prohibited by the scriptures" (ibid., p. 269). This is done so that the yogi can see whether his mind is

indeed steady or not (ibid.). The *Timirodghāṭatantra* says: "O goddess, by eating the body of the beloved, a close friend, relative or benefactor raise up the Maiden of the Sky [and so elevate consciousness]." (quoted in Ś.Sū., vi., p. 33). Kṣemarāja explains that this is an injunction to assimilate embodied subjectivity into universal consciousness (ibid.).

121. Kūrma, 1/11/257.

122. Ibid., 1/11/265.

123. Ibid., 1/11/275.

124. Ibid., 1/13/30; 1/19/61; 2/37/104-5.

125. Ibid., 1/50/24; 2/37/147.

126. Ibid., 1/13/48-9.

127. Ibid., 2/37/140-2.

128. Ibid., 2/37/145-6.

129. *Studies in Devī Bhagavata* by P. G. Lalye, Popular Prakashan, Bombay, 1973 p. 125, with reference to DB, 12/11-12.

130. *Śivamahāpurāṇa kī dārśanik tathā dhārmik samālocanā* by Ramāśaṅkara Tripāṭhī published by the author, Benares 1975, p. 321-2 with reference to *Śivapurāṇa*, 7/1/32/11-13.

131. See above, p. 21.

132. TĀ, 37/10-14.

133. See note 92.

134. Abhinava links the various Pāśupata sects and the groups collectively called *'atimārga'* (see below) with the Kaula traditions. He says: "Once they attain liberation there is no difference at all between those men who have been properly initiated into the Atimārga Krama, Kula, Trika or other currents (*srotas*) in the Supreme Lord's scripture." MVV, I/192b-193. See also TĀv on TĀ, 13/305.

135. *Prabodhacandrodaya*, act III, v. 12-3, Lorenzen, p. 60.

136. Ibid., p. 13.

137. See, for example, the *Bṛhatsaṃhitā*, 9/25; 87/22 and *Bṛhajjātaka*, 15/1.

138. *Āpastambīyadharmasūtra* with Haradatta's *Ujjvala* commentary. Edited by Mahādeva Śāstrī and K. Raṅgācārya, Mysore Government Press, 1898. Haradatta, commenting on sūtra 1/29/1 refers to the *Kāpālikatantra*. The context, however, indicates that by the word "tantra" we should here understand "school" or "teaching" rather than a sacred text. I know of no other possible reference to a specific early Kāpālika scripture.

139. *Obscure Religious Cults* by S. B. Dasgupta, Firma K. L. Mukhopadhyay, 2nd edition, 1962, p. 90.

140. Ibid., p. 58 ff.

141. These insignia—technically called *"Mūdrā"*—are equated in the Buddhist *Sādhanamālā* (p. 489) with the six perfections (*pāramitā*) of the Bodhisattva. In the *Hevajratantra* (1/3/14) the insignia are five, corresponding to the five Buddhas. Yāmunācārya describes the six Śaiva Kāpālika insignia in his *Āgamaprāmāṇya* (p. 93) and is followed by Rāmānuja in the Śrībhāṣya on Bṛ.Sū.2/2/35-7. See *A Review of Rare Buddhists Texts*, vol. I, Central Institute of Higher Tibetan Studies, Sarnath, Benares 1986, p. 103. It is worth noting in passing that the modern Nātha Yogi wears a sacred thread (*janeo*) made of brown

wool. The thread indicates that the wearer is an initiate, but not necessarily a brahmin.

142. *Sacrificial Death and the Necrophagous Ascetic* J. Parry, pp. 88-9.

143. *Gorakṣasiddhāntasaṃgraha* edited by Janārdana Pāṇḍeya, Sarasvatībhavanagranthamālā, no. 110, Benares 1973, pp. 14-15.

144. One colophon in a manuscript of the *Śābaratantra* calls it the *Gorakṣasiddhisopāna*. (Asiatic Society of Bengal MS. no. 8355). Another manuscript of the same work ascribes it directly to Gorakhanātha (Asiatic Society of Bengal MS no. 10542). Kāśinātha Bhaṭṭa (eighteenth century) tries, in his *Kāpālikamatavyavasthā*, to show that there is a historical link between the *Śābaratantra* and the Kāpālikas. See *Hindu Tantric and Śākta Literature* by Teun Goudriaan and Sanyukta Gupta, *A History of Indian Literature*, edited by J. Gonda, vol. II, fasc. 2, Otto Harrasowitz, Wiesbaden, 1981, p. 121. See also ibid., pp. 120-22 for Goudriaan's discussion of the *Sābaratantras* which he classifies amongst the Tantras dealing with magic. For lists of the eighty-four Siddhas and nine Nāthas see S. B. Dasgupta, pp. 202-10.

145. S. B. Dasgupta, pp. 208, 377, 383 and 391.

146. The Prakrit drama, the *Karpūramañjarī* by Rājaśekhara (ed. Sten Konow and translated by C. R. Lanman, Harvard Oriental Series vol. IV, Cambridge, Mass.: Harvard University, 1901) written in the tenth century features a master magician named Bhairavānanda who "follows the Kula path" (act I, v. 22-5; IV v. 19). The author of the *Rucikaraṭīkā* on Kṛṣṇamiśra's *Prabodhacandrodaya* mistakes Rājaśekhara's, Bhairavānanda, for a Kāpālika.

147. Vāmana, 2/17, 4/1.

148. *Śaṅkaradigvijaya*, 15/12-14. The compound sa + umā = soma, implies the Kāpālika's creed, i.e., Somasiddhānta, which affirms that the liberated condition is analogous to the bliss (*ānanda*) experienced in sexual union which reflects that of the union of Śiva with his consort Umā. The word *"soma"* also means moon and so the Kāpālikas have accordingly been associated with the moon. See Bhaṭṭotpala's commentary on Varāhamihira's *Bṛhajjātaka* 15/1.

149. *Śaṅkaradigvijaya*, 15/24-5.

150. Ibid., 15/1-7. See also above p. 29.

151. Lorenzen, p. 20.

152. Ibid., p. 21.

153. Ibid.

154. See above p. 6.

155. See S. N. Ghosal Sastri's *Elements of Indian Aesthetics*, vol. II, part IV, Chaukhamba Oriental Series, Benares 1983, p. 19 ff. Sastri here briefly outlines some phases in this ritual as it is found in the BY, fragments of which he has studied in manuscript along with the *Piṅgalāmata*.

156. TĀ, 27/20b-9. Abhinava's sources are the BY and the *Siddhayogeśvarīmata*.

157. Lorenzen, p. 74 ff. demonstrates that the Kāpālika's vow corresponds to the penance prescribed in Hindu law for killing a brahmin. He makes a mistake, however, when he distinguishes a *"brahmahan"* from a *"bhrūṇahan"* as one who has killed an ordinary brahmin rather than a learned brahmin. *"Bhrūṇahan"*

actually means "one who has killed a fetus" that is, a person who has induced or consented to an abortion. (See Pāniṇi's *Aṣṭādhyāyī*, 3/2/87).

158. The *Jayadrathayāmala* (NA, MS no. 5/4650, fl. 186a) says:

śuddhaṃ saṃśuddha(ṃ) buddhaśca tathā pāśupatavratam |
nagnavrataṃ muṇḍadharaṃ parivrājvratam uttamam ||

159. U.Kā., 24/90 says:

XXX puruṣāj jātas tvatimārgam praṇītavān |
pañcārthaṃ lākulaṃ cānyat tathā pāśupataṃ matam ||

160. SvT, 11/182-4.

161. U.Kā., 24/82 ff.

162. SvT, vol. VI, p. 34-5.

163. One such Kālāmukha teacher was Someśvara who is praised in several inscriptions. Thus, for example, in an inscription found at Belgāve dated 1103 A.D., Someśvara is eulogized as: "he who is gracious to learned men, he who is a very sun to (open) the great cluster of water-lilies (blooming in the daytime) that is the *Nyāyaśāstra*, and who is a very autumn moon to bring to full tide the ocean of *Vaiśeṣikas*; he who is the very ruby ornament of those who are versed in the *Sāṃkhyāgama*, and who is a very bee on the water-lilies that are the feet of his teacher; he who is a very spring to the grove of mango trees that is the *Śabdaśāstra* and who gave new life to the *Lākulasiddhānta* by the development of his wisdom." (Ed. and trans. by Fleet EI V, 220 quoted by Lorenzen, p. 113). Such terms as "*Lākulāgama*" or "*Lākulasiddhānta*" recur frequently in Kālāmukha epigraphs (ibid., p. 110). I believe, as does Lorenzen, that these names, or even the expression "*Paramātmāgama,*" refer equally, according to the context, both to the doctrines of the Lākulīśa Pāśupata and the Śaivāgamas in general.

164. Thus Nārāyaṇabhaṭṭa says:

tathā hi sargādau parameśvaraḥ ūrdhvaprāgdakṣiṇottarapaścima-srotaḥ pañcakabhedabhinnaṃ jñānam |

(Mṛ.Vṛ.Vidyāpāda, p. 7).

165. Jayaratha says: "śivaśāsane iti pañcasrotorūpe pārameśvaradarśane ityārthaḥ | etad hi sarvatraivāviśeṣeṇoktam |" (TĀ, vol. I, p. 73).

166. For a detailed account of how the five faces of Sadāśiva combine to produce the scripture according to the ŚKS quoted in TĀ, 1/18 see *Luce delle Sacre Scritture* by R. Gnoli, Classici Utet, Torino 1972, p. 70, fn. 17.

167. MVV, 1/170-171a.

168. XXXX idaṃ jñānaṃ siddhāntaṃ paramaṃ śubham |
ūrdhvasrotodbhavam aṣṭāviṃśatitantrakam ||

(*Mukuṭāgama*, 1/22b-3a.).

As the 'upper current' of scripture, the Śaivasiddhānta considers itself to be the crown of all Śaiva doctrines. See *Pūrvakāraṇāgama*, 26/19; *Suprabheda*, 1/56/16, 1/24/4, 2/1/12 and *Kāmikā*, 1/1/113 and 1/1/119. See SŚP, vol. I, p. 11.

169. For a list of the twenty-eight Āgamas and their Upāgamas see intro-

duction to the *Rauravāgama* edited by N. R. Bhatt Pondicherry, 1961. Also LĀS, vol. II, intro. pp. 86-90.

170. *Pratiṣṭhālakṣaṇasārasamuccaya* in two parts edited by Bābu Kṛṣṇa Śarmā, Nepāla Rāṣṭriyābhilekhālaya, Kathmandu, vol. I, 1966, vol. II 1968, verses 3/108-127 quoted in LĀS, vol. II, intro. pp. 91-3.

171. See PLSS, intro., vol. II, pp. ka-cha for an extensive discussion about the authorship and date of the PLSS.

172. Mṛ.T. (*caryā*), 1/35-6a.

173. The *Kāmikā* is usually said to possess three Upāgamas, namely the *Vāktara*, *Bhairavottara* and *Narasiṃha*. Nārāyaṇabhaṭṭa in his commentary of the *Mṛgendra* identifies it with the *Narasiṃha:* "śrīmatkāmikākhyaṃ cāsmai parameśvara upadideśa | yatścendrasya nṛsiṃharūpiṇaḥ samupadiṣṭam idam umāpatinā tato mṛgendrasya srotṛtvān mṛgendrasaṃjñayā prathitaṃ |" (Mṛ.vṛ. (*vidyāpāda*), p. 7). The *Mṛgendra* itself characterizes itself as an abridgement of the *Kāmikā*, (ibid., 1/25-27).

174. dvividhaṃ tantram udbhūtaṃ bhairavaṃ dakṣiṇāsyataḥ |
asitāṅgādibhir bhūmau kathitaṃ tad anekadhā ||
(P.Kā, 1/27).

175. nayasūtrādibhedena vāmaṃ vāmād vinirgatam |
caturviṃśatisaṃkhyākam avatīrṇaṃ śivājñayā ||
(P.Kā, 1/25b-6a).

176. See *Studies in the Tantras*, part I by P. C. Bagchi, Calcutta 1975, p. 6.

177. Ibid.

178. Ibid., p. 1 fn. 2. See also Goudriaan, p. 25.

179. NT, 9/11a reads:

> śivaḥ sadāśivaścaiva bhairavas tumburus tathā |

Kṣemarāja comments:

> sarveṣu srotassu ujjvalo bhrājamānaḥ śivo bhāvabhedenāśaya-viśeṣaucityena sadāśivādirūpatayā dhyātaḥ siddhāntavāmadakṣiṇā-diśāstroktaṃ phalaṃ pradadāti |
> (NTu, vol. I, p. 215).

180. For the *dhyāna* of Tumburu see NT, 11/2b-7.

181. See *The Vīṇāśikhatantra: A Śaiva Tantra of the Left Current*, edited with an introduction and translation by Teun Goudriaan, Motilal Banarsidass, Delhi, 1985. Goudriaan has made a chart of the forms of Tumburu, his attendants and Mantras found in a variety of Purāṇic and Tantric sources on pp. 47-50 of this book to which the reader is referred. Tumburu is well known in lexicons and Buddhist works as a Gandharva and musician. (Bagchi, p. 12) He is often associated with Nārada as an attendant of the gods (Goudriaan, p. 18). He also figures as an authority on music in the *Saṃgītāloka* and the *tambura* may well have got its name from him (Bagchi, p. 13). The god Tumburu described in the *Vīṇāśikhatantra* has nothing to do with music, nor is he associated with the *vīṇā* despite the title of the Tantra. He is also devoid of these associations in the

sources Goudriaan has consulted. However, a description of Tumburu, white in colour with two arms and one face, wearing a tiger's skin sitting on a bull playing the *vīṇā* is recorded in the PLSS. (See line drawing on p. 39 in vol. I). A more extensive description of Tumburu is found in the fifth chapter of the first *ṣaṭka* of the JY (NA, no. 5/4650, fl. 22a ff.). Here Tumburu's association with music is clearly evident.

According to the JY, Tumburu is the Lord Himself (*prabhu*) and is called the Great Fierce One (*mahāvyāla*), the crest jewel (*śiroratna*) of all the gods as their Topknot (*śikhā*)—a term used in these Tantras to refer to *Kuṇḍalinī.* He has two aspects, one without form (*asakala*) and the other with form (*sakala*); it is the latter which is described here. He has four energies (*kalā*) which reside in the Cave of the Heart of His universal consciousness. These are: *Śāntikalā*, *Vidyākalā*, *Nirvṛtikalā* and *Pratiṣṭhakalā.* They correspond to the goddesses Jayā, Vijayā, Ajitā and Aparājitā who generate the phenomenal universe (*kārya*) while He Himself is the fifth and highest energy—*Śāntyatītakalā*—which transcends all manifestation. Thus He resides in the Abode of Tranquility (*saumyadhāma*) which is full of the savour of countless Mantras. His entire body is illuminated by the circle of His light and the rays of the jewels of His many Vidyās. He smells sweetly with the scent of many garlands and His body is stained with blood. He makes the gesture of the *Śaktipīṭha* and His *maṇḍala* is that of *Candradurdaṇḍa.* He has four hands in which he holds a noose, hook, trident and makes the gesture of bestowing boons. He has four faces which are white, red, yellow and dark blue (*kṛṣṇa*). His body is like a blazing light shining brilliantly like mount Meru. His principal face is like that of a human being whose lotus-like eyes are blooming and is most beautiful. He wears an earring and its rays cover His face in a network of light. His neck is like a precious gem and His hand is adorned with a ruby ring set in emerald. He wears emeralds and rubies and His broad hips are covered with Kāśmirī cloth. From His mouth comes a deep sound like the rumble of a storm cloud. Of His remaining faces one is that of a crocodile while the two others are those of swans singing sweetly. The pollen of His lotus feet bestows bliss to the *Vīras.* The hook He holds is the goad of the universe. His noose is the abode of all the fetters (*pāśa*) which bind beings as they rise to higher levels or descend. The trident He playfully carries has for its three prongs persistence, arising and destruction. He bestows all that men desire with His wish-bestowing gesture.

Tumburu resides in the circle of the fourteen powers of the Great Fetters (*mahāpāśa*) and is surrounded by a host of female attendants (*dūtī*) and servants. His hosts laugh and shout terribly and their forms are hideously disfigured while He is the Great Hero who can destroy the entire universe by the mere thwang of His bow. At the same time He is the source of all phenomenal existence (*bhava*) and its saviour. He is the cosmic breath (*haṃsa*), the Great Lord of Time and the Fire of Time.

He stands (or sits?) on a lotus of four petals. On the eastern petal is seated Jayā, on the southern Jayeśvarī, on the northern Jitā, while Parājitā is in the west. They are the sisters of Tumburu and all play *vīṇās.* Tumburu's association with music—particularly the *vīṇā*—is also brought out by a number of goddesses amongst the many that surround Him who are said to be skilled in playing this instrument. See below also p. 39.

182. See Goudriaan, p. 48.
183. See footnote 181 above.
184. VŚT, v. 100-8.
185. Ibid., v. 4.
186. Ibid., v. 305.
187. Ibid., v. 317.
188. X XXXX siddhyartham uktaṃ tad avatārakaiḥ |
nayasūtrādibhedena vāmaṃ vāmād vinirgatam ||
(P.Kā., 1/25).

The *Ratnamālā* quoted in TĀ, 37/27 says:

XXXXXXXX vāmaṃ siddhisamākulam |

189. Goudriaan, p. 24.
190. Ibid., p. 25.
191. VŚT, v. 10.
192. Ibid., v. 223, cf. v. 309, 326 and 333.
193. Ibid., v. 362.
194. Ibid., v. 147-9; 254-7.
195. Ibid., v. 116.
196. Ibid., v. 396.
197. See below, p. 198n. 27.
198. See below, p. 113.
199. See below, p. 113.
200. VŚT, v. 317.
201. See below, p. 113.
202. TĀ, vol. XIb p. 40.
203. dvādaśasāhasre śrīmadānandeśvare TĀ, vol. IX, p. 139.
204. TĀ, 37/10-11.
205. The others are the *Bhargaśikhā, Gamaśāstra, Saṃkarṣiṇīyāmala, Navanityāvidhāna, Bhūtakṣobha* and *Nandiśikhā.* These Tantras are certainly not all *Vāmatantras.*
206. TĀ, vol. IX, pp. 138-40.
207. vāmapāṇau jayantyāśca tumbaroścāpi melake |
dātavyaṃ vipruṣāmātram uparyupari kalpitam ||
(TĀ, vol. IX, p. 139).
208. TĀ, vol. IX, p. 281.
209. aṣṭāviṃśatibhedaistu gāruḍaṃ hṛdayaṃ purā |
(Quoted in TĀ, vol. I, p. 44).
210. The printed edition reads: kaulādiviṃśatsaṃkhyātaṃ bhūtatantraṃ sadyataḥ | P.Kā., 1/26b. The reading "Kaula" is probably incorrect, as "Kaula" is a term of reference for a group of scriptures not a single text. This is so even in the *Kāmikā* itself. Perhaps the reading is better emended to *"halādi"* which would agree with *"Halāhalam,"* the first Tantra in our list of *Bhūtatantras.*
211. XXXXXX prācyaṃ trotalādi suvistaraṃ |
(Mṛ.T., ca.1/35).

212. The reading in Dvivedi's edition is *Trotalam* and *Tratalottaram.* MS B.Sak. records the variants *Tottalam* and *Tottalottaram.*

213. muktipradasiddhānta - sarvaviṣaharaṇagāruḍa - sarvavaśīkaraṇavāma - bhūtagrahanivārakabhūtatantra - śatrukṣayakarabhairavasaṃjñakam iti |

(ŚRS, p. 9 quoted by Dvivedi in the intro. to the NSA, p. 55 and also in LĀS, vol. II, p. 114).

214. G.P., 3/8 expressly says that "Garuḍa is Viṣṇu" (garuḍaḥ sa hariḥ). For Garuḍa's sincere devotion, Viṣṇu grants him the boon that he will become Viṣṇu (ibid., 2/55a) and the mere sight or recollection of him will destroy serpents (ibid., 3/7b). In other places he is said to be Śiva Himself, e.g., ibid., 197/51.

215. G.P., 2/52 ff.

216. Ibid., 2/51-57. The *Kāśyapasaṃhitā* of the Pāñcarātra (ed. by Śrī Yathirāja Sampathkumāramuni, Madras 1933) is concerned entirely with the exposition of the Gāruḍamantra. It is a text on snake bites and cures. It is, however, a unique work in the Pāñcarātra corpus so much so that this has led to the suspicion that it is not canonical even though the worship of Garuḍa as a cure for snake bites is counselled in certainly genuine Pāñcarātra texts (e.g., *Bṛhadbrahmasaṃhitā* II, 3, 36-57). See *The Smith Āgama Collection: Sanskrit Books and Manuscripts Relating to Pāñcarātra Studies* by David H. Smith, Syracuse 1978, pp. 21-23.

217. TĀ, 37/12b-13.

218. This preliminary identification with Bhairava is interesting. The purpose of it here seems to be to reinforce the efficacy of the adept's identification with Garuḍa. Bhairava is also depicted as a powerful being who can counter the effect of hostile planets, protect fields, defeat ghosts and *rākṣasas* as well as counter the effects of poison (G.P., 20/14).

219. G.P., 197/46-54.

220. MS no. 3/392; 5/4949; 5/4947; 5/4946 and 5/4948. The oldest MS appears to be 3/392 which is dated N.S. 304, i.e., 1184 A.D. NTu, vol. II, pp. 148; 151; 157-158; 196-199.

221. na śrutaṃ gāruḍaṃ kiñcit sadyaḥ pratyayakārakam |
tam ācakṣasva suraśreṣṭha mama bhaktaśca śaṃkara ||
lakṣaṇaṃ nāgajātīnāṃ garbhotpattim aśeṣataḥ |
rūpakaṃ sarvanāgānāṃ vyantarāṇāṃ ca jātakam ||
grahayakṣapiśācānāṃ śākinīnāṃ ca lakṣaṇam |
bālagrahāśca ye krūrāḥ pīḍyante nityanirghṛṇāḥ ||
(BSP Tantra, vol. I, p. 96).

222. NT, vol. II pp. 150; 151-2; 199.

223. Possibly *Vimalam* which is no. 17 of the *Bhūtatantra* group corresponds to the *upāgama* of that name belonging to the *Vijayāgama.* Again, if we accept the variant reading *Pañcāmṛtam* for *Pañcabhūtam*, which is no. 16 in the *Gāruḍa* list, it may correspond to no. 48 in the NSA list, although it is more likely to be the same as the *Pañcāmṛtam*, which is no. 27 in the list of *Dakṣiṇatantras.* There

are a number of cases where we notice that a text travels from one group to another or, to put it another way, is appropriated by other groups.

224. "bhairavāgameṣu dakṣiṇasrotaḥ samuttheṣu svacchandacaṇḍatriśiro-bhairavādiṣu bheditam |" (NTu, vol. I, p. 225). These three Tantras are No. 1, 2 and 24 in the list of the *Dakṣiṇatantras.* Also SvT, vol. I, p. 8.

225. Abhinavagupta exalts the *Bhairavatantras* which he considered to be the highest of the five currents of scripture:

XXXXXX srotaḥ pañcakaṃ yat tato'pyalam |
utkṛṣṭaṃ bhairavābhikhyaṃ XXXXXXXX

(TĀ, 37/17).

226. At the Institut Français D'Indologie in Pondicherry, transcripts have been made of all twenty-eight Siddhāntāgamas. MSs of many of the two hundred-odd *upāgamas* have also been collected.

227. So, for example, the *Netratantra* says:

sarvāgamavidhānena bhāvabhedena siddhidam |
vāmadakṣiṇasiddhāntasauravaiṣṇavavaidike |

(NT, 9/2).

228. In certain MSs (e.g., NA, 1/285) the colophons describe this tantra as: sarvasrotasaṃgrahasāraḥ | i.e., "the essence of the summary of all the currents of scripture."

229. NT, 9/11.

230. Thus the goddess says:

yad uktaṃ dakṣiṇaṃ srotaṃ vāmaṃ caiva tathā param |
madhyamaśca tathā srotaṃ coditaḥ pūrvam eva hi ||

(BY, MS no. NA 1/296, fl. 187b).

(Philological note: the word *srotas* is a neuter noun ending in the consonant "s." Here it is treated as if it were a neuter noun ending in "a." Accordingly, the form of the nominative singular is *srotam* rather than *srotas.*)

231. These energies constitute a standard triad of will, knowledge and action. Their iconic forms in the BY are portrayals of the goddess in the three ages of life, namely, youth, maturity and old age. (See Ghosal Sastri, vol. II, part IV p. 13. Sastri bases his brief account of this triad on a MS of the BY deposited in the library of Visvabharati University, no. śil. 16/3, fol. 6a). It seems that we have a prior parallel here for the Trika identification of the three currents with Parā, Parāparā and Aparā who are the three goddesses that are the focus of Trika ritual. This identification is made in the *Śrīkaṇṭhīyasaṃhitā* although there the three currents are differently defined.

232. "aśeṣamalasaṃdoharañjitaḥ madhyamāśrayaḥ |" (BY, ibid., fl. 188a). Note: The rules of euphonic combination have not been observed here; *ranjitaḥ* should be *rañjito.*

233. *Śivajñāna* is here expressly identified with the *Śiva* and *Rudrabheda* of the *Madhyamasrotas*; thus the *parajñāna* of the Siddhānta becomes just a part of *jñānaugha.*

234. It is certainly not at all clear whether we can, in fact, make such clear-cut distinctions, although generally speaking the *Siddhāntāgamas* do tend to be dualistic, unlike the *Bhairavatantras* which are predominantly monist. Even so, it is certainly not possible to distinguish the *Śivāgamas* from the *Rudrāgamas* on the basis that the former are dualist while the latter conceive reality to be a unity-in-difference.

235. Abhinavagupta goes further by making all the Śaivāgama ultimately a part of Trika. The god who utters the scripture is not the five-headed Sadāśiva of the Siddhānta. The Supreme Lord who spoke the three types of scripture (of the Left, Right and Siddhānta) is in fact three-headed. He is Triśirobhairava, the Trika form of Śiva:

tad vibhāvayati bhedavibhāgaṃ tat sphuṭatvakṛd athoktam anantam |
saṃgrahiṣṇu parameśvararūpaṃ vastutas triśira eva nirāhuḥ ||
(MVV, 1/397).

236. This state of affairs is peculiar to the *Śrīkaṇṭhī* which does anyway, in a sense, retain the *Vāmatantras* as a part of the same standard, older division into *srotas* although it is relegated to the lower level of a secondary, subsidiary classification. Other *Trikatantras* such as the *Bhargaśikhā* and *Niśisaṃcāra* sustain the continued existence of the *Vāmatantras* although they integrate them into Trika. There was, however, certainly a tendency for the *Vāmatantras* to lose their identity in the ambiance of Kashmiri Śaiva Trika.

237. The *Śikhābheda* in the ŚKS consists of the following eight Tantras: *Bhairavī* called Śikhā, *Vīṇā*, *Vīṇāmaṇi*, *Sammohanam*, *Ḍāmaram*, *Atharvakam*, *Kabandha* and *Śiraścheda*. In the *Vāmatantra* list *Vīṇā* is the seventh, *Sammohanam* may correspond to the fourth called *Mohanam* and *Vīṇāmaṇi* to the fourteenth called *Cintāmaṇimahodayam* (although this identification is certainly more tenuous than the previous one). Also worth noting is that the *Śiraścheda*, which is the *Jayadrathayāmala*, finds itself in this, rather than in the *Yāmala* group, possibly indicating its closer affiliation to the *Vāmatantras*.

238. That there was some problem here is confirmed by the fact that the correspondent member in the *Bhairavāṣṭaka* is called simply "*Bhairava.*"

239. P.Kā, 1/27a.

240. Thus *Jhaṅkāra* is no. 31 and *Śekhara* no. 21.

241. dakṣiṇe dakṣiṇo mārgaś caturviṃśatibhedataḥ |
śaivās sarveṣu kurvanti ye gṛhasthā dvijottamāḥ ||
(TĀ, vol. I, p. 44).

242. yāmale mātṛtantre ca kāpāle pāñcarātrake ||
bauddhe cārhamate caiva lākule vaidike'pi ca |
anyeṣvapi ca mārgeṣu tat tac chāstraiḥ svaśāstrataḥ ||
śaivāḥ kurvanti dīkṣādyaṃ tal liṅgasthāpanādikam |
(P.Kā, 1/122b-4a).

243. The *Yāmalas* listed here are *Rudra*°, *Kanda*°, *Brahma*°, *Viṣṇu*°, *Yama*°, *Vāyu*°, *Kuvera*° and *Indra*°.

244. The names of these *Yāmalas* are listed in the *Ṛjuvimarśinī* (p. 43):

Brahmayāmala, Viṣṇu°, Rudra°, Jayadratha°, Skanda°, Umā°, Lakṣmī° and *Gaṇeśa°*. A part of the *Umāyāmala* appears to be preserved in a collection of fragments in a Nepalese MS (NA, MS no. 3/575). The colophon of this fragment reads:

> iti śrībhairavasrotasi sārasaṃgrahe śrī umāyāmale dvādaśasāhasre umāprabodhe śrīsiddhilakṣmīvidhānaṃ caturviṃśatitaḥ saptadaśākṣaroddhāraḥ samāptaḥ |

245. The *Brahmayāmala* knows the *Yoginīhṛdaya* which is closely related to the NSA. There can be no doubt that the *Yoginīhṛdaya*, which mentions the NSA in many places and has been even considered to be the second part of it, is at least contemporaneous with it.

246. Amongst the eight *Yāmalas* noted in the ŚKS the following are not named above: *Svacchanda°, Ruru°, Atharvaṇa°* and *Vetāla°*. We know of others from references; thus the *Devyāyāmala* is an important scripture quoted in the *Tantrāloka* and elsewhere (see LĀS, vol. II, pp. 84-90). There is also the *Saṃkarṣiṇīyāmala* (quoted in TĀ, vol. IX, p. 139).

Again, although the *Yāmalas* which have been preserved—namely, the JY, BY and fragments of the *Umāyāmala*—belong to the *Bhairavasrotas, Yāmala* was considered by Trika to be higher than the *Dakṣiṇasrotas*. Thus Abhinava writes in the TĀ, probably quoting from the SYM:

> vidyākalāntaṃ siddhānte vāmadakṣiṇaśāstrayoḥ |
> sadāśivāntaṃ samanāparyantaṃ matayāmale ||
>
> (TĀ, 15/319).

247. See above footnote no. 92.

248. The lists of sixty-four Tantras in Lakṣmīdhara's commentary on the *Saundaryalaharī* and Bhāskara's *setubandha* commentary on the NSA as well as the one in the *Kulacūḍāmaṇitantra* are almost the same as that of the NSA. There can be little doubt that they adopted it wholesale as a standard canonical list. Other later lists of sixty-four Tantras are indeed different and probably do present an actual account of the Tantras at the time of their compilation. Even so, the Tantras were listed as a group of sixty-four on the basis of the older, traditional system of classification to which the NSA subscribed. For these lists see LĀS, vol. II, pp. 94-III.

249. The Goddess says at the beginning of the NSA:

> nityāḥ ṣoḍaśa deveśa sūcitā na prakāśitāḥ ||
> idānīṃ śrotum icchāmi tāsāṃ nāmāni śaṃkara |
> ekaikaṃ cakrapūjāṃ ca paripūrṇāṃ samantataḥ ||
>
> (NSA, 1/22b-23).

250. These are numbers 51, 52 and 53 in the list. The *Kulasāra* is quoted by Kṣemarāja in the Ś.Sū., vi., p. 67. It is also named in the *Ciñcinīmatasārasamuccaya* of the *Paścimāmnāya*; see NA, MS no. 1/767, fl. Ib. The *Kulacūḍāmaṇi* listed here is probably different from the published *Kulacūḍāmaṇi*,

which appears to belong to a later strata in the development of the Tantras. Another work of the same name which is more likely to be the same as the Tantra listed here is quoted by Kṣemarāja in Ś.Sū., vi., p. 29.

251. These are numbers 24, 12 and 26 in the list. The *Triśirobhairavatantra* is one of the Tantras Abhinavagupta quotes the most. We know from Kṣemarāja that it was considered to be a *Dakṣiṇasrotatantra:* "bhairavāgameṣu dakṣiṇasrotaḥ samuttheṣu svacchandacaṇḍatriśirobhairādiṣu bheditam |" (NTu, vol. I, p. 225).

There can be no doubt that this is also a *Trikatantra* because Abhinava refers to it at length in chapter 30 of his *Tantrāloka* where he deals with the Mantras of the three goddesses Parā, etc., and their consorts, which is a characteristic feature of Trika. Indeed, the exposition is based essentially on the MVT and SYM, which are *Trikatantras* par excellence. Here the *Triśirobhairava* is referred to as presenting a number of variant forms of these Mantras. The *Triśirobhairava* is again referred to at length in TĀ, 31 where the drawing of the *Triśulamaṇḍala* is described, the knowledge of which, according to Abhinava, is the mark of the true Trika master (TĀ, 31/50b-52). We know that the *Niśisaṃcāra,* (also called *Niśācāra* and *Niśāṭana*) must have been a *Trikatantra* because it considered Trika to be the highest school (see quotations in TĀ, vol. I, p. 49 and PTv, p. 92). A single incomplete and very corrupt MS of a *Niśisaṃcāratantra* is deposited in the NA at Kathmandu (MS no. 1/1606). This is a palm leaf MS and the text is written in old Newari script probably belonging to the twelfth century A.D., if not earlier. The content and style is certainly of the type one would expect of a Tantra of the older group. Even so, its esoteric exposition of the *pīṭhas* does not agree with that found in references from the *Niśisaṃcāra* quoted in Kashmiri works, although the treatment is conceptually similar. Possibly the fragment in Kathmandu was the original *Dakṣiṇatantra,* although it does not affiliate itself to it or any other group anywhere in the text or the colophons. Three MSs of the SYM have been located, all of them incomplete. One is deposited in the NA—MS no. 5/2403 (23 fl.); the other two are in the Asiatic Society in Calcutta, viz. MS no. 3917D (2 fl.) and 5465 (72 fl.). The first of these two Calcutta MSs contains only the fifth chapter called *"Karṇikāpaṭala."* The second MS contains 31 chapters. Although the fragment preserved in the first MS is a part of this Tantra, it has not been traced in the second MS. Again, although a number of verses have been traced in the second MS which are quoted in Kashmiri works, it seems that this is a shorter recension than the one known in Kashmir. Perhaps this shorter recension was called *"Bhairavavīrasaṃhitā"* which is the name given to this Tantra in the colophon of chapter 21. The SYM is known to the NSA (no. 51 in the list) and the BY, clearly indicating that this is an old and well-established scripture. It itself confirms that it is a *Bhairavatantra:*

mahābhairavatantre'smin siddhayogeśvarīmate |

(fl. 15a).

252. proktaṃ bhagavatā kila samūhaḥ pīṭham etac ca |

(TĀ, 37/18).

253. vidyāśritāni yāni syū vidyāpīṭhaṃ varānane |
mantrāśritāni yāni syū mantrapīṭhaṃ tathā caiva ||
mudrāśritāni yāni syū mudrāpīṭhastu suvrate |
maṇḍalapīṭhakāni syū maṇḍalapīṭha ucyate ||
(BY, fl. 188b).

(Philological note: I take the neuter plural forms *"vidyāśritāni"* etc. to agree with *"tantrāṇi,"* which is clearly implied although not directly stated. *"Tāni,"* the correlate pronoun of *"yāni,"* should be understood to refer to *vidyāpīṭhaṃ*, etc., in each line. The third plural of the optative of the root *"as"* is normally *"syuḥ;"* here the form is *"syū."* The gender of the word *"pīṭha"* is neuter and so the nominative singular should be *"pīṭhaṃ"* as it is in the first two lines. In the last two lines, however, it is treated as if it were a masculine noun).

254. Abinava says: "Mantra is that which thinks and saves. It is strengthened and nourished by knowledge (*vidyā*) which illumines that which is to be known. *Mudrā* is a reflected image of *Mantra* and is nourished by *Maṇḍala*. The term *'maṇḍa,'* implicit in *'maṇḍala,'* refers to the essence itself, that is, Śiva. In this way, insofar as the four *pīṭhas* penetrate each other mutually, everything is in reality present in its essence in every individual *pīṭha*." (TĀ, 37/19b-22a).

255. adhunā maṇḍalaṃ pīṭhaṃ kathyamānaṃ śṛṇu priye |
maṇḍalānāṃ śataṃ proktaṃ siddhātantre varānane ||
(quoted in TĀ, vol. XII p. 227).

256. The final colophon of the BY clearly states that it belongs to the *Vidyāpīṭha:*

iti bhairavasrotasi mahātantre vidyāpīṭhe brahmayāmale . . . . .

For the SYM see below, fn. 282.

257. catuṣpīṭhaṃ mahātantraṃ catuṣṭayaphalodayam |
(SvT, 1/5a).

Kṣemarāja explains that these four *pīṭhas* are the most important *Vidyās*, *Mantrās* and *Maṇḍalas* described in the SvT. The *Sarvavīratantra* similarly claims that it consists of all four *pīṭhas*.

258. eṣā sā samayā devī atra sarvaṃ pratiṣṭhitam |
catuḥ pīṭheṣu samayā atra sarvavinirgatā ||
vāmadakṣiṇatantreṣu sāmānyā samayā parā |
kubjikā nāma vikhyātā samayasthā kuleśvarī ||
yatra viśveśvaraṃ sarvaṃ samayādyaṃ vinirgatam |
mantramudrāgaṇo hy atra vidyāmaṇḍalakādikam ||
(KMT, fl. 30b-31a).

259. yasmād bhāṇḍaram ityevaṃ sarvasvaṃ yoginīkule |
atha ca sarvapīṭheṣu mate'yaṃ samayātmikā ||
(Ibid., 31b).

260. KRU, fl. 5a.

261. KMT, fl. 30a.

262. ācāraṃ kulācāraṃ mudrāpīṭham |
(NA, MS No. 1/228, fl. Ia.; BSP, vol. II, p. 67).

263. See Jayaratha's commentary in TĀ, vol. XIb, p. 114. How these rituals, and the texts which are their sources, are associated to these *pīṭhas* is not explained. I am not too clear in my mind about this at present.

264. iha vidyāmantramudrāmaṇḍalātmatayā catuṣpīṭhaṃ tāvac chāstram |
(TĀ, vol. XIb, p. 114).

265. NA, MS no. 1/35 is dated N.S. 307, the equivalent of 1188 A.D.

266. namāmi catuḥpīṭhapīṭhadevyā(ḥ) kuleśvaraṃ |
(Ibid., fl. 1a).

267. mantrākhyaṃ tatra vidyayā upodbalanam āpyāyaḥ |
(TĀ, 37/19b-20a).

268. mantramārgānusāreṇa mudrābhedaḥ sahasraśaḥ |
(BY, fl. 199b).

269. mantrapratikṛtir mudrā XXXXXXXX |
(TĀ, 37/20b).

270. The order in the *Sarvavīratantra* is different:

mudrā maṇḍalapīṭhaṃ tu mantrapīṭhaṃ tathaiva ca |
vidyāpīṭhaṃ tathaiveha catuṣpīṭhā tu saṃhitā ||
(SvT, vol. I, p. 10).

Kṣemarāja enumerates these *pīṭhas* in the following order: *Vidyā, Mantra, Maṇḍala* and *Mudrā* (ibid.). Abhinava however says:

XXXXXXXX maṇḍalaṃ mudrikā tathā ||
mantro vidyeti ca pīṭham utkṛṣṭaṃ cottarottaram |
(TĀ, 37/23b-24a).

271. BY, fl. 188a.
272. TĀ, 37/18b-9a.
273. BY, fl. 188a.
274. See appendix C.
275. BY, fl. 188a.
276. See footnote 270.
277. SvT, vol. I, p. 10.
278. See above footnote 257.
279. See below p. 105.

280. We come across the term *"mantrapīṭha"* in the Siddhānta but here it refers to the seat of the deity (*pīṭha*) which is transformed in the course of the ritual into Mantra (see Mṛ.T., Kr. 8/196b-197). *Vidyāpīṭha* in the Siddhānta refers to the Āgama in general viewed as an object of veneration. The worship of the sacred scripture is a way of worshipping Śiva. The Āgama the disciple studies is an object of his veneration; it is therefore, on occasion, worshipped with flowers and incense, etc., as is the teacher (see SŚP, vol. I, p. 226, 290). During certain rites of atonement prescribed in the *Triśirobhairavatantra*, a sacred thread (*pavitra*) is offered to all the places of worship on the site where the ritual is performed, including the *Vidyāpīṭha* which is presumably where the Āgama is

worshipped (TĀ, 28/156b). Paścimā ritual also provides for the worship of scripture. According to the MBT (Y), the *Kulāgama* is to be worshipped in a specially prepared *maṇḍala* called *Vidyāpīṭha* (fl. 86a). Similarly, at the beginning of the GS the manner in which the master and then the Āgama are to be worshipped is described (p. 5), while the ṢaṭSS explains how the Tantra of the Kubjikā tradition is to be worshipped before the master teaches the disciple its meaning (ṢaṭSS, 3/98-102).

281. vidyāpīṭhapradhānaṃ ca siddhayogeśvarīmatam ||
tasyāpi paramaṃ sāraṃ mālinīvijayottaram |
(TĀ, 37/24b-5a).

The MVT itself states its own close affiliation to the SYM. Thus the god says to the goddess:

śṛṇu devi pravakṣyāmi siddhayogeśvarīmatam |
yan na kasyacid ākhyātaṃ mālinīvijayottaram ||
(MVT, 1/13).

282. In the SYM (fl. 72b) we read:

siddhayogeśvaraṃ tantraṃ vidyāpīṭhaṃ yaśasvini |

283. The BY allocates the 'eight times eight' *Bhairavatantras* along with the *Yāmalas* to the *Vidyāpīṭha*, as well as the following Tantras: *Yoginījñāna, Yoginījāla, Yoginīhṛdaya, Siddhā, Mantramālinī, Aghoreśī, Aghoreśvara, Krīḍāghoreśvarī, Lākinī,* ? , *Śārīra*(?) *Mahāmarī, Ugravidyā, Gaṇa, Bahurūpa* (of two kinds) and *Aghorāstra.*

284. See below p. 114.

285. *Tantric Cult of South India* by R. Nagaswamy, Agam Kala Prakashan, Delhi, 1982, p.34.

286. TĀ, vol. XII, p. 398.

287. See below p. 105.

288. See above footnote 267.

289. TĀ, 37/25b-39.

290. TĀ, vol. XII, p. 399; cf.

mudrāmaṇḍalamantraughaṃ vidyāpīṭhopalakṣitaṃ |
(BY, fl. 1a).

291. NA, MS no. 1/1693. This is a palm leaf MS only two folios long.

292. NA, MS no. 3/379 (161 folios) and NA, MS no. 1/53 (157 folios). The colophons of the latter MS read:

iti lakṣapadādhike mahāsaṃhitāyāṃ dvādaśasāhasre vidyāpīṭhamatasāre . . . . . .
(BSP, vol. II, pp. 210-212).

293. Part of the lengthy colophons of the *Yogakhaṇḍa* of the MBT read:

ityādyāvatāre mahāmanthānabhairavayajñānvaya . . . . ādyāpīṭhāvatārite vidyāpīṭhamārge ......

(MBT (Y), no. 3/165).

294. The god asks the goddess:

lekavīrā katham vidyāpīṭhadevyā katham katham |

(MBT (Y), fl. 22b).

295. See footnotes 258 and 259.

296. A typical colophon of the *Śrīmatottara* reads:

iti śrīmatottare śrīkaṇṭhanāthāvatārite candradvīpanirgate vidyāpīṭhe yoginīguhye .....

(NA, MS no. 2/279; BSP, vol. II, p. 206).

297. The colophons of the *Gorakṣasaṃhitā* clearly state that it is affiliated to the *Vidyāpīṭha* revealed by Śrīkaṇṭhanātha:

.... kādibhede kulakaulalinīmate navakoṭyavatārabhede śrīkaṇṭhanāthāvatāre vidyāpīṭhe yoginīguhye ......

(GS, p. 418).

298. *Abhinavagupta: An Historical and Philosophical Study* by K. C. Pandey, Chowkhamba, Benares, 1963, p. 138.

PART TWO

1. According to the NT (chapter 12), the presiding deity of the *Kulāmnāya* is Bhairava. His form differs only in minor details from the Bhairava who, according to chapter 11 of this same Tantra, presides over the *Dakṣiṇasrotas*. The *Gorakṣasaṃhitā*, a *Paścimāmnāya* Tantra, opens with a hymn to Bhairava (pp. 1-3) who is said to be "born of Kula and Akula, [although] free of the emergence of Kula" (ibid., p. 162). He is, in other words, both transcendent Śiva (*Akula*) and immanent Śakti (*Kula*) and at the same time free of all cosmic manifestation (*Kula*). Maheśvarānanda says of Kuleśvara, the deity every Kaula school venerates as supreme, that "in the *Kaulikātantras* he is generally called Bhairava" (MM p. 172).

2. evam etat kulamārgānupraviṣṭena sarvathā svātmānanda-vyañjakatāmātraparatayā sevyaṃ na tu tad gardhena |

(TĀ, vol. XIb, p. 67).

According to Jayaratha, the Kaula's wife is not the ideal Tantric consort for him because ritual intercourse with her is attended by the danger of his succumbing to lust. Abhinavagupta, however, does not consider this to be a problem and so, according to him, ritual union (*melāpa*) can be of two kinds, depending on whether it takes place with one's own wife or with any other woman initiated into Kaula ritual.

3. Jayaratha quotes from an unnamed Tantra:

He who is dedicated to Kula practice (*kulācāra*) but is not touched by wine should practice penance, be he a brahmin or a kṣatrīya.
(TĀ, vol. XIb, p. 11).

4. layodayaś citsvarūpas tena tat kulaṃ ucyate |
svabhāve bodham amalaṃ kulaṃ sarvatra kāraṇam |
(TĀ, vol. XIb, p. 4).

5. kulasyaiva sarvaviśrāntidhāmatvam uktam |
(quote in TĀ, vol. XII, p. 373).

6. "Kula is the Supreme Bliss . . . . " (TĀ, vol. XIb., p. 4).

"It is from whence this [cosmic] picture arises and where the universe comes to rest" (TĀ, vol. XII, p. 373).

7. "For the emission of the Lord of the Absolute is the Mistress of Kula" (Ibid., 5/67).

"The absolute is the Supreme Abode and it is that which is called Akula. The emission of this Lord is said to be the power Kaulikā" (TĀ, 3/144).

"His inner intention is called Kaulikī, the Supreme" (TĀ, 3/137).

8. śāntoditaṃ sati kāraṇaṃ paraṃ kaulam |
(TĀ, 29/117a ff).

9. "Therefore it is free of all obscuring coverings and so extroverted consciousness is awareness in the form of the means of knowledge while the object of knowledge is the object of awareness such as 'blue' or 'pleasure', at one with it. All this, be it subject or object, etc., is the essence of this expansion. The point is that there is nothing apart from that" (TĀ, vol. XIb, p. 7).

10. In the economy of the Trika of the *Tantrāloka,* the *Niśisaṃcāratantra* is constantly referred to as the authority for this view. Doubt is the Kaula's greatest obstacle; doubt constitutes the firm bars of the prison of *saṃsāra* and it is this doubt he must overcome (see TĀ, 12/18b-25).

11. ata eva hi naikaṭyād vāmadakṣiṇaśāstrayoḥ ||
dhārā prāntadhārāprānte kaulikī pravijṛmbhate |
(MVV, 1/394b-5a).

12. puṣpe gandhas tile tailaṃ dehe jīvo jale 'mṛtam |
yathā tathaiva śāstrānāṃ kulam antaḥ pratiṣṭhitam ||

Abhinava quotes this verse from the *Kālīkula* in TĀ, 35/34, after he has said that: "The supreme goal of (all the scriptures) is the Abode named 'Trika'. That alone is said to be Kula because [only] that which is at one with all things [and unconditioned by time and space] is perpetually manifest. Just as life is one and the same in every individual limb of the body, whether major or minor, similarly Trika is present in all things as scripture itself confirms." Abhinava is here clearly equating Trika with Kula in order to establish that it is present in all the scriptures *as Kula.* Jayaratha similarly quotes this verse to suggest that Trika is Kula. Trika, Jayaratha says, is the sixth current of scripture that consists of the *Siddhānta, Vāma* and *Bhairava* Tantras. The three goddesses, *Parā, Parāparā* and *Aparā,* reside in Trika and so it contains all the scripture and "floods them with the nectar of Supreme Monism (*paramādvaya*)" thus rendering them effective (TĀ, vol. I, p. 45). Maheśvarānanda equates Kula with the Krama absolute (*mahārtha*) and so quotes this verse (M.M., p. 170) to suggest that Mahārtha is the highest esoteric doctrine hidden, and everywhere present, in the scriptures. Maheṣvarānanda is not, however, really much at odds with Abhinava because his Krama tradition is that of *Anuttara* which is the absolute Abhinava's Trika treats as Trika, the supreme principle itself. Accordingly, Maheṣvarānanda does not see much difference between Trikadarśana and Mahārtha (ibid., p. 92).

13. athātaḥ saṃpravakṣyāmi kulāmnāyanidarśanam |
yāgaṃ homaṃ japaṃ kāryaṃ yena sarvam avāpnuyāt ||
(NT, 12/1).

14. Ibid., vol. I, p. 253.

15. Ibid., p. 252.

16. Brunner, in an article on the NT, says in a footnote: "One could ask oneself why Kṣemarāja deems it necessary to explain the characteristics of this school insofar as he has said almost nothing about the others, and why he stresses the fact that it is essentially similar to them. Is it perhaps because it was not popular in his time? Or described? Or not yet integrated into the great Śaiva family? One defends oneself with difficulty from the impression that this integration is achieved at the cost of a certain amount of effort. One frequently comes across references in the *Netra* to the triad *Vāma Dakṣiṇa Siddhānta* which seems to form a solid block: if in these cases reference is made to Kula, it is because it is not a constant fixed group; it is like an addition, in another movement of discourse." *Un Tantra du Nord: Le "Netra Tantra"* in BEFEO, Tome LXI, Paris, 1974 pp. 154-5.

17. After the *Uttarakāmikā* has described the five *srotas* we read:

paścimād vāmasaṃjñaṃ tu vāmād dakṣiṇam uttamam |
dakṣiṇāt kaulikaṃ śreṣṭhaṃ mahākaulaṃ tataḥ param ||
pūrvāmnāyaṃ tatas śreṣṭhaṃ tasmāt siddhāntam uttamam |
(U.Kā, 24/92-93a).

In the *Mṛgendrāgama,* the Siddha—and Yoginī—Kaula which, as we shall see, are important divisions in the *Kulāgama,* are referred to as *upasrotas* of the five *srotas.* (Mṛ *caryāpāda,* 1/37, 1/40-1).

18. antaḥ kaulo bahiḥ saivo lokācāre tu vaidikaḥ |
(quoted in TĀ, vol. III, p. 27).

antaḥ kaulo bahiḥ saivo lokācāre tu vaidikaḥ |
sāram ādāya tiṣṭheta nārikelaphalaṃ yathā ||
(Ibid., p. 278).

19. ekaikakoṭidhābhinnaṃ kulaśāstraṃ suvistaram |
(CMSS fl. 2b).

cintāmaṇisamaprakhyaṃ vistaraṃ kulabhairavam |
(Ibid.).

20. ūrdhvavāmatadanyāni tantrāṇi ca kulāni ca |
(MVV 1/398; also TĀ, vol. I, p. 46).

This is probably a quote from the *Śrīkaṇṭhīyasaṃhitā*.

21. *"Sampradāya"* is defined as follows:

> saṃpradāyairiti tat tac chāstrokta jñānayogarūpaiḥ |
> (NT, vol. II, p. 3).

22. tasya maṭhiketi kulam iti cābhidhānadvayam |
(TĀ, vol. III, p. 296).

In a different, more restricted sense, "Kula" was the name given to the particular group or 'family' to which a demon or malevolent spirit belonged. It was important to determine the spirit's Kula in order to invoke the Lord of that Kula to free those who were possessed by it:

> yasmin kule yadaṃśena mudritaḥ kīlitaḥ kvacit |
> tat kulenaiva ceṣṭena sarvadosaiḥ pramucyate ||
> (NT, 19/80b-1a).

Yakṣiṇī, Yoginī, Mātṛkā, Śākinī, Ḍākinī and other potentially malevolent spirits belonged to these Kulas. Their exorcism and propitiation is a part of Kula practice, which in some of its phases included a number of exorcistic cults.

23. Matsyendranātha (variously "called Macchanda," "Macchagnapāda," "Mīnapāda," "Mīnanātha," "Macchendra" and "Macchagna") is an important founder figure who is mentioned in various contexts in diverse Kaula works. The Kashmiri Trika Kaulas consider him to be the originator of the *Kulāgama*. For an extensive treatment of the legends concerning this figure, the reader is referred to Bagchi's introduction to the *Kaulajñānanirṇaya*. Also G. Tucci, *Animadversiones Indicae* JASB, N.S., XXVI, 1930 p. 131 ff.. Kṣemarāja tells us that the worship of the four Kaula masters, called *"Yuganāthas,"* namely, Khagendranātha, Kūrmanātha, Meṣanātha and Matsyendranātha who taught in the four Ages (*yugas*) is a necessary part of all Kaula ritual. Although the *Paścimāmnāya,* like every Kaula school, had its own masters, it advocated the worship of the *Yuganāthas* (Schoterman p. 7). Here, however, Matsyendranātha and the others are associated, as we shall see, with the *Pūrvāmnāya* with which the *Paścimāmnāya* had close affiliations. A number of works are attributed to Matsyendranātha although it seems highly unlikely that they are in fact his own. Almost all the MSs are in Nepal. Bagchi has edited a number of them and notes others in his KJN. Another work which he has not noticed is the *Kulapañcāśikā* of which there is only one MS, deposited in the NA in Kathmandu (no. 1/1076). The last colophon of this short tract on Kaula yoga reads:

> iti kulapañcāśikāyāṃ śrīmatsandapāvatāre pañcamaḥ paṭalaḥ samāptaḥ |

Clearly "śrīmatsandapā" is a corruption of a homonymn of Matsyendrapāda. This work is quoted twice by Kṣemarāja. (Ś.Su. vi. p. 54 and NTu I p. 191; fl. 4a and 3b in the MS). There is no indication in the text that it is by Matsyendra. Bagchi notes the existence of MSs of the *Śrīkāmākhyaguhyasiddhi* (also called just *"Guhyasiddhi"*). A list of eight *siddhamātṛkā* found in this work constituting the *"Kulāṣṭaka"* also occurs in a number of texts belonging to the *Paścimāmnāya*. Indeed, Bagchi himself notes that he has come across it in the KNT, a *Paścimāmnāyapaddhati*. It is possible, therefore, that it is in fact a work of the *Paścimāmnāya,* attributed to Matsyendranātha. That these and other works could wrongly be attributed to Matsyendranātha is not difficult to explain in view of the fact that many individuals were given this name as initiates. For example, according to the KNT this name was given to a Bengali brahmin initiated into the *Paścimāmnāya*. Quoted by Bagchi, p. 68: varaṇā vaṅgadeśe janma jātir brāhmaṇo viṣṇuśarmā nāma . . . markkaṭanadyāṃ yadā karṣitā tadā śrīmatsyendranāthaḥ |

24. For a table of *Rājaputras* and *Yuganāthas,* etc., see Gnoli's *Luce delle Sacre Scritture* Appendix X, pp. 876-880. Also below p. 69, 70, 80.

25. kulāni mahākaulakaulākulakulākulākhyāni |

(TĀ XIb p. 155).

26. *Bhairavakulatantra* quoted in TĀ, vol. VIII, p. 182:

vāmamārgābhiṣikto'pi daiśikaḥ paratattvavit |
saṃskāryo bhairave so'pi kule kaule trike'pi saḥ ||

cf: vedāc chaivaṃ tato vāmaṃ tato dakṣaṃ tato matam |
tataḥ kulaṃ tataḥ kaulaṃ trikaṃ sarvottamaṃ param ||

(quoted in commentary on TĀ, 13/300b-301 also in commentary on 13/347-8).

27. kuṇḍānāṃ lakṣaṇaṃ vakṣye kule kaule tu paścime ||

(MBT(Y), fl. 8b).

Also: ye kecid devatāś canye kule kaule tu paścime |
tiṣṭhanti kuṇḍamadhye tu bhairavo bhairavī saha ||

(Ibid., fl. 9a).

(The indeclinable *"saha"* meaning "with" normally governs the instrumental. *"Bhairavo bhairavī,"* which are both nominative singular, are therefore anomalous forms. If the two words are conjoined and the compound inflected to form *"bhairavībhairavena saha"* the metre would be disturbed. For the same reason the forms *"bhairavena bhairavyā saha,"* although grammatically correct, would not fit in this verse. Moreover, it appears that both words are here in the nominative to indicate that they carry equal weight. The gods can be either with Bhairava or Bhairavī as well as with both together).

28. anyathā kulakaule 'smin śāmbhave na spṛśanti te |

(Ibid., fl. 29b).

Once the goddess has described the Wheel of Mahābhairava and its sixty-four energies she says in the same Tantra:

catuḥṣaṣṭhikalā proktā bhairavasya kuleśvara |
vidyārūpāḥ smṛtāḥ sarvāḥ kulakaule tu siddhidāḥ ||

(Ibid., fl. 8a).

29. sampradāyam idaṃ kaulaṃ śāmbhuśaktipadānugam |
(GS, 8/164a).

30. śivavīryaṃ (vi)niṣkrāntaṃ śivaśaktisamanvitam |
ubhayānandasandohaṃ pāramparyavijṛmbhitam |
kulamūlānvayaṃ devi kulakaulaṃ vinirgatam ||
(CMSS, fl. 3a).

31. The *Paścimāmnāya,* in common with other Kaula schools, views itself and other traditions not just as doctrine, scripture or school but also as an essential expression of metaphysical principles. "Kula" and "Kaula" are in this context interchangeable terms reflecting the close interaction between Kula and Kaula as divisions within the *Kulāgama* as well as expressions of Kula itself as the power of Speech (*vācchakti*) incarnate in doctrine. Accordingly, the MBT explains that the lower, grosser metaphysical principles merge progressively into the higher, subtler ones in such a way that the entire series ultimately disappears into the Nameless (*anāmaka*) absolute beyond all differentiation. The Nameless is Kula identified with Kuleśvara who is the essence of Kaula, the ocean of consciousness in which the god and his consort, the goddess, fuse (MBT(Y), fl. 26b). Thus Kula—the goddess—has become the god while he is the essence of both the god and goddess where both dissolve and disappear. In other words, Kula is Kaula at the level of the mysterious Nameless, the supreme reality. At the same time, Kaula is the source of creation and its power is *Kulaśakti,* the supreme goddess, the 'Neuter' (*napuṃsakā* in the feminine!) who is the mother of all doctrines:

kaulaṃ nāma mahādeva yena sṛṣṭi carācaram |
tasy(ec)chā nirgatā śaktir aṅkurākārakaulinī ||
darśanānāṃ ca mātā sā parā devī napuṃsakā |
(MBT(Y), fl. 33b).

The Supreme Goddess (*Parādevī*) is Kubjikā, the goddess of the *Paścimāmnāya* which represents itself in this way as higher than Kaula doctrine. It is an independent system in its own right which both integrates and goes beyond these categories.

32. kaulaṃ tu ṣaḍvidhaṃ satva ṣaṭkūṭapatitaṃ dhruvam |
ṣaṭsaṃjñā ca samudbhūtaṃ prasarāt paścimānvayam ||
(CMSS, fl. 3a).

(Read *"śrutva"* for *"satva." "Saṃjñātaḥ"* instead of *"samjñā ca"* would be grammatically correct. Note also that the word *"anvaya"* is masculine; here as often happens in these texts, it is treated as neuter).

33. pūrvapaścimabhedena śailarājasutā nume |
ānandāvalībhedena prabhu yogikena tu ||
atītapādasaṃjñā ca ṣaṭprakāram idaṃ kulam |

(Read -*"sūte"* for -*"sūtā"* and *"avali"* for *"avalī."* "Prabhu" should be in the instrumental, i.e., *"prabhunā."* This is probably a scribal error as the present form cuts short the metre by one syllable. *"Saṃjñā ca"* should be *"Saṃjñayā"*;

in that case, however the seventh syllable would be short instead of long as the metre demands).

In TĀ, 29/36 the order is 1) Bodhi, 2) Prabhu, 3) Pāda, 4) Ānanda, 5) Yogin, 6) Avali. The order in the KMT, (fl. 3a) is the same as the KRU; the latter, however, arranges these six into three groups of two: 4) + 6); 2) + 5) and 1) + 3), thus allowing the *Paścimāmnāya* to be free, in a sense, to have its own line of teachers without losing its essential connection to the original *Siddhasantāna*. The KRU then links one group to the *Pūrvāmnāya* and the other to the *Paścimāmnāya* and so aligns them through their common Kaula heritage and stresses their intimate connection with each other. However, in the KMT, which is older than the KRU, no such distinction is made. The six Kaula traditions are collectively called the *Siddhakrama* which has been transmitted along the Siddha path (*siddhamārgakramāyātam*) (KMT, fl. 3a). The CMSS assigns the Kaula traditions to the *Pūrvāmnāya* which it integrates into the *Paścimāmnāya* (see below).

34. The Kaula schools display a marked tendency to exclusivity (as indeed do all Hindu sects and cults in general). The *Ūrmikaulatantra*, for example, expressly prohibits contact with those who follow other scriptures (TĀ, 15/573b-4). A Kaula does not distinguish himself from other Kaulas on the basis of caste but according to the Kaula group to which he belongs. The Kaula tradition prohibits commensuality outside its circle as a whole and enjoins measures for atoning defaults in this respect (TĀ, 15/272). Voicing the Kaula view, Abhinava says: "In order to attain a state of identity (with Śiva and one another) one must follow one's own spiritual tradition and neither worship nor enjoy the fruits of a Tantric gathering (*cakra*) along with those who belong to a different spiritual lineage." (ibid., 4/268b-9a).

Even members of one or other of the six schools (*ovallī*) affiliated to Matsyendranātha could not worship together and went as far as to devise a system of signs by which they could recognise members of their own group in order to avoid others (TĀ, 29/37). Once within a group, however, no distinction between its members was admissible. Caste and social status ceased to be operational in this society; once in the fold the members become one with Śiva and so indistinguishable from one another. He who viewed the others or talked of them in terms of former caste distinctions ran contrary to the Rule (*samaya*) (ibid., 15/576). In this respect, the Kaula traditions were perfectly in agreement with many other Tantric cults (see for example, SvT 4/414 and 4/545).

35. In an important passage in the *Tantrāloka* (4/221-270) Abhinava comments on part of chapter 18 of the MVT (18/74-81) which he presents as typifying the Trika view and which he contrasts with that of the Śaivasiddhānta, on the one hand, and Kula on the other. Thus, whereas the former enjoins the performance of rituals and the observance of vows and rules governing outer conduct, the Kula position is seen to be one of denying their validity and rejection of these outer forms in favour of inner spiritual discipline. Kula doctrine is essentially based, from this part of view, on an exclusivist monism (*advaya*) intolerant of contrasts, which thus rejects all forms of spiritual discipline that are 'external', that is, 'outside' in the state of duality. The Trika view, however,

excels this because it is a supreme monism (*paramādvaya*) in which nothing needs to be pursued or even abandoned. Even if ritual is performed, it does not break up the integrity of the absolute consciousness of the subject (TĀ, vol. III, p. 288 ff.). Nothing is here prohibited or enjoined insofar as whatever is pleasing is fit to lead to union with Śiva:

> muktikāmasya no kiñcin niṣiddhaṃ vihitaṃ ca no ||
> yad eva hṛdyaṃ tad yogyaṃ śivasaṃvidabhedane |
> (TĀ, 15/291b-2a).

One could say that Trika is in this respect more intensely Kaula than the Kula schools and so, in the same spirit, rejects the view that the divisions between Kaula traditions are important. According to the *Trikaśāsana,* there is an essential equality among all these traditions insofar as they are all ultimately Śaiva (ibid., 4/274-5a). Indeed, according to Abhinava, these distinctions are denied in all the Trika scriptures starting with the SYM because they break up the unity of ultimate reality (ibid., 4/269). Trika Mantras are applicable in all circumstances (ibid., 11/38) but, even so, one should take care not to be misled by following the teachings of other schools (TĀ, vol. III, p. 279 ff; TĀ 25/563).

36. The god says to the goddess at the beginning of the *Yoginīhṛdayatantra* of the *Śrīvidyā* school: "Listen, O goddess, to the great secret, the Supreme Heart of the Yoginī; out of love for you I will tell you today that which is to be kept well concealed, that which has been taught from ear to ear and so reached the surface of the earth." (YHṛ, 1/2b-3). Similarly in the *Kaulajñānanirṇaya* which was revealed, as tradition would have it, by Matsyendranātha: "O goddess, it is heard as residing in the ear (not in books) and has come down through the line of teachers; this, O goddess, is Kaulika [doctrine] transmitted from ear to ear" (KJN, 6/8b-9a).

37. After explaining in a veiled, cryptic manner how to construct a mantra, the KMT says: "This method is hard to acquire, it can be obtained only from the mouth of a master" (fl. 37a).

38. XXXXXXXX kiyal lekhyaṃ hi pustake |
(TĀ, 6/33b).

39. kathitaṃ gopitaṃ tebhyas tasmāl lekhyaṃ na pustake |
guruvaktrāt tu labhyeta anyathā na kadācana ||
(TĀ, vol. III, p. 73; ibid., 26/20-4a; also ibid., 26/28).

40. "O mistress of the gods! [treasure] always in [your] heart [the teaching transmitted] from ear to ear. That which comes from the master's mouth and enters the path of hearing abides [in one's own] heart. A Mantra extracted (from a book) is like one written on water. The *Vidyā* that bestows both enjoyment and liberation should never be written in a book." (Parāt., 8/27-8).

41. "Five are said to be [important] in the Siddhānta, four in the teachings of the Left, three it is said in the Right, in the tradition of the East two, while in the Western liturgical tradition (*paścimakramāmnāya*) of the *Kulāgama* it is the master alone [who matters]" (MBT(Y), fl. 24a; also fl. 87b).

42. "Now I will therefore tell [you] the doctrine of the master knowing

which the Tradition of the Master is transmitted" (Ibid., fl. 24b).

43. "This is the meditation, hard to obtain [even] by the gods, which belongs to the tradition of the Mouth of the Master; he who knows this, O Śambhu, is a Kaula master (*ācārya*)" (Ibid., fl. 96b).

44. XXXXXXXX śrīgurum paścimeṣvaram |
(Ibid., fl. 26b).

45. strīmukhe nikṣipet prājñaḥ strīmukhād grāhayet punaḥ | ityādyukteḥ kulaprakriyāyāṃ dūtīmukhenaiva śiṣyasya jñānapratipādanāmnāyāt iha gurutaddūtyoḥ samaskandhatayā upādānam |
(TĀ, vol. I, p. 35; see also TĀ, vol. XIb, p. 88).

46. See TĀ, 29/40. Also:

yoginyaś ca pravakṣyāmi siddhidā(ḥ) kulaśāsane |
(KRU, 4/30a).

("*Yoginyaḥ*" as the object of "*pravakṣyāmi*" should be in the accusative, i.e., "*yoginīḥ*").

47. TĀ, vol. XIb, p. 19; TĀ, 29/40.

48. yoginī daiśkendreṇa antaraṃ naiva vidyate |
(MBT(Y), fl. 51b).

(In order to convey the intended meaning of this statement in a grammatically correct form, "*yoginī*" should be in the genitive, i.e., "*yoginyāḥ*" and "*daiśikendreṇa*" should not be an instrumental but an ablative, i.e., "*daiśikendrāt*").

49. rahasyaṃ sarvaśāstrāṇām āmnāyahṛdayaṃ param |
vaktrā(t) vaktragataṃ jñānaṃ yoginīmukhasaṃsthitam ||
(CMSS, fl. 14b).

50. yoginī paramā śakti(ḥ) sahajānandadāyinī |
bhairavecchā tu sā vartte tena sā dvividhā na hi ||
(MBT(Y), fl. 51b).

51. TĀ, vol. II,. p. 104.

52. TĀ, 28/147 states that there are four types of Śaivas, namely those who divide the knowable into: 1) Nara, Śakti and Śiva (i.e., the Trika); 2) The five faces of Sadāśiva with their five powers: Vāmeśvarī, Khecarī, Gocarī, Dikcarī and Bhūcarī (i.e., the Krama-influenced Trika of the *Niśisaṃcāratantra*); 3) into the ten and eighteen divisions (i.e., the Siddhānta) and 4) six currents (*srotas*)—these are the Kaulas who add an extra lower current, that of the *Kulāgama,* to Śiva's five faces. See TĀ, 28/147 and Jayaratha's commentary.

53. vaktraṃ hi nāma tan mukhyaṃ cakraṃ uktaṃ maheśinā |
yoginīvaktraṃ XXXXXXXXXXX ||
(TĀ, vol. XIb, p. 89. See also TĀ, 29/124b-5a).

54. See TĀ, 15/206a and commentary.

55. TĀ, vol. IV, p. 160.

56. Monier-Williams notes in his Sanskrit-English dictionary that "Picu" is the name of a Yoginī. Ghosal Sastri (vol. II, part IV, p. 40) notes other meanings of this word. These include "cotton," "a type of soft grain," "a weight," "a leper,"

"the neem tree" and "thorn apple." It is also the name of the Bhairava who teaches in the BY and of one of his eight faces.

57. picuvaktrādyaparaparyāyaṃ yoginīvaktram eva mukhyacakram uktam | patālākhyam adhovaktraṃ sṛṣṭyarthaṃ saṃprakīrtitam | .... adhovaktraṃ sṛṣṭivaktraṃ picuvaktram |

quoted by Schoterman (pp. 86-7) from the ṢaṭSS, a Tantra belonging to the Kubjikā school. He also points out in his commentary to verse 2/37 of this Tantra that this mouth is called *Picuyoni*. *Picuvaktra* is also equated with *Pātālavaktra* in TĀ, 15/206 and commentary. The BY (fl. 201a) also confirms that those Tantras which deal with *Kulācāra* are said to originate from the Lower Current along with others. In the context of describing the content of the Lower Current, the BY states that it is Bhairava who teaches here. The ŚKS's canon is unusual insofar as it equates the Mouth of the Yoginī with the Right Current from which arise the sixty-four Bhairavatantras: "The scripture called Bhairava consisting of eight times eight [Tantras] entered all together into the independent Śaiva [tradition] that is, the [current of the] Right, that of the Emission of the Heart" (TĀ, vol. I, p. 41).

Jayaratha comments that "the Bhairava group consisting of sixty-four [Tantras] is predominantly monist and belongs to the Right Face which corresponds to the [single] non-dual inner nature of the union of Śiva and Śakti, also called the Mouth of the Yoginī." In other words, the *Bhairavatantras* are here understood to be vitally linked with the *Kaulatantras* through their common source. The BY is a good example of how this works. Its very name—*Picumata* (the Doctrine of Picubhairava)—subtly implies its hidden connection with the *Kaulatantras*. Accordingly, Abhinava quotes it along with other Tantras belonging to the *Bhairavasrotas* in the course of his exposition of Kaula ritual in the *Tantrāloka*. One chapter (56) of this work is devoted to *Kulācāra* while another (69) deals with the *Picubheda*. The overall Kaula character of this work is unmistakable, although it does not consider itself to be such. Certain passages, however, refer directly to the attainment of *Kaulasiddhi* and union with Kula (see quote in TĀ, vol. III, p. 64). The Kaula character of other Tantras belonging to the *Dakṣiṇasrotas* is also evident, particularly of those Tantras which teach Trika doctrine. Thus, according to the MVT, the SYM teaches the method by which *Kulacakra* is to be worshipped (MVT, 19/48). Abhinava quotes *Triśirobhairava*, a *Trikatantra* belonging to the *Dakṣiṇasrotas*, when defining the meaning of *"Kaula"* as a metaphysical principle (TĀ, vol. XIb, p. 6). He also refers to it several times while describing Kaula ritual in the *Tantrāloka*, including one passage which deals with the characteristics of the ideal Tantric consort (TĀ, vol. XIb, pp. 69-70). That not all Tantras of the Bhairava group are so markedly Kaula-oriented becomes apparent when we consider the character of the *Svacchandabhairavatantra* whose ritual programme is in many respects similar to that of the *Siddhāntāgama* in which Kaula rituals and practice are largely absent. It seems that the *Vidyāpīṭhatantras* of the *Śaivāgama* were, in this sense, extensively Kaula in character, and it is to this *pīṭha* that the *Trikatantras* generally belong. Moreover, it is to this *pīṭha* that most of the Tantras of the *Paścimāmnāya* affiliate themselves and so do many other *Kaulatantras*. Thus the god says in the *Yoginīhṛdaya:* "The Secret Doctrine I have hidden which bestows immediate understanding . . . resides in [those Tantras] associated with the *Vidyāpīṭha.* It bestows divine yogic accomplishments and [is attained] by those dedicated to *Kulācāra"* (see YHṛ., 2/76-80).

58. See Schoterman, p. 87, who has drawn up a table of these correspondences according to ṢaṭSS, chap. 42.

59. See Schoterman, p. 87.

60. yoginyo lebhire jñānaṃ sadyo yogāvabhāsakam |
yena tad yoginīkaulaṃ nottīrṇaṃ tābhya eva tat ||
(Mr.T.*caryāpāda*, 1/40b-1a).

śaivam māntreśvaraṃ gāṇaṃ divyam ārṣaṃ ca gauhyakam |
yoginīsiddhakaulaṃ ca srotāṃsyaṣṭau vidur budhāḥ ||
(Ibid., 1/36b-37a).

61. kāmarūpe idaṃ śāstraṃ yoginīnāṃ gṛhe gṛhe |
(KJN, 22/10b).

The Kashmiri tradition also associates Matsyendranātha with Kāmarūpa; it was here that he learned the doctrine and practice of Kaula yoga which Bhairavī had heard from Bhairava. See TĀ, vol. I, pp. 24-6.

62. See Bagchi KJN, intro. p. 35.

63. uktaṃ ca siddhasantānaśrīmadūrmimahākule |
(TĀ, 14/31a).

śrīmadūrmikaulasiddhasantānarūpake ityanena pādovallyāṃ pāramparye'pyamlānatvaṃ darśitam |
(TĀ, vol. Ib, p. 39).

64. "In the Yoginīkula, one should know the cremation ground to be the place of the Heart, the Wish-granting Tree to be *Kuṇḍalinī* and the centre between the eyebrows to be the meeting ground of the yoginī."

(TĀ, vol. XIb, p. 51) Here *"Yoginīkula"* may not, however, refer to a Kaula group but to the inner mystical body of the Kulayogi, as is the case in the following reference in MVT, 19/24b-26a:

"Or else the Wheel of Meditation, the nature of which is Kula, should be mentally made to rotate in the wheel of the navel following the sequence of universal Time after which in six months arises, without a doubt, the *Yoginīkula* within the body which illumines one's consciousness." References are certainly rare to the *Yoginīkula* as a Kaula group in Kashmiri works, despite the fact that the Kashmiri Trikakaula tradition affiliates itself to Matsyendranātha.

65. yoginīkulagarbhastha(ḥ) kulavīrāṅge saṃbhavaḥ |
siddhāṅgasiddhasantāna(ḥ) ṣaṭpadarthān sa vindati ||
(KMT, fl. 61a).

(*"Kulavīrāṅge saṃbhavaḥ"* would be better as a single compound, i.e., *"Kulavīrāṅgasambhavaḥ."* The fifth syllable will then be short as the metre demands.)

66. yoginīmatasārantu āmnāyaṃ kulaśāsanam |
(CMSS, fl. 15a).
67. MBT(Y), fl. 50a.
68. mukhāmnāye rahasyan tu yoginīsampradāyakam |
(CMSS, fl. 14b).
69. paścimāmnāyasiddhānāṃ santānaṃ paścimaṃ vada |
tad ahaṃ śrotum icchāmi matānāṃ matam uttamam ||
(GS, 4/9).
70. siddhakaulābhipannānām itarāṇāṃ na darśitaḥ |
(KMT, fl. 83a).

(The word *"itara"* is a pronoun; therefore *"itarāṇāṃ"* should be *"itareṣām."*)

71. The Devī says in MBT(Y), fl. 30b that she will explain the mantras belonging to the *Yoginīkula* indicating that it is being integrated into the main body of Kubjikā doctrine.

72. yasmād bhāṇḍāram ityevaṃ sarvasvaṃ yoginīkule |
atha ca sarvapīṭheṣu mate'yam samayātmikā ||
(KMT, fl. 31b).
73. rūpātītaṃ tatas cordhvaṃ niḥsaṃdigdhaṃ paraṃ padam |
bahunoktena kiṃ devi pūrvaṃ vyāvarṇitaṃ mayā ||
sadguroś ca prasādena labhyate paramaṃ padam |
(KMT, fl. 88a).

kim abhyāsaḥ punas tasya yasya sarvaṃ purassaram |
yasya saṃbhavitaṃ śambhum anantaguṇadāyakam ||
yogātmā ca sa sarvatra pūjyate yoginīkule |
(Ibid.)

74. In the following reference, from the Mat.P. of the Siddhānta, *"svāmnāya"* simply means "one's own tradition"—it does not refer to the *āmnāya* system of classification we are about to discuss:

samayācārasadvādasthitiḥ svāmnāyalakṣaṇaḥ |
(Mat. P., 2/13).

75. For this generic usage of the term *"Kulāmnāya,"* see, e.g., TĀ, 15/533; also ibid., 15/572.

76. The earliest *Trikatantras,* such as the *Triśirobhairava* and even the *Siddhayogeśvarīmata,* do not know themselves to be Trika although they expound Trika doctrine and ritual. The same is true of the *Mālinīvijayottara* to which Abhinava refers as the essence of the SYM which is, to all intents and purposes, the root Tantra of the Trika and indeed, probably, the first Tantra to expound the essentials of Trika, namely the worship of the three goddesses—Parā, Parāparā and Aparā—and their Mantras.

77. The *Paścimāmnāyatantras* to which I have had access so far, which are but a fraction of those extant in Nepalese MSs, all refer to the KMT and so undoubtedly postdate it. Thus the CMSS refers to itself as the essence of the KMT which had been previously expounded extensively:

kathitaṃ devadeveśi saṃkṣepān na tu vistaram |
śrīkubjikāmatasāro'yaṃ vistaram kathitaṃ mayā ||

(CMSS, fl. 24a).

(The word *"vistara"* is masculine so *"vistaram"* should be *"vistaraḥ."* Accordingly, *"kathitam"* which agrees with it should be *"kathitaḥ."* The third quarter of the verse contains an extra syllable. This is probably due to the addition of the word *"śrī"* made as a sign of respect for the KMT. *"Vistaram kathitaṃ mayā"* in the second line should read *"vistaraḥ kathitaḥ mayā."*)

The *Yogakhaṇḍa* of the MBT refers specifically to the KMT of 3500 verses which corresponds to the length of the recovered text of this Tantra. The *Gorakṣasaṃhitā,* which postdates the MBT, to which it refers in one place (p. 278), also knows the KMT, to which it refers in several places as *Śrīmata* (p. 4, 24, 49, 116, 158, 208, 277, 375) and once as *Kulālītantra* (p. 152). It is closely affiliated to the *Śrīmatottara* (perhaps they may be the same work) which, as its name implies, follows after the KMT. The *Kularatnoddyota* is also a later work as it affiliates itself to the *Kubjikāmata.* The colophons are generally of the type:

ityādināthaviditaṃ pañcaśatkoṭivistīrṇaśrīmatkubjikāmate śrīkularatnoddyote . . . . .

Also the Kubjikā *paddhati* by Muktaka, the KNT, certainly postdates the KMT as does the *Kularatnapañcaka.* Although all these texts are later than the KMT, there is still room to doubt the originality of this Tantra. Thus in one place in the KMT it seems that there is a reference to an earlier Tantra.

On fl. 49a the goddess says: "now explain clearly what you have alluded to in the previous Tantra but not clearly elucidated":

XXXXXXXX idānīṃ kathaya sphuṭam |
pūrvatantre tvayā deva sūcitam na prakāśitam ||

This reference may, however, be construed to mean that the matters which are to be discussed are found in older Tantras which do not necessarily belong to the *Paścimāmnāya.* We have still to study the extant literature to see whether there is any more evidence to decide this issue one way or the other. It seems highly probable, however, that the KMT is not only the root Tantra of the *Paścimāmnāya* but also the first.

78. KMT, fl. 44b. This reference is part of a passage reproduced in the GS, 14/195-206a. Other Tantras referred to in this passage are the *Saṃmohana* and *Svarodaya* which is a Tantric astrological work. The *Svacchandabhairava* is referred to here as "the best of Tantras." Svacchanda Mantras are in fact integrated into the *Paścimāmnāya* (see, for example, the exposition of *Svacchandāstra* in GS, p. 155 ff.). C. Chakravarti notices two after works referred to in the KMT, namely, the *Labdhvītantra* (emend to *"Laghvītantra"*) and *Aghorīḍāmaratantra* (RASB Tantras, cat. II, p. 874).

79. PTv, p. 184. This reference has not been traced in the 3500 verse recension of the KMT preserved in numerous MSs in Nepal.

80. paścimaṃ sarvamārgāṇāṃ tvaṃ tāvatt anuśīlayā |

paścimāmnāyamārgo'yaṃ siddhānām akhilam dada ||
(KMT, fl. 6b).

(For *"tāvatt anuśīlayā"* read, *"tāvad"* and the second person singular imperative *"anuśīlaya."* For *"akhilam dada"* read *"akhilaḥ pradaḥ"* which agrees with *"-mārgo'yam."*)

81. tasya caivottare mārge dakṣiṇāmnāyapūrvakam |
vindate nikhilaṃ jñānaṃ nirahaṃkārī dṛḍhavratah ||
(KMT, fl. 54b).

(The fifth syllable of the fourth quarter is long whereas it should be short. This syllable is shortened, however, if we form the compound *"nirahaṃkāridṛdhavratah"*.)

82. According to the following reference, the KMT presents the doctrines of the *Paścimāmnāya* free of contamination from the *Pūrvāmnāya* represented in later Tantras as a close associate of the *Paścimāmnāya:*

idaṃ ca paścimaṃ deva pūrvabhāgavivarjitam |
(KMT, fl. 6b).

83. They are described as four possible ritual patterns included in the *Paścimāmnāya* in MBT(Y), fl. 36-38.

84. The correspondences are *Pūrva-Kṛtayuga; Dakṣiṇa-Treta; Uttara-Dvāpara* and *Paścima* as belonging to the *Kaliyuga* (MBT(Y), fl. 35b). These Tantras frequently extol the *Paścimāmnāya* as the best path in the Kali Age, e.g.,

paścimam udite veśmaṃ kalikālaṃ tu siddhyati |
(Ibid., fl. 36a).

(The nominative singular of the word *"veśman"* is *"veśma"* not *"veśmam."* Instead of *"kalikālam"* read *"kalikāle"* which agrees with *"udite."*)

paścime tu kule siddhiḥ kalau XXXXXX |
(Ibid. fl. 60a. See also ṢaṭSS 3/86).

85. The correspondences are *Ūrdhva-Prāṇa; Pūrva-Apāna; Vāma-Samāna; Dakṣiṇa-Udāna* and *Paścima-Vyāna.* ṢaṭSS, chapter 47, referred to by Schoterman, p. 86.

86. In the seven-*āmnāya* scheme mentioned earlier (fn. 58) a lower and 'upper above the upper' are added below and above the basic five *āmnāyas* of which the speakers are the five faces of Sadāśiva. According to the *Parātantra* also, the five *āmnāyas* are spoken by Sadāśiva with a sixth, lower one that is assigned to the Bauddhas and so is not spoken by Śiva.

87. Abhinava quotes the *Bhargaśikhātantra* as saying:

ūrdhvasrotodbhavaṃ jñānam idaṃ tat paraṃ priye |
paramadhvaninordhvordhvaṃ saṃvidrūpābhidhāyinā ||
(MVV, 1/162).

Following presumably the same Tantra, Abhinava says that the Tantras are in six groups of which the *Trikaśāstras* are the *"pūrvārdha."* To understand what is meant here we must first draw the following diagram. See Figure 4.

Figure 4. The Spatial Deployment of the Tantras According to the Bhargaśikhā.

Above the Upper — *Trika*

Upper — *Siddhānta*

North — *Vāmatantra*

East — *Gāruḍatantra* — West — *Bhūtatantra*

South — *Bhairavatantra*

The *"pūrvārdha"* seems to refer not to the "half on the west side" but that "in front" which is said to be "half of six" (*ṣaḍardha*), that is, the three "in front" of Trika, i.e., the *Siddhānta- Vāma-* and *Bhairavatantras* of which Trika is the essence.

88. KĀ, 3/5.

89. "The five Traditions have originated from My five faces. These five are said to be the paths to liberation, namely, [the Traditions of] the East, West, South and North along with the Upper. O Fair One, this is indeed true nor is there any need to question this. O Mistress of Kula, there are many traditions originating from subdivisions of the four Traditions I have previously explained to You in this Tantra. O Beloved, You Who are praised by the Vīras, many are they who know the four Traditions but few those who know the nature of the Upper One" (KĀ, 3/7-10).

90. For an account of this text, see Dvivedi, intro. to the NSA, pp. 46-7. Also intro. to LĀS, vol. II, p. 73 and Ta.Sā., p. 671.

91. They are equated with the cycle of manifestation thus: *Pūrva-Sṛṣṭi, Dakṣiṇa-Sthiti, Paścima-Saṃhāra* and *Uttara-Anākhya.* Although we cannot make out much here of importance for the historian, these equations are interesting insofar as only four *āmnāyas* are represented. Moreover, the *Uttarāmnāya* corresponds here to *Anākhya* which is significant insofar as this is the highest principle of the Kālīkrama. The association of the Kālīkrama with the *Uttarāmnāya* is well established in other Tantras (see below).

92. The YHṛ, pp. 100-102. The equations made in this passage between the four *āmnāyas* and moments in the cycle of manifestation are described in detail. Basically *Paścima* is equated with the precosmic seed (*bīja*) state consisting

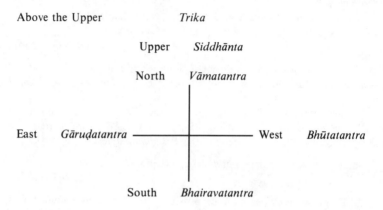

of the couple (*yāmala*), Rudra and His power of action. *Pūrva* is the moment of emanation (*sṛṣṭi*) which includes also persistence (*sthiti*) and withdrawal (*saṃhāra*) and so is three-fold. *Dakṣiṇa* is *Kāmakalā* consisting of the union of the red *Śaktibindu* with the white *Śivabindu* and corresponds to persistence (*sthiti*). The *Uttarāmnāya* corresponds to *Anākhya*. Thus, these equations basically agree with those made in the *Saṃketapaddhati*. Of interest here is the equation made between the *Dakṣiṇāmnāya* and *Kāmakalā*, which implies that *Śrīvidyā* is associated with this *āmnāya*, thus agreeing with the CMSS (see below).

93. Four MSs of this work are deposited in the NA at Kathmandu; there may be others listed in the private collections photographed by the NGMPP which I have not had the opportunity to see. The MSs in the NA are 1/767 (38 folios), 1/199 (69 folios), 1/1560 (34 folios) and 1/245 (36 folios). References are to MS no. 1/767.

94. CMSS, fl. 2a. *Divyaugha* is also referred to as *Divyakaula* (ibid.) or *Divyaughkrama* (ibid., fl. 2b). It is associated with the *Picuvaktra* (ibid., fl. 2a).

95. The Tantras referred to are the *Tantrasāra, Kriyāsāra, Kaulasāra, Trikasāra* and *Yogasāra*. The CMSS also refers to the *Yoginīhṛdaya, Kālacakrodaya* and *Yamala*. Other scriptures and groups are the *Bhairavāṣṭa* and the *Aṣṭāṣṭabheda*, the *Pañcasrotabheda*, the *Gāruḍa-* and *Bhūtatantras*. It then refers to a number of other groups (*bheda*) namely *Mantra, Tantra, Cakra, Hṛdāntara, Sāra, Kalā* and *Nityā- bheda* as well as the *Svacchanda* which it considers to be the highest (fl. 1b). Other works referred to in the body of the text are the *Siddhayogeśvarīmata* (fl. 14a), *Rudrayāmala* (fl. 18a) and KMT (fl. 24a).

96. The CMSS says that *gṛha* is the Inner Dwelling. It is the Wheel of Passion (*raticakra*) which is in the womb of the goddess, sanctified (*bhāvita*) by Kula and Kaula. Yogis reside there in that consciousness, mentally discerning that which is free of being and non-being and playing in the *Kulāmnāya*, the imperishable abode of consciousness (fl. 14b). The *Paścimagṛha* is:

gādha(ṃ) gambhīragahanaṃ tad ānandagṛhasmṛtaḥ |
(Ibid., fl. 4b).

(The word *"gādha"* normally means "shallow." The word *"agādha"*, which is formed from it by adding the negative prefix *"a-"*, means "deep." Although *"agādha"* is derived from *"gādha,"* it is more common in use, particularly in figurative expressions such as this one. The meaning of *"gādha"* has here, it seems, been mistaken for that of *"agādha." "Ānandagṛhasmṛtaḥ"* is not a valid compound. Moreover, "gṛha" is neuter so the correct form would be *"ānandagṛhaṃ smṛtam."*)

97. janmāmnāyarahasyantu catu(r) gharasamanvitam |
(CMSS, fl. 24a).

98. ataḥ parataram vakṣ(y)e caturāmnāyasamsphuṭam |
yena vijñātamātreṇa divyāmnāyaḥ pravartate ||
(MBT(Y), fl. 35a).

99. svasvabhāvaparaḥ kaścit pūrvacakrodaye[1] sthitaḥ |
dakṣiṇottaratam bhedam[2] nityākālīkramodayam ||

sarvaṃ tyaktvā svabhāvena tal layam paścime gṛhe ||
(CMSS, fl. 4b).

(*1. MS A reads *"-odaya"* and MS D *"odayo."* *2. MSs A and B read *"devaṃ."*)

100. Although the *Paścimāmnāya* is, like the other *āmnāyas,* Śakta in the sense that it is the goddess who is the primary focus of worship, Śiva is exalted as the highest principle:

śivāt parataran nāsti ityājñā pārameśvarī |
(CMSS, fl. 25a).

From this point of view the *Paścimāmnāya* is also known as the *Śāmbhavasāra,* i.e., the essence of Śaiva doctrine. It is Śiva who is the ultimate source of the *Paścimāmnāya* and is himself its arising and present in it:

tatrasthaṃ śāmbhavaṃ nāthaṃ paścimāt paścimodayam |
(MBT(Y), fl. 38a).

Indeed all four *āmnāyas* are represented as belonging to 'Śiva's circle' which is identified with Kula doctrine itself:

athātaḥ saṃpravakṣyāmi yāni siddhodayam kule |
paścime dakṣiṇe vāme pūrve vā śāmbhumaṇḍale ||
(Ibid., fl. 40b).

(Emend *"siddhodayam"* to *"siddhodaye".*)

The shift of emphasis from the male to the female principle and vice versa is reflected in the exchange of roles between them as the imparters of *Paścima* doctrine. Thus, most of the *Paścimatantras,* (for example, the KMT, KRU and CMSS) are taught by the god to the goddess who inquires about the doctrine. However, in some cases, such as the *Yogakhaṇḍa* of the MBT, the reverse is true—it is the goddess who instructs. The *Paścimatantras* themselves take note of this and explain that the teaching is transmitted in this two-fold manner. In the KRU the god (*Ādinātha*) says: "I, O goddess, have explained [the doctrine] which was established in the beginning. In this case I, O goddess, am your teacher [that is], O Supreme Goddess, [in the imparting of the original] terms of reference (*saṃjñā*)."

"In the second one of my pervasive eras you will be my [teacher]. So according to this order of succession [the *Kulakrama*] is brought down into this world by the revelation of it part by part [by me as well as by you]."

mayā tu kathitam devi ādisiddhaṃ yathāsthitam |
atrāhaṃ tvad gurur devi saṃjñāḥ parameśvarī ||
dvitīye vyāpake kalpe mama tvaṃ ca bhaviṣyasi |
anena kramayogena aṃśamātrāvatāraṇaiḥ ||
madīyaiśca tvadīyaiśca avatārya kulakramam |
(KRU, fl. 71b).

(Emend *"saṃjñāḥ"* to *"saṃjñāyāḥ".*)

Also:

tvayā mahyaṃ mayā tubhyam tvayā mahyaṃ punar mayā ||
kathitaṃ tava suśroṇi tvat saṅgānyeṣu mokṣadam |
(GS, 15/299b-300a).

In the KMT, which presents the doctrine at its origins, it is indeed Bhairava who speaks, even so, as the embodiment of the Word held within consciousness (*śabdarāśi*). He is forced to acknowledge his dependence on the goddess who, as Mālinī, is the power of his speech by virtue of which the Word can become manifest. Again, it is by virtue of the goddess travelling and manifesting herself in the sacred places throughout India that the doctrine is spread. She, and not he, is the chief protagonist as, indeed, is generally the case with the non-dualist Tantras whether they consider themselves to be specifically Kaula or not.

101. śāmbhavaṃ yatra līnaṃ tu vyāpakaṃ sarvatomukham |
akulā ca kulaṃ jñānaṃ vividhaṃ paścimaṃ gṛham ||
(MBT(Y), fl. 35b).

(Emend *"akulā"* to *"akulaṃ"*.)

102. vimalaṃ paścimaṃ vesma sarveṣāṃ uparisthitam |
viśeṣaṃ tena viditaṃ dharmādharmavivarjitam ||
(Ibid.).

(The word *"viśeṣa"* is a masculine noun; even so it is treated here as if it were an adjective governed by the word *"veśman."* The sixth syllable in the third quarter is not long as it should be).

103. idam eva dakṣiṇānvayarūpaṃ śrīkāmarājamadhyāste |
raudrātmakastu rudraḥ kriyāmayī śaktir asya rudrāṇī ||
yugalam idaṃ tārtīyaṃ bījaṃ palayati paścimāmnāyam |
(quoted in YHṛ, p. 101).

See chapter 2 of the *Saubhāgyasudhodaya* published with the NSA, pp. 311-313.

104. For a schematic representation of their location see below, fn. 110.

105. "I praise the goddess Parā Śivā whose imperishable form is the letter A which pours forth as the waves of Kula!" (NSA, 1/10).

106. "This Vidyā is the Great Vidyā of the Yoginīs, the great arising, the Kulavidyā, O great goddess, which accomplishes the goal of all that is to be done" (NSA, 1/103).

107. "You (O goddess) afflict with pain the one who sets out to practice according to this doctrine not knowing *Kulācāra* and without having worshipped the master's sandals. Knowing this, O fair one, one should always be intent on *Kaulācāra"* (YHṛ, 3/196-7a). For other references which clearly demonstrate the Kaula character of the Śrīvidyā teachings, see also YHṛ, 1/25-27a; 2/15; 2/51; 2/68; 3/139-142; 3/146-153 and 3/170-1.

108. For the *dhyāna* of Śrīvidyā Mahātripurāsundarī see NSA, 1/130-149.

109. "Kula is Śakti while she is said to be Nityā." Quoted from the *Nityātantra* in TĀ, vol. XIa, p. 51. All the presiding goddesses of the *āmnāyas* are called "Nityā" in the *Parātantra.*

110. This is standard practice in many Kaula schools. The *Paścimāmnāya* also refers to itself as divided into lines (*oli*) originating from masters said to reside in these *pīṭhas*. In the KNT they are the three listed below along with their Lords:

Pīṭha	*Masters*	*Lords*
Oḍiyāna:	Oḍḍīśanātha -	Nandeśvara
Pūrṇagiri:	Śrīṣaṣṭhinātha -	Kārttikeya
Kāmarūpa:	Śrīcaryānandanātha -	Gaṇeśvara

(See Schoterman, p. 36).

In the *Divyakrama* of the Śrīvidyā the four *pīṭhas* are arranged in a triangle, the corners and centre of which correspond to a seed-syllable (*bīja*) and teacher who appeared in one of the four Ages. See Figure 5 below.

Figure 5. The Triangle of the Divyakrama.

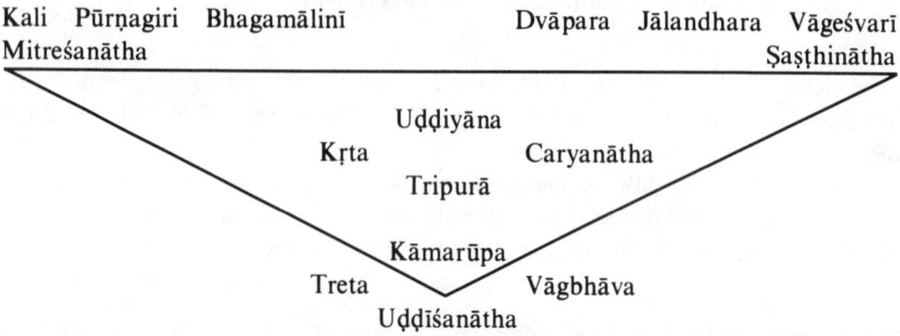

Although the names of the teachers in the various locations do not correspond, the fact that they are the same in these two schools is striking. According to the Śrīvidyā tradition, these four teachers belong to the *Divyaugha* through which the earliest transmission of the teachings took place. The Tripurā and Kubjikā cults share these teachers in common, thus linking them vitally together. However, neither of the two traditions show overt signs of being conscious of this connection between them. As the KMT makes no reference to these teachers, it seems likely that this is a later development in the *Paścimāmnāya*. Rather than say that the Kubjikā tradition has simply borrowed this from that of Śrīvidyā, it may perhaps be more accurate to say that it happens to find common roots with it in an 'original' transmission of Kaula doctrine conceived to be the same for every Kaula tradition. Again, that the CMSS defines itself as a Tantra belonging to the *Divyaugha* is a sign that major Kaula schools attempt to appropriate this 'original tradition' in order to appear to be the first, and hence, most genuine recipients of the Kaula teachings.

111. Maheśvarānanda in his *Mahārthamañjarī* takes over the same division into four lines of doctrine found in the NSA and calls them *srotas*. His purpose is to identify Mahārtha, the Krama absolute worshipped as Kālī, with Tripurā. He does this by comparing the four *srotas* to oceans churned by Manthānabhairava who although associated, from his point of view, particularly with the Kālīkrama is considered to be the Bhairava of all the *Kaulatantra* (MM, v. 68 pp. 170-2). Thus Maheśvarānanda appears to be integrating the four-fold *pīṭha* division of the Śrīvidyā with the four *āmnāyas* of the *Kulatantras*. In the process, he makes Manthānabhairava the Lord of them all, thus demonstrating that the highest tradition and the essence of all the scriptures (MM, p. 171) is the Mahārtha or Krama which, as he himself says, is the Kaula *Uttarāmnāya* (ibid., p. 6, 143, 186). Maheśvarānanda thus knew and supported the division into four *āmnāyas* which must therefore have persisted in this form up to his time (mid-thirteenth cent.) along with the original Kaula Tantras which adhered to this classification.

112. iyam ca vidyā caturāmnāyasādhāraṇyapi dakṣiṇapakṣapātinīti (NSA, p. 41).

113. Schoterman p. 36. In the *Parātantra*, where the *āmnāyas* are six, the goddesses presiding over the *āmnāyas* are fearful in form except Kubjikā and Tripurāsundarī who are both seated on Sadāśiva's lap and described as young and beautiful.

114. The term "Kramadarśana" is not common in the original Tantras. They generally refer to their doctrinal and ritual system as "Kramanaya," "Atinaya," "Mahārtha," "Mahārthakrama," "Mahākrama," "Kālīkula," "Kālīkulakrama," "Kālīkrama," "Kālīnaya" or "Devīnaya" (see Rastogi, pp. 16-30).

115. CMSS, fl. 23b.

116. Jayaratha refers to a number of authorities in his commentary on TĀ, 4/148-170 where Abhinavagupta expounds the order of the twelve Kālīs constituting *Saṃviccakra*. Amongst them are the *Devīpañcaśatikā, Śrīsārdhaśatika,* and the *Kramasadbhāva* which have been edited from Nepalese MSs by Mr. G. S. Sanderson but, as yet, unfortunately not published. The *Kramasadbhāva* enjoins the worship of seventeen Kālīs in *Anākhyacakra* whereas the other sources usually speak of thirteen (apart from the *Kramastotra* where they are twelve). In the *Śrīsārdhaśatika* (quoted in TĀ, vol. III, p. 161) the thirteen Kālīs are listed in the following order:
1) Sṛṣṭi° 2) Sthiti° 3) Saṃhāra° 4) Rakta° 5) Svakālī 6) Yamakālī 7) Mṛtyu° 8) Rudra° 9) Paramārka° 10) Mārtaṇḍa 11) (Kālāgni) Rudra 12) Mahākālī and 13) Mahābhairavacaṇḍograghorakālī who is in the centre. *The Tantrarājabhaṭṭāraka* (quoted in TĀ, vol. III, p. 189) also lists thirteen Kālīs. The eighth Kālī is called Bhadrakālī, as it is in the CMSS, while the name of the thirteenth Kālī, Mahābhairavakālī, is a variant of *Mahābhairavacaṇḍograghorakālī* which is the commonly accepted form of her name. The order of the Kālīs in the *Devīpañcaśatikā* as quoted by Jayaratha is listed below:
1) Sṛṣṭi° 2) Rakta° 3) Sthiti° 4) Yama° 5) Saṃhāra° 6) Mṛtyu° 7) Rudra°

8) Mārtaṇḍa° 9) Paramārka° 10) Kālāgnirudra° 11) Mahākālī° 12) Mahābhairavacaṇḍograghorakālī and 13) Sukālī.

The order of the Kālīs Abhinava presents follows the *Kramastotra,* a work on which he wrote a commentary called the *Kramakeli.* This is as follows (TĀ, 4/148-170):

1) Sṛṣṭi° 2) Rakta° 3) Sthitināśa° 4) Yama° 5) Saṃhāra° 6) Mṛtyu° 7) Bhadra° 8) Mārtaṇḍa° 9) Parmārka° 10) Kālāgnirudra° 11) Mahākālakālī 12) Mahābhairavacaṇḍograghorakālī.

Abhinava rejects the sequence of thirteen Kālīs and leaves empty the space in the centre of the rotating circle of Kālīs, where the thirteenth Kālī is usually located. Thus he agrees with the *Kramastotra* as opposed to the generally accepted pattern by the Tantras which take Mahābhairavacaṇḍograghorakālī to be the thirteenth (see TĀ, vol. III, p. 189). He does this, again following the lead of the *Kramastotra,* by eliminating *Sukālī* who is usually the fifth in this sequence. This, Jayaratha tells us, the *Pañcaśatikā* does not do (ibid.). Moreover, it seems that Mahābhairava Kālī was the thirteenth according to this text as well. It is therefore probable that Jayaratha has altered the original order of the Kālīs it enumerates to fit with that of the *Kramastotra.* Another Tantra Jayaratha quotes arrives at the number twelve by eliminating Sukālī. It appears, therefore, that Paramadevī, who is located in the centre of the twelve Kālīs according to the CMSS, is Mahābhairavacaṇḍograghorakālī. Thus there can be doubt that the Kālīs to which the CMSS refers are those of the Kālīkrama as presented in the majority of the Āgamas of the Krama school prevalent in Abhinava's time.

117. santi paddhatayaś citrāḥ srotobhedeṣu bhūyasā |
anuttaraṣaḍardhārthakrame tvekāpi nekṣyate ||

(TĀ, 1/14).

Gnoli's translation of this verse into Italian reads in English: "Many are the manuals in use in the different currents. For the school of that of which there is none higher, for the Trika and for the Krama, there is however not a single one."

In a footnote he writes that the "school of that of which there is none higher" (*anuttara*) is probably an allusion to the Kula school. He adds, however, that the first part of the compound (viz. *"anuttaraṣaḍardhārtha-"*) could also be translated to mean "for the method concerning Trika, that is, the school of that of which there is none higher." It seems to us that this translation is more satisfactory. The original translation implies that Kula is a separate system which differs substantially from Krama and Trika and has an independent identity similar to them. It seems, however, that "Kula" is, in Abhinavagupta's works, a much broader term of reference than "Trika" or "Krama," as it is in the original Āgamic sources. In one sense, the term "Kula" refers to a *type* of doctrine and liturgical pattern. This use of the term is well exemplified by the contrast posited in the TĀ between the Kula method or liturgy (*kulaprakriyā*) and the Tantric Method (*tantraprakriyā*). The former denotes Trika and Krama Kaula ritual in general; the latter all Tantric ritual that is free of Kaula elements, notably, the use of meat, wine and ritual intercourse. Again, "Kula" denotes a type of Tantric tradition; there are, as we have seen, a number of Kula schools.

Therefore, the expression *"Anuttaraṣaḍardhārthakrama"* is best not taken to be a copulative compound but read to mean "the liturgy (*krama*) of the *Anuttaratrikakula* school (*artha*)." Jayaratha also takes the word "Krama" here to mean "liturgy" (*prakriyā*) and not the Krama school (*anuttaratrikārtha-prakriyālakṣaṇam* TĀ, vol. I, p. 33). The Anuttaratrika Kula is the highest form of Trika. It is also known as the *"Anuttarāmṛtakula"* which Abhinava invokes in the first verse of his *Tantrāloka* and which Jayaratha says is the supreme principle that contains, and yet is beyond, the Triad (Trika) of Parā, Parāparā and Aparā (see commentary on TĀ, 1/1).

118. kaulārṇavānandaghanormirūpām unmeṣameṣobhayabhājam antaḥ |
nilīyate nīlakulālaye yā tāṃ sṛṣṭikālīṃ satataṃ namāmi ||
(quoted in TĀ, vol. III, p. 158).

119. TĀ, 4/170. For the nature of Akula see TĀ, 3/67.

120. See TĀ, vol. III, p. 185.

121. We notice here how, as with other Kaula schools, Śiva figures as the supreme transcendental principle. He is the ultimate end of all the sequences of states of consciousness, ritual acts and their macrocosmic counterparts, namely, the stages of manifestation and withdrawal. As in the *Paścimāmnāya*, Śiva is called Śambhu in the *Kramasadbhāva* where he is identified with Bhāsā—the principle of pure illumination, equivalent to the "expanse of the glory of the light of consciousness" (*prakāśavibhavasphītham*) referred to in the *Kramastotra* as Kālī's supreme abode (TĀ, vol. III, p. 185). In the *Kramasadbhāva, Anākhya* is Śakti who follows after creation, persistence and destruction.

jñānaṃ sṛṣṭiṃ vijānīyāt sthitir mantraḥ prakīrtitaḥ |
saṃhāraṃ tu mahākālamelāpaṃ paramaṃ viduḥ ||
anākhyaṃ śaktirūpaṃ tu bhāsākhyaṃ śambhurūpakam |
(quoted in MM, p. 94).

122. See K. C. Pandey's *Abhinavagupta*. He refers to these practices on pp. 491-493, in a section entitled: "the problem of moral turpitude in Krama ritual."

123. Goudriaan writes: "Of many texts, the adherence to the Kula standpoint appears from the fact that they have been referred to in the twenty-ninth chapter of the *Tantrāloka* which deals with secret (Kula) ritual." *Hindu Tantric and Śākta Literature* by Teun Goudriaan and Sanjukta Gupta. *A History of Hindu Literature* edited by J. Gonda, vol. II, fasc. 2, Otto Harrassowitz, Wiesbaden, 1981, p. 49.

124. TĀ, 29/2.

125. Ibid., 29/14-16.

126. Ibid., intro. to 29/43.

127. Ibid., 29/43.

128. Ibid., 29/56-63.

129. TĀ, vol. XIb, p. 44.

130. Ibid., pp. 68-9.

131. See TĀ, 29/56.

132. Ibid., 29/2b-3.

133. It is standard practice to commence a ritual by worshipping the divinities in the east which is the direction the worshipper is facing, and then to proceed clockwise round to worship the deities in the other quarters.

134. Jñānanetra received the original transmission from the goddess Maṅgalā (also called Makāradevī) in the Uttarapīṭha, also called "Oṅkārapīṭha" identified with Oḍḍiyāna in which the cremation ground called Karavīra was located (MP, pp. 49-50, 107; also MM, p. 92). (For Śivānanda and his works see Rastogi. Page numbers are listed extensively in the index on p. 287. Also Pandey, index p. 1004). Although Jñānanetra is referred to as the master who brought Krama doctrine to earth (*avatārakanātha*, TĀ, vol. III, p. 195) he was not the original propagator of Krama doctrine but the founder of a branch of the Krama tradition which associated itself with the Uttarapīṭha.

135. A unique MS of this work is deposited in the ASB (MS no. 10000). It has been edited by Mr. G. S. Sanderson, although not published.

136. khagendrādyādisiddhānāṃ kathitā gurusantatī |
ete vai kulamārge'sya rahasyaṃ śivanirmitam ||
(quoted in RASB Tantra, cat. I, p. 108).

137. sa kālīkulasambhūto bhāvanāṃ bhāvayet sphuṭam |
(quoted in TA, vol. XIb, p. 41).

138. kramakulacatuṣṭayāśrayabhedābhedopadeśato nāthaḥ |
(TĀ, vol. III, p. 195).

139. Goudriaan (*Hindu Tantric and Śākta Literature,* p. 50) points out that "the exact position of the Krama system within the Kashmiri tradition and its relationship to Kula are, however, difficult to assess." When Goudriaan discusses the Krama school he, quite rightly, regularly refers his reader to N. Rastogi's excellent study, *The Krama Tantricism of Kashmir,* Motilal Banarsidass, Delhi, 1979. He says however that "Rastogi seems to lay too much emphasis on the Krama school as a separate entity. We are inclined to think of a method of initiation or self-realization which could be followed by adherents of the Kula view point." The history of Āgamic Krama, its structure and relationship to other Tantric traditions, is another of the many subjects we can hope to understand only by carefully studying what remains of the original Āgamic sources.

140. In the opening benedictory verses of his commentary he says: "May that imperishable Auttara non-dual principle which is rooted in A [i.e., the absolute] unfolding, be victorious!" (MM, p. 1).

141. Ibid., p. 189.

142. In the concluding section of his book (p. 180 ff), Maheśvarānanda tells us of the tradition, also recorded in Abhinava's commentary on the *Kramastotra*, that the Mahārtha, i.e. Krama, doctrine was taught by Kṛṣṇa to Arjuna in the *Bhagavadgītā.* Maheśvarānanda goes on to say that this doctrine is that of the Auttara Krama. For other references see ibid., p. 6 and 176.

143. Ibid., p. 170, 176.

144. Ibid., p. 129. *"Anuttarāmnāya"* could equally well refer to the Trika

tradition as formulated in Kashmir, particularly in the works of Abhinavagupta (see fn. 119 above). The implication, therefore, seems to be that Maheśvarānanda (like Abhinava) sees Trika and Krama as intimately connected in a single doctrinal tradition. Accordingly, he says that he sees little difference between them (MM, p. 92).

145. The *Parātantra* says that the *Uttarāmnāya* originated from the Kālīkula (4/10). Perhaps the *Uttarāmnaya* is a part of the Kālīkula, (or a development of it) which, as an independent tradition, precedes it. Apparently we are dealing here with a later development in the Kālīkrama schools. It seems that Krama, like Trika, acquired an identity as a system only gradually.

146. ityuttarāmnāya śrīoṃkārapīṭhavinirgate śrīcaṇḍabhairave
ṣoḍaśasāhasre udite yonigahvaraṃ samāptam |
(RASB Tantra, cat., I, p. 109).

147. mahāśāsanasampradāyam | .... kaulottarasārabhūtam |
(Ibid., p. 108).

148. The *Devīpañcaśatikā*, an important Krama work well-known to the Kashmiris (see fn. 116 above), was copied by a South Indian sannyasin called Vimalaprabodha and is preserved in Nepal. The colophon (NA, MS no. 1/255) reads as follows:

iti śrīparaṃhaṃsasya kule kālīkākramapañcaviṃśatyadhikaśatadvayaṃ
śrī uttarānvāyagataṃ samāptam |

149. KRU, 1/399.

150. See fn. 117 above.

151. In the Tantras of the Kubjikā school, the *Paścimāmnāya* is called a "Kulakrama." We came across expressions such as the following: "he is a master belonging to the *Paścimāmnāya* [a master] in Kulakrama".

XXX paścimāmnāyaḥ sa ācāryaḥ kulakrame |
(MBT(Y), fl. 26a).

Compare also the following expression found in the KMT and recorded in a quote from this Tantra in the BSP, vol. I, p. 60 from NA, MS no. 3/378:

XX kramakulasakalaṃ maṇḍalotthānapūrvam |

The KRU does refer to the school to which it belongs as the *Paścimāmnāya* in a few places but generally prefers to identify itself as belonging to the Śrīkrama, Kramānvaya or Kulakrama. In the KRU the terms Kula and Krama are freely interchanged. For example, in one place the *Yuvakrama* of Kubjikā as a young maid (*yuvatī*) is said to be worshipped according to the *"Kulapaddhati"* (3/63) which a little further on is called *"Kramapaddhati"* (3/67). This is in accord with the *"Śrīkulakramamārga"* (3/85). We also come across cognate expressions such as *"Divyakramapaddhati"* (3/174) or *"Śrīkulapaddhati"* (fl. 58a).

152. Abhinava's *Tantrāloka* can be viewed as an extension of this same phenomenon. One essential difference is that this is a work of known authorship which makes no claim to being an original scripture. Even so, however, it is

venerated by Kashmiri Śaivites as a sacred text which transmits the doctrines of the Trika taught by an enlightened master.

153. kālacakrodayaṃ yatra tatra bhakṣayate param |
evaṃ kramavicāreṇa dvaitañcādvaitalakṣaṇaṃ ||
(CMSS, fl. 7b).

(The noun *"udaya"* is masculine, not neuter; so read *"-odayo"* in the place of *"-odayam".*)

154. This process of realization is described in CMSS, fl. 5b-6a.

155. KMT, fl. 43b-44a.

156. This appellation appears in a verse quoted from the KNT NA, MS no. 1/269 in BSP, vol. I, p. 58.

157. The Asiatic Society of Bengal preserves possibly unique manuscripts of two works by Akulendranātha. We know nothing about the author except that he was a follower of "Akulamahādarśana" which in the colophons to one of these works is defined as a *"bauddhāmnāya"* although both works are entirely Śaiva. One text is called the *"Pīyuṣaratnamahodadhi"* (ASB, MS no. 10724 B); the title of the other has been lost but is labelled *"sārasaṃgraha"* (ASB, MS no. 1074 D). The latter work consists entirely of extracts from *sāra* Tantras amongst which is the CMSS (eighth *adhyāya*, fl. 24b-6a). The text is written on palm leaf in a form of Newarī script, not younger than the thirteenth century, which thus sets the upper limit for the CMSS's date. The date of the MBT is discussed in appendix C.

158. kālasaṃkarṣaṇī devī kubjikā parameśvari |
(MBT(Y), fl. 73a).

159. spṛṣṭāspṛṣṭi vinirmuktaṃ paścimaṃ kramaśāsanam |
(MBT(Y), fl. 34a).

Following the same form of expression the Kālīkrama is called "uttarakramaśāsana." Ibid., fl. 38a.

160. See TĀ, vol. XIb, p. 31.

161. *Yonigahvara*, fl. 18a quoted in RASB Tantra, cat. I, p. 108. Two verses quoted from the *Devīpañcaśatikā* (in TĀ, vol. XIb, p. 31) in which these teachers are listed recur in the *Yonigahvara.* Although we might posit that one source has borrowed from the other, it seems more probable that this passage was a standard one.

162. This proves, incidentally, that Jñānanetra alias Śivānanda, the revealer of the *Yonigahvara* and founder of the branch of Krama prevalent in Kashmiri, i.e., that which originated from the Uttarapīṭha, is not to be identified with the Śivānanda who is worshipped along with his consort Samayā in the *Devīpañcaśatikā* as some modern scholars maintain (see, for example, Rastogi, p. 91).

163. See also Rastogi, pp. 91-92.

164. TĀ, 29/18-27.

165. Ibid., 29-40.

166. TĀ, vol. XIb, pp. 28-9.

167. PTv, pp. 222-3.

168. TĀ, 29/46b-8.

169. yad etat paramaṃ deva ājñāsiddhaṃ kulānvayam ||
pūrvapaścimasaṃjñāti(ḥ) sarpitedaṃ sudurlabhāṃ |
(KRU, 1/34b-35a).

(The primary suffix "-ti" is added to roots to form nouns in the sense of verb-action as, for example, *"kṛtiḥ," "sthitiḥ"* and *"matiḥ."* In his case we have "√jñā" + "ti" → *"jñāti;"* by adding the prefix *"sam-"* we get the noun *"saṃjñātiḥ."* This word is feminine as are all nouns formed in this way. The remaining words in this sentence agree with *"saṃjñātiḥ"* and so should be feminine. Thus we have *"sarpitā"* + *"iyam"* (not the neuter *"idam"*) → *"sarpiteyaṃ"* (not *"sarpitedaṃ"*). Also read *"-labhā"* for *"-labhāṃ."* Note also that the word *"-anvaya"* is treated as if it were a neuter noun, whereas it is usually masculine.

170. kathayāmi yathā tathyaṃ śrīsiddhājñākramoditam |
yāgamaṇḍaladīkṣādipūrvapaścimanirṇayam ||
(Ibid., 1/40b-41a).

171. KRU, 3/132-4.

172. tvat santānam idaṃ vatsa pūrvāmnāyeti saṃjñayā |
paścimasya tu mārgasya pratibimbam iva sthitam ||
(Ibid., fl. 87a).

173. KRU, fl. 77b.

174. kathaṃ pūrvānvāyam nātha paścimāt śrīkulānvayāt |
utpatsyate dvitīyaṃ tu ādinātha tathā vada ||
(Ibid., fl. 86b).

175. See Bagchi, KJN, intro. pp. 6-32 for an account of these variant myths and stories related to Matsyendranātha.

176. KRU, 1/10 ff.

177. Ibid., 1/16. Other Tantras are: *Haṃsabheda, Nīla,* Tārā, Gaṇa, Rīmata* (?) *Caṇḍākhya, Rauravākhya,* Ghorākhya,* Bhūtaḍāmara, Saṃcāra, Saṃvāra, Mahāraudra,* Yoginīmata, Haruka, Bhūdhara, Śākinī, Jālasaṃbara, Carcikāhṛdaya, Hāṭakeśa, Mamata, Caṇḍāgra, Dhāraṇī, Kaulikāmata, Karālamata, Kulayoga, Nityā-Nirgākṣa*(?) *Kāmeśvarīkula, Siddhādevīmahātantra, Piṅgalāmata,* Umāgaṇeśvara, Viśvakarmamaya, Kiraṇa,* Pañcarāja, Raurava,* Rurubheda, Caṇḍikākalpa, Kālacakra, Mahāraudra, Ananta,* Vijaya,* Sarvavīra, Mahāyoga, Nīlakaṇṭhapaddhati, Tejīśa, Matula* (or *Atula*) *Cāmuṇḍāmata, Mātṛnāda*(*t*)*rikūṭa, Mātṛkāhṛdaya, Pañjarīmata, Brahmāṇḍavijaya, Kapālinīmata, Raudrapratiṣṭha* and *Pārameśvara.** KRU, 1/10-20.

The Tantras marked with an asterisk are *Siddhāntāgamas* or their *Upāgamas.* The *Bhūtaḍāmara* is no. 50 in the NSA list. *Saṃvāra* may be the Buddhist *Cakrasaṃvāratantra.* The *Harukatantra* may also be the Buddhist *Herukatantra. Dhāraṇī* may be the *Dhāraṇāgama,* an *Upāgama* of the Siddhānta *Vimalāgama. Kālacaka* may be the Buddhist Tantra of this name.

178. At the beginning of the *Kulapradīpa,* a *Paścimatantra* preserved in

Nepal, these three Devīs are revered as the components of Śrīkula, i.e., Paścimāmnāya:

aparaparāparaparamaśaktiḥ śrīkaulikī jayantu |
(NA, MS no. 1/1076, fl. 1a).

179. Dr. Goudriaan has delivered a lecture on the *Samayāmantra* of Kubjikā described in KMT, chapter 18, in which he has incidentally also demonstrated that the Parā, etc., Mantras of the Kubjikā school are those of the Trika as expounded in chapter 30 of the *Tantrāloka.* Conference on Yantra and Mantra at the CNRS, Paris, 22/6/84.

180. These Mantras are dealt with extensively in the KRU in various places. For *Navātmamantra* see KRU, 5/76-78. *Bhairavasadbhāva* and *Ratiśekhara* fl. 53-54. The three Mantras of Parā, etc., are described ibid., 5/119 ff. Not only are these Mantras essentially the same, but the energies associated with them are also similar. There is no need to expect that all the details should coincide as Abhinava himself tells us that there are a number of variants in the form of these Mantras and associated principles even in the one Tantra (here he is referring to the *Triśirobhairava* TĀ, 30/27b-28a). However, we find that the eight energies (*kalā*) of the *Parāparā* Mantra are virtually the same as those we find in the *Triśirobhairava.* In the KRU (5/121-2a) they are Aghorā, Paramaghorā, Ghorarūpā, Ananā, Bhīmā, Bhiṣaṇā, Vāmanī and Pivanī. In the passage quoted from the *Triśirobhairava* in TĀ, vol. V, p. 11 and TĀ, vol. XII, p. 341 the names and order are the same, except that Ananā of the KRU is called Ghoravaktrā. In the MVT, 1/19b-20 these same eight energies are said to create, sustain, destroy and offer grace. They are associated with the Mantreśvaras and Mahāmantreśvaras from which the seven *koṭis* of Mantras which constitute the cosmic order are created.

181. So, for example, it is said in the CMSS, (fl. 4b): "He who knows the three Kulas, that which is beyond the three Kulas, the three states and that which is other than the three states, the three wombs and that which has no womb is the follower of the tradition". In the MBT(Y), fl. 72a-b *Paścima* is described as the "divine tradition, which removes all impurities and is established in the three principles." Groups of three are then listed.

182. These three recur persistently in the *Paścimatantras* as three *Kramas* through which the goddess is worshipped. According to the MBT, in her child (*bālā*) form, Kubjikā is called "Umābhagavatī" and is described as having six faces, five of which are named here: Upper (Mālinī), East (Siddhayogeśvarī), South (Mahālakṣmī), North (Mahākālī) and West (Kubjikā). (MBT(Y) fl. 93a ff.) Mālinī, which is important in the Trika, is here given pride of place as the upper face, while Siddhayogeśvarī is located in the east which reminds us of Trika's association with the *Pūrvāmnāya*, the Eastern Tradition.

183. śatakoṭipravistīrṇaṃ vyākhyātaṃ khañjinīmatam |
evaṃ sā śāmbhavīśaktir anantā anantatāṃ gatā ||
tasyā(ḥ) saṃpreraṇā yātaṃ śāṃbhavaśākt(ākta)m āṇavam |
icchājñānakriyāsyā(s) ca saṃsthitā bhuvanatrayām ||
(MBT(Y), fl. 70a).

(The last half of the third line reads: *"śāmbhavaśāktam āṇavaṃ."* The copyist has written *"-ākta-"* twice by mistake. In the last line read *"-traye"* for *"-trayām."*)

184. See GS, 8/121. CMSS, fl. 8a-8b furnishes an example of how this works.

185. An account of these three initiations is found in the KRU, fl. 68b. ff.

186. For an extensive account of *Śabdarāśi* and *Mālinī* see A. Padoux's standard work: *Recherches sur La symboliques et L'Énergie de la Parole dans certains Textes Tantriques,* Paris 1963. For an account of how these operate as codes in the Tantras of the Kubjikā school, see Schoterman, pp. 182-221.

187. śabdarāśiśca mālinyā vidyānāṃ tritayasya ca |
sāṅgopāṅgasamāyuktā trikatantraṃ kariṣyati ||

(KRU, fl. 78b).

(For *"śabdarāśiś"* read *"śabdarāśeś."* For *"-samāyuktā"* read *"-samāyuktaṃ"*).

188. For example, the CMSS acknowledges that it has derived the *pīṭhasaṃketa* from the *Siddhayogeśvarīmata:*

saṃketa eṣa vikhyātas siddhayogeśvarīmate |

(fl. 14a).

According to this account, there are four *pīṭhas*, namely, Oṅkāra, Jālandhara, Pūrṇa (*giri*) and Kāmarū. The first is located in the mouth, which represents the circle of the Sky of Consciousness as the state of withdrawal and suspension of all extroverted conscious activity. Jālandhara and Pūrṇa are in the right and left ears respectively while Kāmarū resides at the end of the flow of the vital breath (*prāṇānte*).

189. The original *Trikatantras*, such as the SYM and *Triśirobhairava*, as we have already had occasion to remark, were *Bhairavatantras.* Moreover, none of the *Trikatantras* I have had access to, namely, the published *Mālinīvijayottara*, a part of the SYM and *Śrītantrasadbhāva* (NA, MS no. 1/363) ever refer to Trika as a school. The last two simply affiliate themselves to the *Vidyāpīṭha* of the *Bhairavasrotas.* Another unexpected feature of these Tantras is that they are not *Kaulatantras* although their doctrines, metaphysical presuppositions and rituals are of a Kaula type. Where Kula is referred to as a ritual pattern, doctrine or tradition, it figures as an element in the broader context of the Tantra as a whole. However, the later *Trikatantras*, which did think of themselves as belonging to a Trika tradition, such as the *Niśisañcāra, Kularatnamālā, Bhairavakula* and *Trikasāra,* define Trika in Kaula terms as the highest Kaula school which as such is, in a sense, beyond the Kula tradition. These facts along with the absorption of Krama doctrine in some form are fundamental features of the history of the development of Āgamic Trika before Abhinavagupta.

190. The *Paścimatantras*, it seems, are so conscious of having absorbed many Trika elements that at times it becomes necessary for a Tantra in the course of its exposition of a topic to distinguish what it is going to say about it from what the Trika and others have said. Thus, for example, the MBT proclaims that it will explain the characteristics of the sacrificial hearth according to the Paścima Kula/Kaula tradition (see above p. 62) as explained in the *Mahārṇava-*

tantra(?) and the common ritual which concerns it, free of Trika and Dakṣiṇa elements:

kuṇḍānāṃ lakṣaṇaṃ vakṣye kule kaule tu paścime |
mahārṇave lakṣapāde uktaṃ te sarvakāraṇā ||
olināthas tu sāmānyaṃ trikadakṣiṇavarjitam |

(MBT(Y), fl. 8a).

(Read *"-kāranaṃ"* for *"-kāranā"*)

Similarly the goddess proclaims the purity of the *Paścima* doctrine taught in the KMT by saying that it is free of the Eastern portion:

idaṃ ca paścimaṃ deva pūrvabhāgavivarjitam |

(KMT, fl. 6b).

It is quite common in these Tantras, as it is in others, for the speaker to let us know that what he has said or is about to say is new in some respect. The god may say to the goddess: "Now I will tell you of a matter I have never revealed before," or "Hear now the tradition which up to now has been transmitted only by word of mouth," or "Now I will clarify that which has been kept hidden in previous Tantras" or "Know that this form of the deity has never been spoken of before," etc. Again, at times, we are told that a topic has been dealt with only cursorily, in which case the god may say something like "Now I will explain at length that which was told to you before concisely." Such remarks are clear indications that the tradition is conscious of drawing from external sources (whether these be Tantras which have been set to writing or oral tradition) as well as contributing something new of its own.

191. Judging from the colophons recorded in the BSP, many chapters of the JY are dedicated to accounts of the worship of Kālī in diverse forms. The names of the Kālīs mentioned in the colophons are, in the second *ṣaṭka:* Kālasaṅkarṣaṇī, Yamakālī, Gahaneśvarī, Raktakālī, Indīvarīkālikā, Dhanadakālī, Īśānakālī, Vīryakālī, Raktakālī and Saptārṇakālī. In the fourth *ṣaṭka:* Mohakālī, Amareśvarī, Parāntakālī, Meghakālī, Priyakālī, Stambhakālī, Kālarātri, Melāpakālī, Nityakālī, Śāntikālī, Netrakālī, Jagatkṣobhakālī, Ghaṭṭanakālī and Hṛdayakālī. It is interesting to note in passing that one chapter of this *ṣaṭka* is concerned with the worship of Siddhayogeśvarī. Seven chapters in this same section are specifically labelled as dealing with Kālīkulakrama rites (see BSP, Tantra I, p. 119 ff.).

192. See Goudriaan and Gupta, 1981, p. 52; also Schoterman pp. 5-6.

193. Apart from the sacred geography peculiar to these Tantras, we find combined with it the general pattern of sacred places referred to in the *Kaulatantras* and cognate texts as a whole. Representative lists of the latter are found in references in the *Tantrāloka.* Nepal hardly ever figures in these lists (an exception to this general rule is YHṛ, 3/37). The reason for this is probably that Kaula-oriented Tantra was introduced into Nepal only after the original redaction of these works. The oldest MSs of these Tantras do not pre-date the eleventh century. Before then the type of Śaivism popular in the Kathmandu valley seems to have

been of the Siddhānta and Purāṇic type which prescribed *liṅga* worship and consisted of cults such as that of *Umāmāheśvara* described in works like the *Śivadharma, Śivadharmottara* and *Śivopaniṣad.* An early tenth century MS of these texts (NA, no. 4/531) is preserved in Nepal. Similarly early Nepalese MSs of the *Kiraṇāgama* and other *Siddhāntāgamas* also exist. Although the earliest Śaiva cults in Nepal were not Kaula-oriented, a reference to Nepal as one of eight *upapīṭhas* occurs in the MBT(Y), fl. 15b. Another reference has been traced in a MS of the *Niśisañcāratantra* (NA, MS no. 1/1606) which is written in early Newarī characters probably not younger than the twelfth century. Here Paśupati is mentioned as residing in Nepal along with his consort Guhyeśvarī. These references suggest that Nepal did not become a centre of Kaula Tantricism much before the eleventh century.

194. See Schoterman, p. 6, 37.

195. Schoterman, p. 6.

196. Practically the only reference to Kubjikā apart from in her Tantras is a brief description of her worship in the *Agnipurāṇa.* See Schoterman's article *A link between Purāṇa and Tantra: Agnipurāṇa 143-147* in ZDMG suppl. IV Wiesbaden 1980. See also *Les Enseignements Iconographiques de L'Agnipurāṇa* by Mth. de Mallman Paris 1963 pp. 159-60, 206-207.

197. See Schoterman, p. 10, fn. 4.

198. Dr. Kiśoranātha Jhā in his Hindī introduction to the first part of the *Guhyakālīkhaṇḍa* of the *Mahākālasaṃhitā* (p. 18, fn. 1) informs us that the late Parmeśvara Siṃha, who was a Maithili Tantric, had a statue of Guhyakālī in her ten-faced form made and installed in a temple in the village of Madhubanī in the Bhauragadhi district of Behar. This is the only example he knows of a representation of this form of the goddess in India. There is, however, an old image of Guhyakālī carved in black marble preserved in the Rājputāna Museum in Ajmer (No. 193, 268). See article by P. K. Majumdar, *Śakti worship in Rajasthan* published in the *Śakti Cult and Tārā*, Calcutta 1957, p. 68.

199. Schoterman, p. 6.

200. Kuiper, F. B. J. *Proto-Muṇḍā Words in Sanskrit*, Amsterdam 1948, p. 42. ff.; referred to by Schoterman, p. 11.

201. Kubjikā is also called "Kukāradevī" which is not only an abbreviated form of her name but also the seed-syllable corresponding to the Earth Principle. The word *"ku"* means "earth" and so"Kujā" which is one of Kubjikā's common names means "born of the earth" and "Kujeśvarī"—"the goddess born of the earth."

202. tathā sa kuṭilā vakrā madhyamolyāṃ kuleśvara |
kubjikā ṣaṭprakārā ca vṛddharūpeṇa devatā ||
(MBT(Y), fl. 95a).

203. The KMT, fl. 69b says: "She in whose centre the universe resides and who resides in the centre of the universe is thus called Khañjikā; she who is subtle and present in subtle things." These names give rise in their turn to various names for the Kubjikā school such as *"Khañjinīmata," "Khañjinīkula," "Vakrikāgama," "Vakrikāmata"* as well as *"Ciñciniśāstra"* or *"Ciñcinīmata"* and *"Kulālikāmnāya"* (for Kubjikā as Ciñcinī see below, and as Kulālikā the potteress,

see Schoterman, pp. 7-9).

204. KRU, 1/72-78.

205. prabuddhā vrīḍayākuñcya gātraṃ svasthāsyati priye |
(KRU, fl. 77b).

206. saṃsārasāgare ghore duṣṭācāro'tidāruṇe |
vikalpakoṭivakre mahāmāyāmahārṇave ||
(MBT(Y), fl. 69b).

(The end of the third quarter is one syllable short. This deficiency could be remedied by adding "tu" or some such particle to complete the metre.)

207. KMT fl. 69b also Schoterman p. 11.

208. svanābhimathanād devi svakīyarasanā purā ||
brahmāṇḍaṃ garbhatas tasyā jatidivyena yoninā
tad ārabhya maheśāni kubjādevīti viśrutā ||
(Parāt., 3/2b-3).

209. "The Wheel of Energy consisting of consciousness and the unconscious resides in the wheel of the navel which is the Great Matrix. It is supremely divine, the illuminator of the *Brahmanāḍī* which, by its upwards and downward flow, pervades [all things] and faces in every direction. Piercing through the path of the palate it causes the nectar of the power of consciousness to flow. This, O fair one, is the door to liberation" (CMSS, fl. 5b).

210. Kubjikā is extolled as the Divine Light of consciousness in a hymn in MBT(Y), fl. 67a-69b.

211. MBT(Y), fl. 81a.

212. Ibid., fl. 67a.

213. śrīśāsane parā devī kuṭilā divyarūpiṇī |
parāparāparāśakti(r) yā parā paramā kalā ||
mantramātā parāyonir nādiphāntasvarūpiṇī |
(Ibid., fl. 69b).

The fifty goddesses which embody the energies of Mālinī are extensively described as part of *Mālinīcakra* in GS, pp. 29-45 where they are said to belong to the *Vāmamārga*. In this Wheel are located the three goddesses Parā, etc. and worshipped there as aspects of Mālinī. The *dhyānas* of these three are found in verses 8/159-163 (*Parā*), 8/113 (*Parāparā*) and 8/171-8 (*Aparā*).

214. CMSS, fl. 1a.

215. A hymn dedicated to Kubjikā as *Bhaga* is found in the CMSS, fl. 10.

216. CMSS, fl. 1a.

217. Ibid.

218. Kubjikā is nowhere referred to as Ciñcinī in the KMT. She is called this quite commonly, however, in later *Kubjikātantras* such as the MBT and KRU as well as in the CMSS. This is clearly, therefore, a new element that has evolved in the *Paścimāmnāya* in the later phases of its development.

219. CMSS, fl. 11a.

220. KRU, fl. 77b. Possibly this new development in the *Paścimāmnāya* (see fn. 218 above) was initiated by this yogi. Goddesses are still quite commonly

associated with sacred trees. One exorcist (*ojha*) I met in Benares told me that he had gained the power to propitiate the goddess śītālā (who causes smallpox and other skin diseases) when he had a vision of her sitting on her sacred neem tree.

221. CMSS, fl. 1a.

222. Ibid., fl. 1a-b, 13a-b.

Ciñcinī is also one of the ten forms of 'unstruck sound' which resound in the yogi's cosmic body, figuratively called "the belly of the machine of Māyā" (*māyāyantrodara*). These ten are in order: 1) Cini 2) Ciñcinī 3) The sound of a pleasing voice 4) Conch 5) Stringed instrument 6) Flute 7) Cymbals 8) Rumble of storm clouds 9) Sound of a running stream 10) Sound of a kettle drum. KMT fl. 50. The same verses, in a slightly variant form, are quoted from the BY in TĀ, vol. III, p. 410.

223. ādāv eva mahādevi ādināthena nirmitam |
paścimaṃ kramasantānaṃ svayaṃ yeṣṭam tataḥ priye ||
(KRU, 2/12).

(Read "jyeṣṭaṃ" for "yeṣṭam")

224. The derivative status of the goddess is variously expressed in the KRU; thus, for example, she is called "the one who is born of Akula" (ibid. 3/32).

225. KRU, 2/30-32.

226. Ibid., 2/13-15.

227. evam uktvā jagaddhātā śrīnātha ādisaṃjñākaḥ |
(KRU, fl. 94a).

228. MBT(Y), fl. 60a.

229. tvat prasādena śrīnātha aśeṣaṃ kulanirṇayam |
(GS, 21/176).

230. See above p. 91.

231. śrīkaṇṭhaṃ prathame pūjyaṃ śaṃkaraṃ ca dvitīyake |
(KMT, MS 1/229; BSP, vol. I, p. 58).

According to the KRU (fl. 73a ff.) three lines of teachers are established in *Śivatattva*. The first of these starts with Śrīkaṇṭha who produced twenty-four propagators of the doctrine, the second starts with Ajeśa who produced sixteen, while the third begins with Mahākāla. According to the colophons of the GS, Śrīkaṇṭha brought down to earth the *Kādibheda* (i.e., the Kubjikā group) of the Kulakaulamata.

232. See Schoterman, pp. 36-38.

233. In, for example, MBT(Y), 8a *"Oli"* is a synonym of *"Ovallī"* which term is defined in TĀ, vol. XIb, p. 28 as "the current of doctrine" (*"ovallyo jñānapravāhāḥ"*).

234. See ṢaṭSS, 3/90.

235. svabhāve kubjikākārā divyadehāṃ kujāmbikāṃ |
candradvīpapure kubjā śrīkaṇṭhasya anugrahe ||
(Ibid., fl. 94b).

(Read "-dehā" for "-dehāṃ" and "kujāmbikā" for "kujāmbikāṃ". The last quarter is defective by one syllable; "tu" for example, may be added to complete the metre so we read "tvanugrahe" in the place of just "anugrahe").

236. candrapīṭhapure rāmye devī cākhandamaṇḍalaṃ |
(MBT(Y), fl. 77a).

237. Schoterman, p. 37.

238. meroḥ paścimadigbhāge gandhamālyasamīpataḥ |
(KMT, fl. 3b).

239. ṢaṭSS, chapter 47 referred to by Schoterman, p. 35.

240. santānaṃ paścimāmnāyam etac candragṛhaṃ smṛtam |
(ṢaṭSS, 1/26a).

241. Schoterman, p. 35.

242. nādānte trisrajatam himagiriśikhare khañjinī ṣaṭprakārā |
kālī tatrāvatāraṃ kaliyugasamaye bhārate dvāparānte ||
(MBT(Y), 76a).

(This is the second half of a verse in *sṛgdharā* metre which has seven plus seven plus seven syllables per line.)

243. kailāśaśikharāntasthā śikhā devī maheśvarī |
kukārā (saṃ)smṛtā tat ta(c) cakreśī siddhanāyikā ||
(Ibid., fl. 80b).

244. manthānānandadākhyātā śikhā tasya maheśvara |
eṣā caitanyamūrtis tu parākhyā vakrikā mahā ||
tasyā adhikāram āyātam śrīm(ac) candrapure gṛhe |
(Ibid., fl. 83b).

245. śṛṅgatrayatrikūṭasthā śikhā devī maheśvarī |
kukārājñā smṛtā tatra cakreśī siddhanāyikā ||
sā ca merukramayātā pañcāśākṣarabhūṣitā |
(Ibid., fl. 80b).

246. Part of a typical colophon of the MBT reads "ityādyāvatāre mahāmanthānabhairavayajñe anvaye saptakoṭipramāṇe merumārgavinirgate lakṣapādādhike ādyapīṭhāvatāre |."

247. KRU, 2/44-48.

248. KMT, fl. 41a.

249. MBT(Y), fl. 62b.

250. GS 13/163. Birch bark is also referred to on p. 134, 143 and 292.

APPENDIX A

1. *A Catalogue of Palmleaf and Selected Paper Manuscripts belonging to the Durbar Library, Nepal.* By Haraprasāda Śāstrī with a historical introduction by C. Bendall, Calcutta, 1905. Volume II came out in 1915. See preface to volume I, p. LXXVII ff..

2. The *Kaulajñānanirṇaya*, edited by P. C. Bagchi, Metropolitan Press, Calcutta 1934. p. 68.

3. *Yearbook of the Royal Asiatic Society of Bengal,* 1937 pp. 158-9.

4. See K. R. van Kooy, *Die sogenannate Guptahandschrift des Kubjikāmatatantra* in ZDMG, Supp. III-2, Wiesbaden, 1977.
5. *A Descriptive Catalogue of the Sanskrit Manuscripts in the Government Collection under the care of the Royal Asiatic Society of Bengal*; Vol. VIII A and B, revised and edited from Haraprasāda Śāstrī's notes. Chintāharan Chakravarti, 1939 and 1940.
6. *Caṇḍī*, sixth year. *Saṃvat* 2004 (i.e., 1947 A.D.) *'32 sāla kā anubhava'* by Major General Dhana Saṃśer Jaṅgabahādur Rāṇā, Nepal p. 221-225, 276-284, p. 324-33, p. 347-354 (*Paścimāmnāya*) and p. 376-384.
7. *Les Enseignements Iconographiques de l'Agni-Purāṇa* by Mth. de Mallmann, Paris, 1963, p. 159-60, 197-8, 206-7.
8. *A Critical Edition of the Kujbikāmatatantra* in BSOAS vol. XXVI-3, London by K. R. van Kooy, 1973.
9. *Gorakṣasaṃhitā* (part I) edited by Janārdana Pāṇḍeya Sarasvatībhavanagranthamālā, Vol. 110, Vārāṇasī, 1976.
10. *Some Remarks on the Kubjikāmatatantra* by J. A. Schoterman in ZDMG, supp. III, Wiesbaden, 1977.
11. *A link between Purāṇa and Tantra: Agnipurāṇa 141-143* by J. A. Schoterman in ZDMG, Supp. IV, Wiesbaden, 1980.
12. *The Ṣaṭsāhasrasaṃhitā*, Chapters 1-5 edited, translated and annotated by J. A. Schoterman, Leiden, 1982.

APPENDIX B

1. *Caturviṃśatisāhasrikatāntrābhidhānaḥ* is the name given to this Tantra on the title leaf of a manuscript deposited in the ASB (no. 10841).
2. See H. C. Ray, *Dynastic History of North India,* vol. I, p. 204.
3. See RASB Tantra Cat., vol. I, pp. 23-24.
4. See colophon of the *Kumārikākhaṇḍa* of the MBT NA, no. 1/241; BSP, vol. II, p. 59.
5. *The Parātantra,* 1/7.
6. śrīmatkalaṃkanāthena anītam avanītale |
caturviṃśatisāhasre durlabhaṃ khaṃjanīmatam ||
sārdhastrīṇi sahasrāṇi anitā tumbureṇa tu ||
niveditaṃ dakṣine mārge tantraṃ śrīkulālikāmatam ||
ratnasūtram iti proktaṃ siddhan tu dakṣiṇe pathe |
(MBT(Y), fl. 70a-b).

(Read *"sāhasram"* for *"-sāhasre"* and *"anītam"* for *"anītā."* The fourth line is too long by two syllables. If we read *"kubjikāmatam"* for *"śrīkulālikāmatam"* the metre is preserved).

7. īdṛśaṃ cintayed rūpaṃ kaulīśaṃ śrīkuleśvaram |
āgamaṃ śrīmataṃ haste mahāyogadharaṃ śubham ||
(Ibid., fl. 86a).

8. For Dharmakīrti's date and life see Warder, *Indian Buddhism* pp. 469-472. The reference in the MBT reads: "dharmakīrti(r) bhavet tarkaṃ prajñāpāramitākriyā |" (MBT(Y), fl. 34b). This Tantra appears to be well aware of the existence of Buddhism and refers specifically to the Sautrāntika, Vaibhāṣika, Yogācāra and Mādhyamika (Ibid.). It also knows that foreigners practise Buddhism:

kṛtvādau uditāḥ so hi mlecchā yatra upāsakāḥ |

(Ibid.).

(The metre is defective by one syllable in the second half unless we take *"mlecchā"* to be *"malecchā"*).

9. cathurthe tu yuge svānte dharmocchede samāgate |
mleccharājyekachatre ca bhuñjate pṛthivīmahān ||
rāvaṇasyāvatāre tu siṃdhos tīre XXXX ||

(MBT(Y), fl. 91b).

There appears to be another possible reference to an invasion in the ṢaṭSS. Here it is described as one of the many horrors of the Kali Age. It says:

kṣatriyā āhave bhagnāḥ kariṣyanti prabhutvatām |

(3/79b).

10. MBT(Y), fl. 70a.

11. Colophon of the *Kumārikākhaṇḍa* of the MBT NA, no. 1/241; BSP, vol. II, p. 59.

APPENDIX C

1. The manuscript is NA, no. 5/4650 Śaivatantra 431. It is 275 folios long and written in Devanāgarī script. The relevant section starts on folio 165b. It extends from chapter 35 to 45. The colophons all begin as follows: iti bhairavasrotasi vidyāpīṭhe śiraś chede śrījayadrathayāmale mahātantre caturviṃśatisāhasre prathamaṣaṭke śrīkālasaṃkarṣiṇyāṃ . . . Then the name of the chapter (*paṭala*) and its number follows. These are chapter 35 (fl. 163b-68b) nityāhnikācāra yoṭhā (?) saṃbandhāvatārākhyāvarṇanaṃ; chapter 36 (fl. 168b-170a) svacchandasūtranirṇayaḥ; Chapter 37 (fl. 170a-171a) bhairavasūtranirṇayaḥ; Chapter 38 (fl. 171a-2a) krodhabhairavasūtranirṇayaḥ; Chapter 39 (fl. 172a-3b) mantrapīṭhavinirṇaya; Chapter 40 (fl. 173b-181a) brahmayāmalanirṇaya; Chapter 41 (fl. 181a-2a) viṣṇusūtranirṇaya; Chapter 42 (fl. 182a-3a) umāyāmalādisūtranirṇaya; Chapter 43 (fl. 183b-4a) unnamed; Chapter 44 (fl. 184a-5b) sadāśivāṣṭāṣṭakanirṇaya; Chapter 45 (fl. 185b-197b) cumbakacaryā.

2. See *Studies in the Tantras* by P. C. Bagchi, reprinted, Calcutta 1975. See pp. 109-114 for notices of the *Jayadrathayāmala*.

3. bhītānāṃ sarujārtānāṃ duṣṭānāṃ cāpi śāsanāt |
bhayānāṃ ca paritrāṇāc chāstram uktam hi sūribhiḥ ||

(JY, fl. 165b).

cf. śāsyate trāyate yasmāt tasmāc chāstram udāhṛtam |
(quoted from the *Piṅgalāmata* in Bagchi, p. 106).

4. See also Bagchi pp. 110-11 where this passage is quoted. The JY also accepts the standard division of the *śāstras* found in the Āgamas into five groups, viz., Laukika, Vaidika, Ādhyātmika, Atimārga and Āṇava which stands for Mantratantra (see above p. 49). This division of the *śāstras* into five corresponds to five fruits they are supposed to yield (JY, fl. 166a).

5. The Vaimala along with the Lākula, Mausula and Kāruka is one of a standard group of four Pāśupata sects mentioned in the Āgamas and elsewhere. See SvT, 11/69-74 and Kṣemarāja's commentary. Also Jayaratha on TĀ, 1/33. There are eight *Pramāṇas* according to SvT, 10/1134-35. They correspond to eight Rudras that have incarnated as Pāśupata teachers who founded the following eight Pāśupata schools: Pañcārtha, Guhya, Rudrāṅkuśa, Hṛdaya, Lakṣaṇa, Vyūha, Ākarṣa and Ādarśa. (Ibid., 10/1134-5; cf. also TĀ, 8/328-9).

6. The text (fl. 166a) simply reads *Guhyādi* which I have taken to be a reference to the *Guhyasamājatantra*. It is interesting that the JY classifies the Vajrayāna *śāstras* as belonging to this group, thus distinguishing them from other Buddhist scriptures which are assigned to the previous one. We should not, however, understand this to mean that the Buddhist Tantras are aligned with the Bhairava and other similar Śaivatantras on an equal footing.

7. This account largely agrees with the way the genesis of scripture is generally described in the Āgamas. According to the *Kulamūlāvatāra*, out of Śiva, who is the supreme cause, tranquil and transcendent, emerges the power of will, followed by those of knowledge and action. Through them, the worlds are created, as is speech in all its expressions (MM, p. 39). Similarly, according to the *Svacchandabhairava* (quoted in YHṛ, p. 153) a pure and subtle resonance (*dhvani*) emerges out of Śiva, the cause of all things. This is Speech which is the power beyond mind (*unmanāśakti*) that goes on to assume the form of scripture and the spoken word.

8. The Āgamas regularly refer to the types of relationship that form between the teacher and his disciple through which the meaning of the scripture and the realization it conveys are transmitted. The basic pattern is the same although it may vary in individual cases. Abhinava records that according to the *Kula-ratnamālā*, there are five relationships: great (*mahat*), intermediate (*avāntara*), divine (*divya*), divine-cum-nondivine (*divyādivya*) and mutual (*itaretara*) (TĀ, 1/273-4). Bhagavatotpala also refers to five; these are supreme (*para*), great (*mahat*), divine (*divya*), other than divine (*divyetara*) and mutual (*itaretara*). (Sp.Pra., p. 84). Through these relationships formed between the teacher and disciple and taught at different levels, scripture and its meaning are transmitted from and through the divine consciousness which is its source and basis: "The Lord, Sadāśiva, establishing himself on the plane of master and disciple, brought the Tantra into the world through a series of questions and answers." (SvT quoted in VB, p. 7). There is, as Abhinava explains, an essential identity between the disciple who inquires and the teacher who instructs, as both are embodiments of the one consciousness. The disciple represents the aspect of consciousness which

questions (*praṣṭṛsaṃvit*) and the teacher the aspect which responds (TĀ, 1/252-5). Thus as Abhinava says "relationship (*saṃbandha*) is the identity (that is established) between the two subjects who question and reply. Its supreme aspect consists of the revelation of identity in all its fullness. The other relationships mentioned in the scriptures must also be considered in the light of this principle in order that the results one desires etc. may manifest in all their fullness" (TĀ, 1/275-6).

9. Similarly the *Svacchandasaṃgraha* says "this is the Lord Anāśrita who has five faces each of which bears three eyes and who has one, two, four or ten arms. He is Sadāśiva, the God of the gods who utters the worldly and other scripture. [It is He who] has spoken the countless Āgamas divided into superior and inferior" (quoted in Y.Hṛ., p. 271).

10. Mahākāruṇika is probably a Pāśupata sect. The four instruments could also possibly be Pure Knowledge, Sound, the Drop and the metres.

11. See chapter 45 of this section of the JY.

12. We are reminded of Sumati who was Abhinava's grand teacher of Trika Śaivism. He was reputed to have known all five currents of scripture (see commentary on TĀ, 1/213).

13. vāmadakṣiṇamiśreṣu bhinnapīṭhacatuṣṭayam |
vyapadiśyate mukhyavac cchākhā śākhāntare sthitam ||
(JY, fl. 168a).

(The fifth syllable of the third quarter is long and the sixth short. In standard anuṣṭubh metre of the 'śloka' variety the fifth syllable in every quarter should be short and the sixth long).

14. mantravidyāsuharmyāṇām saṅghastomakadaṃbakam |
vratavṛndaṃ ca nikara(ḥ) samūhaḥ saṃhiti(r)valam ||
vicchindo maṇḍalaṃ pīṭhaṃ paryāyair upaśabditam |
(Ibid., fl. 168b).

(Read *"vicchinnaṃ"* for *"vicchindo"*) see above p. 49.

15. yatra yatra tu vidyānāṃ guṇatvam samprayujyate |
yat tad hi paramaṃ tejo mantrapīṭhaṃ hi tat smṛtam ||
tasya bhoktṛsvarūpasya vidyākhyaṃ bhogya(m) iṣyate |
ubhayasyāpi mudrākhyaṃ maṇḍalaṃ triṣvapi sthitam ||
bhūyo bhedaṃ tripīṭhantu maṇḍalaṃ capyabhedagam |
(Ibid., fl. 169a).

16. These Tantras have been discussed above on p. 45 ff. The reader can consult the detailed index for cross references to Tantras in this monograph.

17. The *Sarvavīra* as quoted in SvT, vol. I, p. 10:

svacchandabhairavaś caṇḍaḥ krodha unmattabhairavaḥ |
granthāntarāṇi catvāri mantrapīṭhaṃ varanane ||

In JY, fl. 168b the first line of this verse is the same as above; the second reads:

granthāntarāṇi catvāri mantrapīṭhe sthitāni ca |

18. mantrapīṭham dvidhārūpam XXXXXXXX |
(Ibid., fl. 169b).

19. suvistaram idaṃ devi vidyāpīṭhaṃ svabhāvataḥ |
(Ibid., fl. 169a).

20. Ibid., fl. 182b.

21. It is worth noting that the Lākulīśapāśupata, or at least the branch of it associated with Musalendra, is linked with the *Mantrapīṭha.* Interesting also is their association with the Ṛṣi Gautama because in the Purāṇas he is portrayed as being indirectly responsible for the origin of the 'unorthodox' Tantras. The story is told in the *Kūrmapurāṇa* (1/15/95 fl.) and the *Varāha* (chapters 70 and 71). Once, the story goes, a long drought devastated the country and afflicted the inhabitants with severe famine. Amongst the victims was a group of ascetics who, to save themselves, sought Gautama's hospitality in his hermitage in Dāruvana. Gautama enjoyed their company and so after the famine was over he insisted that they continue to stay with him. Although they did not wish to do so, they felt obliged to accept the invitation and so stayed. Once, when Gautama happened to go away for a few days, they found their opportunity to leave. They created a magic cow which they substituted for a real one in the hermitage. When Gautama returned, the illusory cow died and the ascetics charged him with its death and so, on the pretext that he had committed a sin, left. After the ascetics had gone, Gautama realized that he had been tricked and cursed them to be outside the Vedic fold (*vedabāhya*). The fallen sages, worried by the consequences of the curse, invoked Viṣṇu and Śiva with hymns in Sanskrit (*laukikastotra*) entreating them to free them from their sins. Out of compassion, the two gods revealed the heretical (*pāṣaṇḍa*) and deluding scriptures (*mohanaśāstra*) of the *Kāpāla, Nākula, Vāma, Bhairava, Pūrvapaścima, Pāñcarātra* and *Pāśupata.*

22. *Asitāṅga* is fifth in the *Dakṣiṇatantra* list of the PLSS. It is also fifth in the list of the sixty-four Bhairavatantras in the ŚKS. *Ekapāda* is the twenty-fifth *Dakṣiṇatantra* in the PLSS. An *Ekapādapurāṇa* is listed as the sixth upāgama of the *Cintyāgama. Śekhara* is the twenty-first in the *Dakṣiṇatantra* list. A *Śivaśekhara* is the thirteenth upāgama of the *Cintyāgama. Amṛta* is the name of the sixth *upāgama* of the *Cintyāgama;* this may be the *Mahāmṛta. Bhīma* is the sixteenth *Dakṣiṇatantra.* The *Bījabheda* which is the twenty-fourth Tantra amongst the *Vāmatantras* may be the *Bījatantra.*

23. The *Vīratantra* may be the fifth Rudrāgama or the eleventh upāgama of the Vīrāgama. The *Caṇḍāsidhara* is the ninth *Bhūtatantra.* A *Bhūtatantra* is listed as the fifth upāgama of the *Aṃśumadāgama*; this may be either the *Bhūtogra* or *Bhūtanigraha. Vijaya* is the name of the first Rudrāgama and the eighth upāgama of the *Vijaya.* The ninth *Vāmatantra* in the PLSS list is called *Vijaya* while the *Vijayā* is the twenty-ninth Tantra in the ŚKS list. *Ḍāmaratantras* are said to deal with magic and are often regarded as a group on their own. *Ḍāmara* is the sixty-first Tantra listed in the ŚKS.

24. mokṣāvarodhakaṃ yad yat tasya tasya hi vastutaḥ |
nigrahaikaparaṃ yena tena krodham udāhṛtam ||
(JY, fl. 172a).

(The word *"krodha"* is a masculine noun; here it is treated as if it were neuter).

25. An *Anantatantra* is listed as the first upāgama of the *Vimalāgama*. *Anantavijaya* is listed as the twenty-first *Vāmatantra*. *Parā* is the name of the eighteenth Rudrāgama while *Amṛta* is the sixth *upāgama* of the *Cintyāgama*. *Ānanda* is listed as the seventeenth *Vāmatantra*; it is also the name of the sixth *upāgama* of the *Dīptāgama*.

26. For the *Sarvavīra* and SYM see index. A *Viśvādyamata* is the twenty-fourth in the *Bhairavatantra* list of the ŚKS. *Viśvavikaṇṭha* is thirtieth in the *Dakṣiṇatantra* list while the *Yoginījālaśambara* is the twenty-ninth.

27. The JY says:

> savyasrotasi siddhāni śira(ś)chidrabhayātmakam ||
> nayottaraṃ mahāraudraṃ mahāsaṃmohanaṃ tathā |
> trikam etat mahādevi vāmasrotasi nirgatam ||

We have translated this verse above (p. 36) as follows: "Belonging to the Current of the Left are the perfect [Āgamas including] the frightening *Śiraścheda*. The three: *Nayottara, Mahāraudra* and *Mahāsaṃmohana* have, O goddess, emerged in the Current of the Left." Although this is certainly a possible translation of these lines, the JY does not in fact reckon itself to be exclusively amongst the *Vāmatantras* but prefers to classify itself amongst the *Dakṣiṇatantras*. It does, however, also say that it belongs to both Currents (see above p. 113), although in the detailed description of the contents of these Currents it is amongst those of the Middle Current and so we have listed it there accordingly.

28. The *Ucchuṣmatantra* is eighteenth in the *Dakṣiṇatantra* list, thirty-fourth in the NSA list and seventh in that of the ŚKS. The *Sarvatobhadratantra* is mentioned in VŚT, v. 317 along with the *Mahāsaṃmohana*. It is therefore probably a *Vāmatantra*.

29. These are listed further ahead as the eight Tantras which constitute the *Cakrabheda* of the sixty-four *Bhairavatantras*.

30. A *Bhīmasaṃhitā* is listed as the fifth upāgama of the *Kāraṇāgama* and as the sixteenth *Dakṣiṇatantra*. *Tilaka* may be the *Tilakodyānabhairava* which is the thirty-second *Dakṣiṇatantra*.

31. *Siddhārtha*, the first Tantra in this list, may be the *Siddhāgama* which is the sixteenth *Rudrāgama*; if so this confirms the JY's statement that the six remaining Tantras are still ideal rather than actual.

32. These gods and goddesses are frequently portrayed as given to orgiastic revelry or other chaotic behaviour which threatens to disrupt the cosmic, ethical and divine order. Goudriaan (*Vīṇāśikhatantra*, introduction p. 19) refers us to another example found in the *Yogavāsiṣṭha* (the first half of the *nirvāṇaprakāraṇa* 18/24 ff.). Here Tumburu and Bhairava are described as enthroned together and surrounded by eight Mothers (*mātṛkā*) said to belong to the Left Current and to be associated with Tumburu. Their appearance and activity is intense. Their revelry and drunkenness breaks all limits of cultured behaviour but they are put in their place by Śiva.

33. nīlarudrodbhavānyādyāḥ śiśyās te aṣṭāṣṭakāśritāḥ |
(JY, fl. 177b).

34. *Trottala* is the twenty-seventh *Gārudatantra* in the PLSS list, and the forty-sixth in the NSA list. The *Bindusara* is the third in the *Gāruḍatantra* list while the *Bindutantra* is no. 37 in the ŚKS's list of *Bhairavatantras.* Possibly the *Mahodayatantra* corresponds to the *Cintāmaṇimahodaya* which is the fourth *Vāmatantra* in the PLSS list. The *Bhūtaḍāmara* listed here may be the well-known Tantra concerned wth magic of this name. For the *Vijayatantra* see fn. 23 above. *Nīlaketu* may be the *Nīlatantra* which is the third upāgama of the *Kīraṇāgama* or *Nīlarudraka* which is the eighth upāgama of the *Cintyāgama. Mohana* is the fourth *Vāmatantra* in the PLSS's list. The *Śikhatantra* may be the *Śikhāmṛta, Sikhāyoga* or *Śikhāsāra* which are, respectively, the twelfth, tenth and eleventh in the PLSS's list of *Gāruḍatantras. Karkoṭa* may be the third *Bhūtatantra.* The *Daurvāsāmṛta* may correspond to the *Daurvāsa* listed as the twenty-third *Vāmatantra. Lalita* is the name of the twelfth *Rudrāgama* and also that of its first upāgama. *Bhogineya* may be *Bhoga*, the first upāgama of the *Vimalāgama.*

35. The JY defines *"yāmala"* as the worship which takes place through the union of husband and wife:

dampatyayogataḥ pūjā yāmaleti nigadyate |
(Ibid., fl. 169a).

Abhinava refers to a ritual type in the TĀ which he says is found in a number of Tantras. This involves the projection of Vidyā liturgical formulas on the body of the Tantric consort and Mantric formulas on the body of the Tantric master as a prelude to ritual intercourse. In this way the female partner becomes the embodiment of the brilliant 'Lunar' energy of the sphere of objectivity and the male, the 'Solar' energy of the sphere of cognitive consciousness. These two represent the *Vidyā* and *Mantra-pīṭhas* respectively which fuse when the couple unite (TĀ, 29/166b-8a). In short "Mantra" can also denote the male Tantric partner and "Vidyā" the female, while "yāmala" is the ritual union of the two.

36. yāmalaṃ yugalaṃ nāma mantravidyaikagocaram |
jñānakriyātmakaṃ tac ca anyonyāpeṣkayā sthitam ||
(JY, fl. 182b).

37. Ibid., fl. 174b.

38. These *Matatantras* are virtually those listed below amongst the sixty-four *Bhairavatantras.* Note that *Lampaṭa* which is listed here as an *anutantra* of the *Nīlakeśamata* is listed amongst the *Matatantras* in the ŚKS.

39. *Utphullaka* is a part of the *Śāmbaramata.*

40. arthāvirbhāvabhedena pañcasūtrojjvalaṃ matam |
(JY, fl. 179b).

41. pīṭhabhedavibhinnan tu mūlasūtraṃ pratiṣṭhitam |
(Ibid., fl. 169a).

42. TĀ, 28/385b-407.

43. Ibid., 28/386b-7a.

44. See TĀ, vol. XI, pp. 171-2 where Jayaratha quotes a long passage

from the *Devyāyāmala* in which these correlates are explained.

45. JY, fl. 179a. The *Kālottara* is considered to be an upāgama of the *Vātulāgama.* It has numerous recensions. See the *Sārdhatriśatikālottarāgama* edited with the commentary of Bhaṭṭa Rāmakaṇṭha by N. R. Bhatt, publications de l'Institute Français d'Indology, no. 61, Pondicherry, 1979 p. v ff. The *Mahāmṛtyuñjaya* may be the *Netratantra* published in the KSTS (see bibliography).

46. māpitaṃ tu jagatkṛtsnaṃ trāṇitaṃ ca viśeṣataḥ |
yasyā(ṃ) yayā ca sā cakre mātṛśabdena gīyate ||
tasyā vicitrabhedo yo mātṛbhedaḥ sa ucyate |

(Ibid., fl. 183a).

47. *Aparājita* is the eleventh *Vāmatantra* while *Karoṭinī* may correspond to *Karoṭa* which is the fifth *Bhūtatantra.*

48. kubjikāmatavistīrṇā parvātā(n)nirgatā |

(Ibid.).

49. ŚKS quoted in TĀ, vol. I, pp. 49 ff. Pandey, p. 141 ff.

50. pañcasrotasi śaive'tra vistāraḥ prāk proceditaḥ |

(JY fl. 188b).

Various gods, demigods and sages have revealed the Āgamas of the five Currents:

pañcasrotātmakaṃ śaivaṃ tena tena avatāritam |

(Ibid., fl. 189a).

51. ṣaḍsrotasi mahāśaivapṛthagvastu vinirṇayam |
boddhavyaṃ gurubhedena santānakramasaṃsthitam ||

(Ibid., fl. 185b).

52. pratisrotasi yā vyaktiḥ sarahasyārthavedakaḥ |

(Ibid., fl. 193a).

53. The similarities between this system and that of the modern ascetic orders (particularly those of the Dasanāmī sannyasins) suggests that they were influenced in their formation by it. Thus each Dasanāmī order has its own internal subdivisions called *madhis*, a word which is clearly derived from the word *"maṭha"* of which *"maṭhikā"* is the diminutive. A variant, although not common, form of the word *maṭhikā* is *madhikā* (see, for example, ibid., fl. 188b) from which we get the word *"madhi."* Sinha and Sarasvati writing about the central organisation (i.e., the Ākhāra system) of the Dasanāmī orders say "all the Dasanāmī ascetics, excepting the Dandis, admitted that they are divided into fifty-two Madhis—also known as Dhunis . . . Excepting Ashrama and Tirtha all others in the Ten Names are connected with the Madhi organization." This has also been noted by Ghurye. The term "Madhi" does not signify a recruiting or initiating centre. Etymologically it is a vernacular diminutive of the Sanskrit word *"maṭha,"* and in usage it stands for a lineage in spiritual kinship or what is called *"nada vansa,"* as the ascetics call it. The names of the Madhis indicate persons. The consideration of Madhi for inheritance also indicates its kinship significance." *Ascetics of Kashi* by Surajit Sinha and Baidyanath

Saraswati, N. K. Bose Memorial Foundation, Varanasi, 1978, p. 87.

54. "sa muniḥ mānasān siddhān tryambaka - āmardaka - śrīnāthākhyān advaya - dvaya - dvayādvaya - matavyākhyātṝn maṭhikāsu satsampradāyamārgaṃ pracārayitum nyayuṅkta |". Quoted in *Kashmir Shaivaism* by J. C. Chatterji reprinted by the Research and Publication Department, Srinagar, 1962, p. 6 fn. 1. "Tairambhā" and "Mahātairambhakā" are the names of two of the eight *maṭhikās* of the *dakṣiṇasrotas* according to the JY, (fl. 186b).

55. *"Sammoha"* which normally means "delusion" has a special technical meaning in these Tantras. *"Sammoha,"* far from referring to a state of spiritual ignorance, denotes the knowledge of the liberated condition—kaivalyajñānaṃ saṃmoham XXXXXXXX |" (Ibid., fl. 190a).

56. Ibid., fl. 4a.

57. Ibid., fl. 8a.

58. Ibid., fl. 191a.

59. Ibid.

60. "dakṣiṇam bhuktimuktīnām padam eva sadādvyam |" (Ibid.).

61. śakter ūrdhaṃ samākhyātaṃ XX paradhāmīśvaram |
sā śikhā paramā proktā santānavyaktisādhanī ||
(Ibid.).

62. Ibid., fl. 191a.

63. vāk catuṣṭayasaṅkrāntā paramā bindubhairavī |
(Ibid.).

64. śākhārupā tu vijñeyā vyaktihetuvicitratā |
atra ṣaḍsrotaso' bhinnā yā saktiḥ pīṭhasūtragā |
(Ibid.).

65. haṭhād devas tadā jñeyo haṭhakeśo mahābalaḥ |
prabhu sarvasvaṃ devo' sau kulakaulaviśāradaḥ |
rahasyagrāmam akhilam tasmāt sarvam ihoditam |
śrīpādam prabhur ānandayogaśaktiḥ krameṇa tu |
hāṭakākhyaṃ sadā jñeyaṃ miśraṃ vāme'pi dakṣiṇe |
kvacid anyesvavijñeyaṃ kulaśāsanatatparaiḥ |
gharapallikramaṃ tatra samāsād upavarṇitaṃ |
(Ibid., 191a).

There can be no doubt, on the basis of these statements, that the JY considers the Sixth Current to be that of the Kaula schools.

66. SvT, 10/95b-119.

67. tad asmāt prabhaved devi vaktrāt pātālanāyakāḥ |

68. TĀ, 8/31.

69. Quoted ibid., 8/32b-40.

70. Ibid.

Bibliography

SANSKRIT TEXTS

Āpastambīyadharmasūtra with Haradatta's *Ujjvala* commentary. Edited by Mahādeva Śāstrī and K. Raṅgācārya. Mysore: Mysore Government, 1898.

Karpūramañjarī by Rājaśekhara. Edited by Sten Konow and translated by C. R. Lanman. Harvard Oriental Series vol. IV, Cambridge: Harvard University, 1901.

Kādambarī by Bāṇa. Edited by P. V. Kane. Bombay: Nirnaya Sagar Press, 1913.

Kāmikāgama, Part I (called "*Pūrvakāmikā*"). Edited by Swāminātha Śivācārya. Madras: Dakṣiṇabhāratārcakasaṃgha, 1975; part II (called "*Uttarakāmikā*"). Civaña Napotayantraśālai, Cintātripeṭṭai. Madras: 1909.

Kāśyapasaṃhitā. Triplicane: Yathirāja Sampathkumāramuni of Melkote, 1933.

Kulārṇavatantra. Edited by Tārānātha Vidyāratna. Introduction by Arthur Avalon. Delhi: (reprinted by) Motilal Banarsidass, 1975.

Kūrma Purāṇa (with English translation). Part I by Sri Ahibhusan Bhattacharya; part II by Dr. Satkori Mukherji, Dr. Virendra Kumar Varma and Dr. Ganga Sagar Rai. Edited by Sri Anand Swarup Gupta. Fort Ramnagar, Vārāṇasī: All India Kashi Raj Trust, 1972.

The Kaulajñānanirṇaya. Edited by P. C. Bagchi. Calcutta: Metropolitan Press, 1932.

Garuḍapurāṇa. Reprint of the Veṅkaṭeśvara Press edition. Delhi: Nag Publishers, 1984.

Gorakṣasiddhāntasaṃgraha. Edited by Janārdana Pāṇḍeya Sarasvatībhavanagranthamālā no. 110. Benares: 1973.

Gorakṣasaṃhitā, Part I. Edited by Janārdana Pāṇḍeya Sarasvatībhavanagranthamālā no. 110. Benares: 1976.

Tantrāloka by Abhinavagupta and commentary by Jayaratha. Vol. I. edited by Mukunda Rāma Śāstrī, KSTS no. 23, 1918; vol. II edited by Madhusūdan Kaul Śāstrī KSTS no. 28, 1921. The remaining volumes were all edited by Madhusūdan Kaul Śāstrī. These are vol. III, KSTS no. 34, 1921; vol. IV, KSTS no. 36, 1922; vol. V, KSTS no. 35, 1922; vol. VI, KSTS no. 29, 1921;

vol. VII, KSTS no. 41, 1924; vol. VIII, KSTS no. 47, 1926; vol. IX, KSTS no. 59, 1938; vol. X, KSTS no. 52, 1933; vol. IX, KSTS no. 57, 1936; vol. XII, KSTS no. 58, 1938.

Nityāṣoḍaśikārṇavatantra. With the commentaries *Ṛjuvimarśinī* by Śivānanda and *Artharatnāvalī* by Vidyānanda. Edited by Vrajavallabha Dviveda. Yogatantragranthamālā no. 1, Vārāṇasī: 1968.

Netratantra. With commentary by Kṣemarāja. Edited by Madhusūdan Kaul Śāstrī. Vol. I KSTS no. 46, 1926; vol. II KSTS no. 61, 1936.

Parātantra. Edited by Ghanasum Ser. Prayaga: Kalyan Mandir, 1952.

Parātriṃśikā. With commentary by Abhinavagupta. Edited by Mukunda Rāma Śāstrī, KSTS no. 18, 1918.

Pratiṣṭhalakṣaṇasārasamuccaya. Edited by Bābu Kṛṣṇa Śarmā, Nepāla Rāṣṭrīyābhilekhālaya, Kathmandu, *Devatācitrasaṃgraha* 1963; Vol. I, 1966; vol. II, 1968.

Bṛhatsaṃhitā by Varāhamihira with English translation, notes and comments by M. R. Bhat. Delhi: Motilal Banarsidass, Part I, 1981; part II, 1982.

Brahmasūtrabhāṣya by Śaṅkarācārya. Published together with Vācaspati Miśra's *Bhāmatī*, Āmalānanda Sarasvati's *Kalpataru* and Appayadīkṣita's *Parimala*, 2nd ed. Edited by Bhārgava Śāstrī. Bombay: Nirṇaya Sāgara Press, 1938.

Mataṅgapārameśvarāgama (*Kriyāpāda, Yogapāda* and *Caryāpada*) with commentary by Bhaṭṭa Rāmakaṇṭha. Edited by N. R. Bhaṭṭ. Pondicherry: 1982.

Mahākālasaṃhitā (*Kāmakalākhaṇḍa*). Edited by Kiśoranātha Jhā. Allahabad: 1972. *Guhyakālīkhaṇḍa*, Part I, Allahabad: 1976; part II, Allahabad: 1977; part III, Allahabad: 1979.

Mahānayaprakāśa by Śitikaṇṭha. Edited by Madhusūdan Kaul Śāstrī. KSTS no. 71, 1937.

Mahārthamañjarī by Maheśvarānanda. Edited by Vrajavallabha Dviveda. Yogatantragranthamālā no. 5. Vārāṇasī: 1972.

Mālinīvijayavārtika by Abhinavagupta. Edited by Madhusūdan Kaul Śāstrī. KSTS no. 31, 1921.

Mālinīvijayottaratantra. Edited by Madhusūdan Kaul Śāstrī. KSTS no. 37, 1922.

Mṛgendratantra with *vṛtti* by Nārāyaṇakaṇṭha (*Vidyapāda* and *Yogapāda*). Edited by Madhusūdan Kaul Śāstrī, KSTS no. 50, 1930.

Kriyāpāda and *Caryāpāda*. Edited by N. R. Bhaṭṭ. Pondicherry: 1966.

Yoginīhṛdaya with commentaries *Dīpikā* by Amṛtānanda and *Setubandha* by Bhāskara Rāya. Edited by Gopinātha Kavirāja. Sarasvatībhavanagranthamālā no. 7. 2nd ed. Vārāṇasī: 1963.

Rājataraṅgiṇī by Kalhaṇa. *A Chronicle of the Kings of Kashmir*. Translated with an introduction, commentary and appendices by M. A. Stein in two volumes. 1st ed. 1900. Delhi: (reprinted by) Motilal Banarsidass, 1961, 1979.

Rauravāgama. Edited by N. R. Bhaṭṭ. Vol. I Pondicherry: 1961; vol. II Pondicherry: 1972.

Luptāgamasaṃgraha. Part I collected and edited by Gopinātha Kavirāja. Yogatantragranthamālā no. 2. Vārāṇasī: 1970; part II collected and edited by Vrajavallabha Dviveda. Yogatantragranthamālā no. 10. Vārāṇasī: 1983.

Varāhapurāṇa. Edited by Pañcānana Tarkaratna. Calcutta: Vaṅgavasī Press, 1916.

Vāmakeśvaramatatantra with the commentary of Rājānaka Jayaratha. Edited by Madhusūdan Kaula Śāstrī. KSTS no. 64, 1945.

Vāmanapurāṇa. Bombay: Veṅkaṭeśvara Press, 1908.

Śaktisaṅgamatantra. Edited by Benoytosh Bhattacharya. Three volumes. Gaekwad's Oriental Series, nos. 61, 91 and 104, 1932-47.

Śaṅkaradigvijaya by Mādhvācārya with Dhanapatisūri's *Ḍiṇḍima* commentary. Ānandāśrama Sanskrit Series no. 22. Poona: Ānandāśrama Press, 1915.

Śataratnasaṃgraha by Umāpatiśivācārya with his own commentary, *Śataratnollekhanī*. Edited by Pañcānana Śāstrī with introduction by Swāmī Bhairavānanda. Tantrik Texts vol. 22. Calcutta: 1944.

Śivadṛṣṭi by Somānandanātha with *vṛtti* by Utpaladeva. Edited by Madhusūdan Kaul Śāstrī. KSTS no. 54, 1934.

Śivapurāṇa, Vāyavīyasaṃhitā. Edited by Mallikārjuna Śāstrī. Two volumes. Dattaprasāda Press, 1905-6.

Śivasūtravimarśinī by Kṣemarāja. Edited by A. K. Chatterji. KSTS no. 1, 1912.

Ṣaṭsāhasrasaṃhitā. Chapters 1-5 edited, translated and annotated by J. A. Schoterman. Leiden: E. J. Brill, 1982.

Somaśambhupaddhati. Translation, introduction and notes (in French) by Hélène Brunner-Lachaux. Institut Française D'Indologie, no. 25. Pondicherry: Part I 1963; Part II 1968; Part III 1977.

Skandapurāṇa Seven volumes. Bombay: Veṅkaṭeśvara Press, 1909-11.

Skandapurāṇa, Sūtasaṃhitā with Mādhavācārya's commentary. Edited by V. S. Paṇaśīkara. Three volumes. Ānandāśrama Sanskrit Series, no. 24. Poona: 1893.

Spandapradīpikā. Published in the *Tantrasaṅgraha* vol. I. Edited by Gopinātha Kavirāja. Yogatantragranthamālā vol. III. Vārāṇasī: 1970.

Svacchandatantra with commentary by Kṣemarāja. Edited by Madhusūdan Kaul Śāstrī. Vol. I KSTS no. 31, 1921; vol. II KSTS no. 37, 1923; vol. III KSTS no. 44, 1926; vol. IV KSTS no. 48, 1927; vol. Va KSTS no. 51, 1930; vol. Vb KSTS no. 53, 1933; vol. VI KSTS no. 56, 1935.

MANUSCRIPTS

Kubjikānityāhnikatilaka ASB, MS no. 11282.

Kubjikāmatatantra ASB (govt. collection), MS no. 4733.

Kulapañcāśikā NA, MS no. 1/1076 vi.

Ciñcinīmatasārasamuccaya NA, MS no. 1/767 (MS A); NA, 1/5160 (MS B); NA, 1/245 (MS C); NA, 1/199 (MS D).

Jayadrathayāmala NA, MS no. 5/4650.

Brahmayāmala NA, MS no. 3/370.

Manthānabhairavatantra (*Yogakhaṇḍa*) NA, MS no. 5/4654.

Śrītantrasadbhāva NA, MS no. 1/363 vi.

Siddhayogeśvarīmata NA MS no. 5/2403, ASB MS no. 3917D and no. 5465.

BOOKS AND ARTICLES

The names of authors are recorded just as they are in the book or article. If the text is in Hindī or Sanskrit, the author's name is transliterated.

Agrawal, V. S. *The Vāmana Purāṇa—A Study*. Benares: Prithivi Prakashan, 1983.

Alphabetical Index of Sanskrit Manuscripts in the University Manuscripts Library, Trivandrum. Edited by Suranada Kunjan Pillai. Trivandrum Sanskrit Series no. 186. Trivandrum: 1957.

Bagchi, P. C. *Studies in the Tantras*, Part I. Calcutta: University of Calcutta, 1975.

Banerjee, J. N. *The Development of Hindu Iconography*. 3rd ed. Delhi: Munshiram Manoharlal, 1974.

Banerji, S. C. *Tantra in Bengal: A Study in its Origins, Development and Influence*. Calcutta: Naya Prakash, 1978.

Bhandarkar, R. G. *Vaiṣṇavism, Śaivism and Minor Religious Systems*. Benares: Indological Book House, 1965.

Bharati, Agehananda. *The Tantric Tradition*. London: Rider and Co., 1969.

Bhattacarya, S. C. *Principles of Tantra*. The *Tantratattva* with an introduction by Arthur Avalon and Baroda Kanta Majumdar. Edited by Arthur Avalon, 3rd ed. Madras: Ganesh and Co., 1960.

Bose and Halder. *Tantras: Their Philosophy and Occult Secrets*. Calcutta: Firma K. L. Mukhopadhyay, 1973.

Bṛhatsūcīpatram. Vol. 4. Part I and II dealing with Tantra manuscripts in the Vīra (*Darbar*) Library. Compiled by Buddhisāgara Śarmā. Kathmandu: Vīrapustakālaya, 1964, 1969.

Brunner, H. *Un Tantra du Nord: Le "Netra Tantra"*. BEFEO Tome LXI, Paris: 1974.

Differentes Conceptions du term "Śaiva" dans la litterature āgamique du Sud de l'Inde. Paper presented at the 30th congress on Human Sciences in Asia and North Africa. Mexico: 1976.

Le Śaiva—Siddhānta 'essence' du Veda. (Étude d'un fragment du *Kāmikāgama*). Indologica Tourinensia Vol. VIII-IX (1980-81), pp. 51-66.

Chakravarti, Chintaharan. *Tantras: Studies on their Religion and Literature*. Calcutta: Panthi Pustak, 1963.

Chakraborti, Haripada. *Pāśupata Sūtram with Pañcārthabhāṣya by Kauṇḍinya*. Translated with an introduction on the history of Śaivism. Calcutta: Academic Publishers, 1970.

Dasgupta, S. B. *Obscure Religious Cults*. Calcutta: Firma K. L. Mukhopadhyay, 1962.

A Descriptive Catalogue of the Sanskrit Manuscripts in the Collection of the Royal Asiatic Society of Bengal. Vol. VIII, part I and II, Tantra manuscripts. Compiled by Haraprasāda Śāstrī. Revised and edited by Chintaharan Chakravarti. Calcutta: Royal Asiatic Society of Bengal, 1938, 1940.

Dunwila, Rohan A. *Śaiva Siddhānta Theology*. Delhi: Motilal Banarsidass, 1985.

Dvivedi, V. *Purāṇavarṇitāḥ pāśupatayogācāryāḥ*. Purāṇam XXIV no. 2, July 1982.

Dyczkowski, M. S. G. *The Doctrine of Vibration*. Albany: SUNY Press, 1987.

Gnoli, R. *Luce delle Sacre Scritture*. Torino: Classici Utet, 1972 (This is an Italian translation of Abhinavagupta's *Tantrāloka*).

Goudriaan, Teun and Gupta, Sanyukta. *Hindu Tantric and Śākta Literature*. A History of Indian Literature. Edited by J. Gonda. Vol. II fasc. 2. Wiesbaden: Otto Harrasowitz, 1981.

Goudriaan, Teun. *The Vīṇāśikhatantra: A Śaiva Tantra of the Left Current*. Edited with an introduction and translation. Delhi: Motilal Banarsidass, 1985.

Handiqui, K. K. *The Yaśastilaka and Indian Culture*. Sholapur: Jain Saṃskṛti Saṃrakṣaka Sangha, 1949.

Hazra, R. C. *Studies in the Purāṇic Records on Hindu Rites and Customs*. 2nd ed. Delhi: Motilal Banarsidass, 1975.

Hopkins, E. W. *The Great Epic of India*. Calcutta: Panthi Pustak, 1978.

Karmakar, A. P. *The Vratya or Dravidian Systems*. Vol. I of a projected series *The Religions of India*. Lonavla: Mira Publishing House, 1950.

Kavirāja, G. *Tāntrikasāhitya* (*vivaraṇātmaka granthasūcī*). (in Hindī) Lucknow: Hindī Samiti, 1972.

Kooy, K. R. van. *A Critical Edition of the Kubjikāmatatantra.* BSOAS, vol. XXVI-3. London: 1973.

Die sogenannate Guptahandschrift des Kubjikāmatatantra. ZDMG supp. III-2. Wiesbaden: 1977.

Lalyle, P. G. *Studies in Devī Bhagavata.* Bombay: Popular Prakashan, 1973.

Lorenzen, David N. *The Kāpālikas and Kālamukhas: Two Lost Śaivite Sects.* Berkeley and Los Angeles: University of California Press, 1972.

Mallman, M. de. *Les Enseignements Iconographiques de L'Agnipurāṇa.* Paris: Presses Universitaires de France, 1963.

Nagaswamy, R. *Tantric Cult of South India.* Delhi: Agam Kala Prakashan, 1982.

Padoux, A. *Recherches sur la Symboliques et L'Énergie de la Parole dans certains texts Tantriques.* Paris: Edition E. De Boccard, 1963.

Pandey, K. C. *Abhinavagupta: An Historical and Philosophical Study.* 2nd ed. Chowkhamba Sanskrit Studies no. 1. Vārāṇasī: Chowkhamba, 1963.

Pathak, V. S. *History of Śaiva Cults in Northern India from Inscriptions.* Published by Dr. Ram Naresh Varma. Benares: 1960.

Rastogi, N. *The Krama Tantricism of Kashmir.* Delhi: Motilal Banarsidass, 1979.

A Review of Rare Buddhist Texts I, Central Institute of Higher Tibetan Studies, Sarnath. Benares: 1986.

Sastri, Ghosal S. N. *Elements of Indian Aesthetics.* Chaukhamba Oriental Series. Vol. I 1978; vol. II (parts I-IV) 1983.

Schoterman, J. A. *A Link between Purāṇa and Tantra: Agnipurāṇa. 143-147* ZDMG suppl. IV. Wiesbaden: 1980.

Schrader, F. Otto. *Introduction to the Pāñcarātra and Ahirbudhhya Saṃhitā.* 2nd ed. Adyar: Adyar Library Series, 1973.

Shah, U. P. *Lakulīśa Śaivite Saint* in *Discourses on Śiva.* Edited with an introduction by M. W. Meister. Bombay: Vakils, Feffer and Simons Ltd., 1984.

Sircar, D. C. (editor). *The Śakti Cult and Tārā.* Calcutta: Calcutta University, 1967.

Smith, David H. *The Smith Āgama collection: Sanskrit Books and Manuscripts Relating to Pāñcarātra Studies.* Syracuse: Syracuse University, 1978.

Śukul, K. N. *Vārāṇasī Vaibhava* (in Hindī). Patna: Bihār Rāṣṭrabhāṣā Pariṣad, 1977.

Tripāṭhī, Ramāśaṅkara. *Śivamahāpurāṇa ki dārśanik tathā dhārmik samālocana.* Benares: Published by the author, 1973.

Virānanda. *Constructive Philosophy of India.* Vol. II (Tantra). Calcutta: Firma K. L. Mukhopadhyay, 1973.

Index of Proper Names

A

Ā

U

O

JH

T

D

DH

N

P

B

BH

M

Index of Titles

U

Ū

O

E

K

KH

G

BH

M

Ś

H

Index of Subjects

A

Ādhyātmikaśāstra, 31
Āgamas, creation of, 195n.7; individuality of, 13; as members of canon, 14; worship of, 158n.280
Aghorī, 27-28
Akula, 61, 62, 75, 161n.7
Akulamahādarśana, 184n.157
Āmnāyas, according to *Caṇḍī*, 95; according to Maheśvarānanda, 179n.111; definition of, 66; development of, 87; goddesses of, 179n.113; number of, 67, 173n.86; relation to the breaths, 173n.85; relation to the four ages, 67, 173n.84; relation to phases of manifestation, 174-75n.91, 92; Śākta and Śaiva character of, 176-77n.100; system of classification, 66
Anākhya, 75, 78, 181n.121
Ānanda, 62, 70
Anantasrotas, 112
Āṇava, 84
Anuttara, 162n.12
Anuttarāmnāya, 76, 182n.144
Anuttarāmṛtakula, 181n.117
Anuttaratrikakula, 181n.117
Anuttaratrikakulakrama, 75
Ārhata, 102
Aṣṭāṣṭabheda, 47, 175n.95
Atīta, 62
Auttara, 182n.140
Auttarakrama, 182n.142
Auttarāmnāya, 76
Avali, 62

B

Bahurūpatantras, 46, 47
Bark, birch, 92
Behaviour, antinomian, 22, 24, 26, 28
Beef, 6
Beyond Mind (*unmanā*), 60
Bhairavācārya, 30
Bhairava (sect), 17
Bhairavasrotas, relation to *Kaulatantras*, 59
Bhairavāṣṭaka, 45, 46, 53, 175n.95; contents of, 45-46; as an independent group, 47
Bhairavāṣṭāṣṭaka, 43, 159n.283
Bhairavatantras, 19, 26, 42-49, 86, 102, 110, 123, 153n.225, 154n.234, 197n.21; according to the ŚKS, 32; as authority for Kashmiri Śaivites, 5; cults of, 30; as *Dakṣiṇatantras*, 46-47; development of, 33; early loss of, 7; followed by Kāpālikas, 29; persistence of, 42; rejected the Vedas, 9; rejected by Purāṇas, 10
Bhairavatantras, sixty-four, 44, 114,

T